CHILDREN OF POVERTY

STUDIES ON THE EFFECTS OF SINGLE PARENTHOOD, THE FEMINIZATION OF POVERTY, AND HOMELESSNESS

edited by

STUART BRUCHEY
ALLAN NEVINS PROFESSOR EMERITUS
COLUMBIA UNIVERSITY

A GARLAND SERIES

HOW BLACK DISADVANTAGED ADOLESCENTS SOCIALLY CONSTRUCT REALITY

LISTEN, DO YOU HEAR WHAT I HEAR?

LORETTA J. BRUNIOUS

GARLAND PUBLISHING, INC.
A MEMBER OF THE TAYLOR & FRANCIS GROUP
NEW YORK & LONDON / 1998

Library of Congress Cataloging-in-Publication Data

Brunious, Loretta J., 1945–
    How Black disadvantaged adolescents socially construct
reality : listen, do you hear what I hear? / Loretta J. Brunious.
        p.   cm. — (Children of poverty)
    Includes bibliographical references and index.
    ISBN 0-8153-3235-1 (alk. paper)
    1. Afro-American teenagers—Illinois—Chicago—Social
conditions—Case studies. 2. Afro-American teenagers—Illinois—
Chicago—Education—Case studies. 3. Afro-American teenagers—
Illinois—Chicago—Psychology—Case studies. 4. Poor children—
Illinois—Chicago—Case studies. 5. Chicago (Ill.)—Social conditions—Case studies. 6. Inner cities—United States—Case studies.
7. Social psychology—Illinois—Chicago—Case studies. I. Title.
II. Series.
F548.9.N4B78 1998
305.235—dc21
                                                                98-27138

Printed on acid-free, 250-year-life paper
Manufactured in the United States of America

In memory of Jewell Ann McLaurin

Contents

Tables and Figures

TABLES

FIGURES

Foreword

Occasionally one comes across a book that is both unpretentious and enlightening. Such is the case for Loretta Brunious' *Listen: Do You Hear What I Hear*? Which chronicles the lives of twenty inner-city adolescents in how they experience their lives in and out of school. Using the social construction of reality framework developed by sociologist Peter L. Berger and Thomas Luckmann, Brunious argues that the behavior of these adolescents form a coherent belief system largely based on their day-to-day lives. Focused on what these youngsters especially experience in their school, a fascinating picture of struggle and survival emerges where the formal rules and expectations of the school system confront and are confronted by these seventh and eighth graders. What occurs in this cauldron of tensions, hopes, unfilled dreams and daily survival strategies is the grist of Brunious' work.

From a scholarly point of view, the book is a well-crafted case study within the anthropological tradition. The twenty adolescents become a subculture within a subculture, that Brunious studies with objectivity, insight and also compassion. Through careful documentation and analysis she refutes the still prevalent myths that inner-city African-American youngsters suffer from "cognitive deficits." She finds, rather, that the combination of the despair of school personnel, the poverty conditions of the surrounding community and the survival needs of the adolescents themselves all conspire to produce a less than truthful picture of the black adolescent as an automatic school failure.

The problem is that the various actors have different, and often conflicting, "constructions" of their own realities. Teachers and administrators operate under one set of constructions, families under another, and the adolescents under still others. These constructions are seldom congruent and the result is often anger, apathy, dampened expectations and eventually a sense of hopelessness-not by all, but nevertheless a large number by all those involved in these overlapping social structures. Along these lines, Brunious makes a strong case for arguing that the very existence of spatial boundaries produce powerful constraints on the adolescents which, in turn, significantly shape the content of their "commonsense" realities. For example, gang defined "turf" determines where one can and cannot be. Additionally, Brunious discovers that many youngsters have never experienced the major institutions of Downtown Chicago, such as, the Field Museum or the Adler Planetarium. The lack of exposure to these forms of "cultural capital" places constraints on what can become the content of their constructions of reality.

The major strengths, in my view, of Brunious' book is her willingness to use the actual dialogue of the adolescents to describe their commonsense constructions of social reality. The dialogue becomes a rich source not only of "data" but for an actual feel of how these kids experience *their* lives. They are open in how they express who they are and what their future lives might become. The dialogues give further in-depth insights into such areas as family social structure, the powers of gangs to recruit and socialize, the perceptions of the "system" and how to use it or avoid it and, especially, what "schooling" really means to them.

Those twenty adolescents speaking openly about their lives and the role of schooling in their lives gives us a realistic picture that no large scale empirical study can approximate. Moreover, the theoretical framework, that social constructions of reality are actual things, is concretely grounded in these dialogue: we obtain a clear picture of what these adolescents believe and why they believe the way they do. What emerges, to borrow the philosopher Wittgenstein's phrase, is a "family resemblance"—a complex but definable picture of how life does not imitate reality but becomes reality.

Brunious does, however, give credible interpretations to these dialogues. In very readable and understandable ways she uses the additional frameworks of stage developmentalist theorists, such as Erickson, Piaget, and Kolhberg, to show that even though these kids may not be "typical" adolescents, they are still concerned with and go through these "stages" associated with this period of growth and development; for instance, concerns about how they look, what they wear and what kind of music they listen to and identify with. But as Brunious insightfully describes, these normal adolescent concerns take on a new sense of urgency for this group of twenty kids. For example, clothing is related to gang activity; sexual concerns are highlighted earlier; and "Rap" music becomes a focal point of identity as well as pleasure. What Brunious gives us is a sometimes frightening picture, a picture in "fast-forward" if you will, of how these kids *must* grow up to adapt to and survive the realities they encounter. In turn, their "social constructions of reality" are at once genuine but superficial. That is, their "adult" adaptations to the environment are "translated" through their adolescent stage of development. What Brunious perceptually shows is that these "commonsense" constructions are maladaptive for future functioning as *actual* adults. Nevertheless, they are very real and powerful social constructions that, in one form or another, remain with the adolescents as they become adults.

Brunious makes a strong argument for how the schools must take additional responsibility to change these "commonsense" constructions of social reality. For her, education still remains the crucial factor not in reversing the "cycle of poverty" but in reshaping how reality constructions are made. However, to accomplish this, changes must be made in the social structures that define educational policies. One example she cites is the irrelevance of many teacher training programs to address the unique educational needs of the kids in her study. In this context, she again points out that the social constructions held by these adolescents are not "bad" in themselves, but they are counterproductive in the long run. The teacher's job is not to reject these constructions but use them as a basis for showing how schooling can increase other, less limiting, life options.

I would, finally, recommend this book to all who need an insightful view or reminder, of how our "realities" are formed by who and what we "see." Specifically, it would be a very good introduction to undergraduate and graduate students in education and the social sciences, especially in showing the power and reality of the term "socialization"—a term often used but seldom really understood. Brunious is successful in bringing life to this term by cleverly balancing the academic perspective with the real-life "voices" of these adolescents. What we gain is an opportunity to reconstruct our own (or at least a portion) reality. To do this is in itself a valuable experience.

Stephen I. Miller, Ph.D.
Professor, Educational Leadership and Policy Studies
Loyola University Chicago

Acknowledgments

The writing of this manuscript has been enhanced by Dr. Steven Miller (Loyola University Chicago). Through his guidance, expertise, and support, a probable research study became a reality. I would also like to acknowledge, Dr. Talmadge Wright and Dr. Carol Harding both from Loyola University Chicago, for unselfishly giving of their time.

The completion of this manuscript would have been inconceivable without the support, understanding, and patience of my mother Anice Mobley and son, Courtney.

Finally, I must give recognition to my able and delightful friend, Carmen Tolhurst, for her scholarly assistance.

ARTIST PAYNE

A special acknowledgment and recognition must be given to Dion (*Artist Payne)* Samuels who created the art work for the cover and nine chapter illustrations. *Artist Payne* was born in Chicago Heights, Illinois on November 21, 1957. He attended Southern Illinois University, majoring in Commercial Advertising. He has also worked in some of the best photo studios in Chicago, where he received his first hands on experience in the graphic arts.

In 1990, he moved to St. Thomas, Virgin Islands, where he became known as *Artist Payne*. Throughout the three islands of St. Thomas, St. Croix and St. John, Samuels had established himself as one of the best artist in African, Caribbean and African American Art. *Artist Payne* returned home in 1998 to display his talent for the very first time.

Thank you Dion for unselfishly giving of your talent and time, which gave a soul to *Listen! Do You Hear What I Hear?*

How Black Disadvantaged
Adolescents Socially
Construct Reality

CHAPTER 1

Introduction

Realities are unique to each individual. Peter Burger and Thomas Luckmann (1967) allude to this fact in that,

> Everyday life presents itself as a reality interpreted by men [sic] and subjectively meaningful to them as a coherent world . . . The world of everyday life is not only taken for granted as reality by ordinary members of society in the subjectively meaningful conduct of their lives. It is a world that originates in their thoughts and actions, and is maintained as real (p. 19).

Children's reality is no exception: it is also subjectively created and personally meaningful. But personal realities are not totally internal. Individuals also rely on others' perceptions in order to construct personal realities. For black children, particularly those at economic disadvantage, this is a particularly critical factor in their perception and creation of the self.

To what extent does society function on preconceived ideas about black, disadvantaged children? Can we distinguish between our realities and ways of seeing and theirs? Is it possible to understand and accept that what is "real" to one is not necessarily so to another? An African proverb states, "Let him speak who has seen with his eyes," (Leslau, 1985, p. 18). While this makes common sense, it is not sufficient. To understand black disadvantaged adolescents' notion of the self, it is necessary to understand how they see reality. In the *Handbook of Research on Teaching*,

Frederick Erikson (1986) writes that realities exist in specific contexts, and crucially, that there is a quality of *invisibility* in everyday life. Because everyday life is so familiar, being in and all about us, "The commonplace becomes problematic." But Erikson (1986) also stresses that, "What is happening can become visible and it can be documented systematically" (p. 121). As such, in this ethnographic study, the phenomenon of poverty will be investigated from the cognitive, linguistic, and experiential occurrences of the children being studied. While researchers tend to assume that these children are on the outside of the "mainstream" of society, it is reasonable to wonder whether they see themselves as marginal. Do they believe that they are on the outside of society looking in? Furthermore, how do these perceptions—the larger society's and the children's—affect the way in which they construct their *common sense* world: how they see schooling, its relationship to their lives, what the system means to them and how they define themselves?

Because adolescence is so critical—the stage in which children stand between childhood and adulthood—the social construction of their reality is paramount in their development. This period is characterized by confusion, assertion, and the search for personal identity. Peers crucially create much of their inner and outer reality. Psychoanalyst Erik Erickson ✶ (1950) conceives of this period in the adolescent mind as a time of moratorium, "a psychological stage between childhood and adulthood and between the morality learned by the child and the ethics to be developed by the adult. It is an ideological outlook of a society that speaks most clearly to adolescent" (p. 263). Fifth of the eight stages of human development, this adolescent stage is characterized by opposing forces, identity and confusion. It is in this tension, the period of puberty, that childhood proper comes to an end and youth begins. At this time of awareness and questioning, much of the young adolescents' reality is an expression of the "truth" as they are constructing it. However, psychiatrists James P. Comer and Alvin F. Poussaint (1975) observe that for the black child, adolescence starts early. They state:

> black children who are reared in an environment of poverty and are forced to assume adult responsibilities at an inappropriately early age may be socially advanced for their years. Burdening children with adult

tasks may inhibit their passing through the usual stages of childhood (p. 293).

Many black children have had little of what is commonly termed "a childhood." Unlike most white children, many black children do not enjoy the luxury of a period of playtime and learning which extends into their late teens, since they often assume responsibilities and burdens of adulthood at a very early age (Comer and Poussaint, 1975). An old African proverb, " an elephant's head is no load for a child" (Leslau, 1962, p. 54) makes the point: the advent of this critical period of development is much more complex for children reared in poverty.

Given this perspective, a central question of this study is: what underlying messages are black children who live in poverty communicating, and are we willing to listen to their messages. A preponderance of evidence shows that, historically, the majority of black, disadvantaged children have been unsuccessful in schooling with a significant and still growing dropout rate. Society fails to meet the needs of this group of students. While most of the literature shows that research on disadvantaged students and schooling has been approached from an empirical perspective, it is valid to question whether this method can always provide an adequate understanding of the many facets of poverty that disadvantaged black students face in their daily lives.. In order to understand and interpret the complexities of the social construction of reality of black disadvantaged adolescents, children must be empowered to define themselves and from their definition we can begin to grasp more clearly the factors related to the phenomenon of poverty as it relates to many disadvantaged children in our society.

This exploration will offer insight into the social construction of reality among black, disadvantaged adolescents, focusing on their construction of everyday knowledge and how it relates to their day to day existence. We will come to understand the ways in which they perceive the reality of schooling and its relationship to their lives; how their educational identity is formed; the assumptions which teachers and administrators construct about children in poverty; and the ways that self-perceptions of race, class, and gender have an impact on their school and everyday reality. Such an analysis will hopefully shed new light on why the majority of black, disadvantaged children do not succeed in school.

The data was collected from July of 1994 through June of 1995, six-months of intensive observation and on a more intermittent basis thereafter. A qualitative approach was utilized within a holistic, naturalistic and humanistic framework. Naturalistic inquiry studies real-world situations as they unfold naturally, it is non-manipulative, unobtrusive and non-controlling; it has a characteristic openness to whatever emerges and lacks predetermined constraints on outcomes. The majority of the material was based on observations, and in-depth interviews both in and out of the classroom within the realm of the school boundaries. The students were asked a series of open-ended questions that identified certain aspects of their lives and ways of "seeing" and how they construct their *common sense world.*

The players are 20 African-American students in the seventh and eighth grades, between the ages of twelve and fourteen. The students attend an elementary school located on the south side of Chicago in a predominantly African-American and poverty-stricken neighborhood. The school has a total enrollment of 546 students whose racial/ethnic background is 100% African-American, 86% are classified as low-income students with a mobility rate of 40.6% (School Report Card, 1994). The school is located in a low socio-economic section of the metropolitan Chicago area that has been designated as the most crime ridden community. The median family income is $13,243 Census Report [CR], 1992 and Woodstock Institute Staff [WIS], 1992) 27,183 (CR,1992) persons are at or above the poverty rate and 20,710 (CR, 1992) are below (CR, 1992). There are 5598 of 14857 households that receive Public Aid (CR, 1992). The median home value is $39,700 to $57,199; the median rent is $115 to $294 (CR, 1992).

In selecting the students race, class and gender served as important characteristics. The children selected their own pseudonyms to provide confidentiality and protect their identities. In addition, there is no attempt to describe any disadvantaged African-American children other then those with whom I was in direct communication. To what extent this descriptive and interpretive material is applicable to disadvantaged African-American children in the global society is a matter for further research. However, this is not to suggest that we are dealing with a unique and distinctive population. In fact, the weight of the evidence presented demonstrates quite the contrary. True, the students were not selected by random sampling of other sophisticated selection techniques. In reality, they were not consciously selected at all. They were one of three eighth grade classes within the school. The difference being the seventh/eighth grade split, which eventually became two separate classrooms, one seventh and the other eighth during the year. It is important to remember, however, that this population represents a microcosm of society. It took place in the center of a major city, in the heart of a disadvantaged community, which bears a strong resemblance to disadvantaged areas in this city and other large urban areas and especially black, disadvantaged areas throughout the United States.

Thus, this attempt is not intended to develop generalizations about black, disadvantaged adolescence, but to examine a microcosm of this population, to make sense of the persistent, over-whelming failure of disadvantaged black children to succeed in schooling and in life in our society. It is with hope, that educators will find merit and validity in some of the concepts and test them for applicability. However, the concluding chapter may appear to contradict this intent, by including summaries, general statements, speculations, recommendations and conclusions about black disadvantaged adolescents in our society.

This age group represents a critical stage of development, adolescence, in which children stand between childhood and adulthood. Comer and Pouissant (1975) contend that burdening children with adult responsibilities may inhibit their passages through the usual stages of childhood development. In addition to this burdening, children who live in poverty are forced to cope with negative messages and images such as violence, gang graffiti, warning signs to gangs and drug dealers, over-representation of liquor stores in a one block radius, people of all ages "strung out" and congregating inside and outside of these "establishments," drive-by shooting, and so forth. These "social facts" come to constitute the important elements, cognitively and affectively processed, for the eventual construct of a social reality that is at once realistic and potentially destructive.

Poverty is a highly complex social phenomenon. In the United States, it is pervasive in predominantly black areas and directly influences the cognitive and emotional development of children, as well as the very basic fact of survival. Researchers have argued that such children arrive at school with cognitive, experiential and linguistic deficits (Knapp and Shields 1990). While it has been shown that these children have an overwhelming failure rate in school, this failure cannot simply be dismissed as a result of cognitive, experiential and linguistic deficit. An assumption underlying the current study is that many researchers do not understand and accept that what is "real" from their perspective does not necessarily reflect the reality of those being studied? The type of interpretive insight being proposed is consistent with a statement from Domestic Violence and Juvenile Circuit Court Judge Judy I. Mitchell-Davis (1994):

> the parties appearing before me have been overwhelmingly minority persons . . . I seek to understand what it is that has caused the confusion regarding the legal consequences of the behavior—consequences which I, as a judge of behavior simply explain. Is the confusion caused by apathy? By a lack of self-esteem that has succumbed to apathy or violent behavior? By a lack of a strong, positive, socializing[sic] foundation in early childhood—a foundation most know only, loving, caring, consistent and disciplining parents or surrogates can give? Though "probably" knowing the answer, I do not *in fact* know, since I am personally unacquainted with those whom I preside. I do not in fact know because I have not walked in the shoes of those before me.

Consistent with Judge Mitchell-Davis' self-reflection, much of what is known about black disadvantaged adolescents results from empirical studies developed by researchers who are effectively detached from the phenomenon of poverty and its consequences. This study will examine how the adolescent cognitive, experiential and linguistic "world" is formed, and through these findings attempt to offer insight and clarification of this social construction process.

A major focus of this investigation will be an examination of whether these children have cognitive, experiential and linguistic "deficits" contributing to their observed failure in school or if the causes of failure can be attributed to other sources. It is hoped that the findings of this research may be used by various policy analysts to develop instructional strategies and programs to provide an educational environment that addresses the needs of these children.

The following terms are defined for clarification of specific material.

1. Adolescent: A psychosocial stage between childhood and adulthood, and between the morality learned by the child and the ethics to be developed by the adult (as defined by Erik H. Erikson)

2. At-risk: Children who face social and personal problems which threaten their ability to do well in school and inhibits their progress toward becoming productive members of society (as defined by Chicago Board of Education, Early Intervention Program, 1991).

3. Disadvantaged: Children between the ages of 3 and 18 who do not qualify for the special educational facilities provided for in Article 14 of the School Code but who, because of their home and community environment, are subject to such language, cultural [sic], economic and like disadvantages that it is unlikely they will graduate from high school unless special educational programs and services supplementing the regular public school program are made available to them (as defined by the Illinois School Code 14B-2, 1990)

4. Folks: One of two alliances which forms umbrella groups. The "FOLKS" alliance uses a six pointed star which is actually known as the star of David. They also use various configurations of a pitch-fork (which will always be pointed upward). All gangs allied with folks will "represent" (identify by virtue of some display) to the *right* in similar ways that counter parts represent left. (as defined by the Chicago Police Department, Neighborhood Relations/Preventive Programs, 1994).

5. Gangs: A street gang is a cohesive group of youth, usually between the ages of eleven and twenty-three years, who have recognizable geographical territory (usually defined with graffiti), leadership, a purpose, and various levels of an organized, continuous course of criminal activities (as defined by the Chicago Crime Commission, 1995).

6. Knowledge: the certainty that phenomena are real and that they possess specific characteristics (as defined by Berger and Luckmann).

7. Low-income: students from families receiving public aid, living in institutions for neglected or delinquent children, being supported in foster homes with public funds, or eligible to receive free or reduced-price lunches (as defined by School Report Card, 1994).

8. Mobility-rate: the number of students who enroll in or leave a school during the school year. Students may be counted more than once (as defined by the School Report Card, 1994).

9. People: The second of the two alliances. The "PEOPLE" alliance uses a common 5 pointed star as one of their universal symbols. They "represent" by wearing their hats tilted or shifted towards the *left*. Other ways of representing will usually include something which focuses on the left side of the body such as, rolling up the pant leg on the left, or the sleeve on the left, or shifting the belt buckle to the left and so on (as defined by the Chicago Police Department, 1994).

10. Poverty: As defined by poverty threshold, which is established by the Bureau of Statistics by the size of the family and number of children in the household, e.g., threshold for family of four is $14, 335 (Poverty Threshold).

11. Reality: a quality appertaining to phenomena that we recognize as having a being independent of our own volition ,we cannot "wish" them away (as defined by Berger and Luckmann).

12. Social-constructivism: Reality and knowledge as it pertains to specific social contexts and a sociological analysis of these contexts (Berger and Luckmann).

The setting in which the children live has an interesting historical background, illustrating how a somewhat opulent locale becomes a devastated, poverty-stricken community. Englewood was originally swamp and oak forest located on a ridge running southwest of Chicago, which is now Vincennes Avenue. The community was initially called Junction Grove. Henry B. Lewis, an early settler-realtor suggested that the name be changed to Englewood because of the great oak trees and forest that enveloped the area. Lewis believed the name Englewood to be more eminent than Junction Grove. The following is a chronological listing of the events in Englewood some of which eventually precipitated a once thriving community to become one of the most crime and poverty ridden districts in Chicago:

1840: A station for the Michigan City stage road was built.

1852: The first Michigan, Southern and Northern Indiana Railway (later part of the New York Central line) ran through the district.

1854: The Fort Wayne Railroad was built; a settlement called Junction Grove was developed. German and Irish railroad workers and farmers were the first settlers.

1865: Junction Grove became part of the Town of Lake.

1868: Junction Grove became Englewood. The Cook County Normal School was established (later the name was changed to Chicago State University). L.W. Beck, a prominent developer donated ten acres of land. The area attracted middle-class professionals and businessmen. Established Normal Park, or Normalville.

1869: The Roman Catholic Parish of St. Anne was established.

1872: Streets were created in the area from Wentworth Avenue to Halsted Street south of 55th Street to 71st Street 1873:Oakwood High School was opened.

1880: Standard Oil Company opened on Michigan Avenue, employing 30 men. Population German, Irish and Scotch.

1885: Two small black districts: western boundary of Racine and a mile east to the east along Stewart.

1889: Town of Lake, including Englewood was annexed to Chicago. Columbian Exposition occurred which lead to improvement in transportation and subsequent expansion.

1890: Swedish-Americans moved to area; Many German and Irish moved further south.

1893: South Side elevated line completed to Jackson Park.

1896: Surfaced line were supplied with electric power.

1905: Oakwood had predominantly single-family dwellings; the area had become established. Hamilton Park was opened.

1907: Completion of Englewood branch of the "EL"

1920:   Population 86,619; new construction, apartment buildings were evident. 63rd and Halsted shopping district became readily accessible.

1929:   Sears Roebuck bought out the Becker Ryan store

1930:   Population 89,000

1934:   Sears closed the Becker Ryan store; built a $1.5 million store and leased other properties for its block long building. 63rd Street shopping district became the second busiest commercial area in Chicago

1930s: White-collar workers lived an apartment complexes east of Halsted Street; working-class families lived in small homes west of Halsted Street. Housing was in the decline. Houses on Wentworth Avenue were deteriorating.

1940:   Population 93,000: predominantly Irish, German and Swedish; small pocket of Dutch in the southwest corner; 2% of population was black.

A small group of African-Americans lived in Englewood before the Civil War. They were concentrated in an area called Alden Park at 67th and Racine. The district was once a terminal for the Underground Railroad. Each decade after 1940 brought with it an increase in the black population. Several factors accounted for the emigration: increased and steady wages promised by World War II, and the overcrowding in the Black-Belt areas after the War and subsequent loss of economic opportunity and housing. Englewood's decline in prosperity was caused by a series of events which contributed and ultimately resulted in the area that we know today as one of the highest crime-rate districts in Chicago. These included the lack of housing when construction ceased in the 1930s; the exodus of whites to South and Southwest Chicago; and the new opening of shopping centers, e.g., Evergreen Park and Chicago Lawn business district; demolition of homes for city projects, e.g., Dan Ryan Expressway (1950s). Today, the unemployment rate is extremely high, housing units have decreased and residents live in overcrowded conditions.

1950:   11% of population was black; population 97,000+ (loss of 50,000 whites).

1960:   69% of population was black; slum area had spread.

1960s: Failed attempts made to revitalize shopping concourse: traffic was diverted and a mall was created.

1970:   96% black.

1971:   Kennedy-King City College opened.

1972:   Chicago State University moved further south.

Mid-
1970s: Sears and Wieboldts closed.

1980:   99% black Shops in concourse mostly owned by immigrant Koreans. (The Chicago Fact Book Consortium [CFBC], 1984).

Poverty, poor educational achievement, unemployment and high crime levels have been accompanied with an "infestation"of gangs. According to the Uniform Crime Report for United States, the estimated juvenile gang killings increased form one hundred-eighty-one in 1981 to eight-hundred-fifty-two in 1992. The average age of murder arrestees dropped from thirty-two and one-half in 1965 to twenty-seven in 1992 (1993). In Chicago alone, one-hundred-sixty-nine murders were committed by children under eighteen (Chicago Police department Annual Report, 1993).

The principal gangs in the Englewood community are "GD (Gangster Disciples)" and "BD (Black Disciples)" which are both factions of FOLKS. Gang affiliation at the school is predominantly "GD" (18 of the 20 students studied were admitted gang members). A gang prevention and intervention classroom discussion was held on November 4, 1994. Don Lewis, a gang investigator with the Chicago Police Department was the facilitator. The students were asked, " How can you avoid gangs?" They responded with four different possibilities:

1. You can't!
2. Move out of the neighborhood
3. Stay in the house
4. Get into positive activities e.g. sports

He then asked, "Why do kids get involved in gangs?" The eighth grade students stated:

1. To get help
2. Protection
3. Poor, a way to get money, to buy clothes.
4. Respect

Gangs create and manipulate a mind set about "reality" for the adolescent According to the gang investigator, they are manipulated and brainwashed by a friend, neighbor and/or relative. The tools of manipulation are intimidation, fear and ignorance. Lewis states that the gang offers the path of least resistance and the adolescent succumbs to pressure.

Addressing this very issue, Erikson (1950) conceives of the adolescent mind as ideological. In fact, he claims that it is the ideological outlook of society that speaks most clearly to the adolescent. In other words, adolescent ideology responds to societal ideology. Further, Erikson contends that adolescence is the time for establishment of a dominant positive ego identity. It is then that a future within reach becomes part of a conscious life plan. For Erikson, the danger of this stage is role confusion in which, "delinquent and outright psychotic episodes are not uncommon. To keep themselves together they temporarily over identify to the point of apparent complete loss of identity, with the heroes cliques and crowds" (p. 262). Erikson also points to adolescent propensity for a tribal mentality with an attendant cruelty in their exclusion of those who are "different," perversely testing each other's capacity to be loyal to the group. But this feature of adolescent development is not all negative since it also allows adolescents to assist one another temporarily through the pain of the experience by forming cliques and by stereotyping themselves, their ideals, and their enemies. Erikson (1950) notes that "the adolescent is eager to be affirmed by his peers, and is ready to be confirmed by rituals, creeds and programs which at the same time define what is evil, uncanny and inimical" (p. 263).

Given the psychological turmoil of adolescence and the social reality in which black, disadvantaged adolescents exist, it is little wonder that the academic performance of these youngsters is so precarious. The school's reading and mathematics level of performance falls below state, district and city norms. More than 70% of the student population is not performing at the expected grade level. By the eighth grade, the average reading and math score is already two years below grade level. Traditional curriculum, strategies, low student self-esteem, socio-economic problems and other factors contribute to these low scores, thereby increasing the risk that these students will not complete high school (School Vision Plan, 1994). The nonpromotion rate is 5.8%. There are high rates of discipline problems which include fighting, truancy, gang involvement, teen pregnancy, and drug-related activities. Teacher and student morale as well as academic learning are affected by the high incidence of discipline problems. Clearly, students who exhibit these behaviors are at-risk. Low self-esteem and student alienation are also reflected in the conduct and academic performance of students on a daily basis. Teachers report that the lack of motivation is a problem with many students.

The social reality of black adolescents living in poverty cannot be analyzed without taking into account the routes by which this reality has been constructed. Three elements in particular have had a profound effect on the social construction of reality for these children: the legacy of slavery and the pedagogical "machinery" by which they are educated. In addition, the theoretical framework which attempts to answer the crucial questions about these youths' construction of their reality is part of the account.

CHAPTER 2

The Course of Construction

Literature and studies that define black, disadvantaged adolescents have been a common thread of research among sociologists and educators over the past forty years. Their theories and assumptions have created myriads of practices and programs to alter the phenomenon. Yet, today the majority of these children continue to be unsuccessful in school and in their everyday lives. Black and Hispanic children have the highest drop-out rate among any ethnic group. In 1994 the Chicago drop-out percentages were 45.3% and 42.9% respectively for the two groups. The 1994 Citywide Drop-out Rate for the Chicago Public Schools (CPS) was 42.6%. The comparative drop-out statistics for the CPS from 1989 through 1993 were 47.8%, 45.9%, 51.5%, 45.3% and 42.7% respectively (Chicago Public Schools Department of Research and Evaluation, 1995). The gap between the research insights, the practices, and the daily existence of these children is a dilemma which gives rise to continuing debate.

Although the literature shows that most research on black, disadvantaged adolescents has been approached from an empirical framework, it is valid to question whether numbers alone can provide insight into the many facets of poverty and the reality which black and disadvantaged adolescents construct.

This study examines the relationship of the effects of poverty on the lives of adolescents from the perspective of adolescents. More specifically, how they socially construct the reality of poverty, schooling, race and its correlation to their lives. First, in accordance to a precept that requires participants to define themselves for reasons of empowerment, these adolescents will provide their self-definitions (Hill-Collins, 1990). From their definition the facets associated with the phenomenon of poverty and the construction of self will hopefully offer insight into their reality. Carter G. Woodson (1933) addressed the issue of self-definition in a chapter entitled "The Study of the Negro,"

> The Negro can be made proud of his past only by approaching it scientifically himself and giving his own story to the world. What others have written about the Negro during the last three centuries has been mainly for the purpose of bringing him where he is today and holding him there (p. 194).

According to Woodson, the construction of black identity has been the product of historical and structural forces of exclusion and subordination. Consequently, he believed that to dispel stereotypes and misinterpretations blacks must create their own historical dialogue.

Thus, the social construction of reality of black adolescents living in poverty cannot be analyzed without taking into account the routes by which this reality has been constructed. Three elements in particular have had a profound effect on the social construction of reality for these children: the legacy of slavery and the pedagogical "machinery" by which they are educated. In addition, the theoretical framework that attempts to answer the crucial questions about these youths' construction of their reality is part of the account. The first component relies on accounts of the progression of the black-white relationship taken from the historical perspective, personal narratives of slaves, oral histories, the concept of psychic trauma, the use of stereotypical images, and its impact on childhood development. The second component deals with the pedagogical mechanism under which children in poverty develop and takes its cue from a historical overview of the theories that underline the thinking affecting the education of black children. The final section on theoretical frameworks relevant to the "success" of disadvantaged students and to their construction of reality cites various studies researching factors that conspire against black student success. Particular focus is given to the role of mass media and popular culture to the reality that impoverished black children develop.

THE HISTORICAL PERSPECTIVE

An account of today's black disadvantaged adolescent would be lacking in essence and adequacy without discussing the historical realities of the legacy of slavery. While the experience of slavery has been predominant in the lives of blacks, and as such has produced an overabundance of research on slavery, a certain attitude has developed that there is little to be gained from dwelling on past issues (Akbar 1984). Nevertheless, the history of enslavement still impacts on blacks present day life.

Winthrop Jordan (1974) contends that to understand the full concept of the black-white relationship it is essential to understand its evolution, from its inception of uncomprehending "discovery" of black savages to their racial subjugation from 1550 to 1865. As such, exploration of the various disciplines: psychology, anthropology, genetics, literature and linguistics are critical to this understanding. For, attention to past and subsequent experiences are major components that are a sine qua non to grasping and interpreting current problems and events that is the present is grounded in the past. Accounts of economic exploitation and social degradation are crucial elements in the study of racism, but these factors alone do not provide adequate answers. Attitudes are also discrete and complex entities significant and susceptible of historical analysis relating to the issue of racism. Thus, the complexity of human oppression can be better understood by recognizing and analyzing the various degrees of human attitudes, conscious and unconscious.

A key element to "unlocking" this phenomenon is an understanding of the "peculiar" relationship of the slave master and the slave provide a sense of plantation life. Further, to provide better insight into the personality of the slave, an adequate analysis must use personal records, preferably autobiographies of the slaves which were ignored by historians in the past. In addition, the "traveler" who has an external point of view observes the relation between the slave and the master. John Blassingame (1972) states that slave life must be examined from two different perspectives and three points of view: the slave's, the slave master's and the traveler's (i.e. observer's). He believes that the three perspectives allow for a better interpretation of the complexity of slavery. Without, this analysis a distorted record based on the plantation owners' view will continue to prevail throughout historical records.

Today, much of what is known about slavery is based on written and oral accounts by individuals who endured bondage (Blassingame, 1977; Harris et al, 1974). Frederick Douglass (1968) recounts the horrors of slavery in a biography published in 1845. Studies by James Mellon (1988), Rawick (1971) and Fisk University (1945) use oral histories from former slaves. Pascoe Hill (1848) relates the atrocities and sufferings aboard a slave vessel and the subsequent psychological effect on its "cargo." All documentation bears out that slavery had a cataclysmic effect on African-Americans since its onset in 1619. Researchers recapitulate the significance of those events throughout the many studies devoted to the effects of slavery.

To briefly recount its origin, twenty black Africans arrived in Jamestown, Virginia in August of 1619 aboard a Dutch man-of-war ship whose purpose was to provide free plantation labor, thus the history of black America began (Al-Mansour, 1993; Bennett, 1961; Campbell et al, 1991; Mellon, 1988). Although the status of the Africans was tenuous at this point, surviving evidence alludes to the fact that, in most instances, they were treated as indentured slaves, but, unlike their white counterparts, their term was for life. By 1708, there was a dramatic increase in the number of slaves, many times outnumbering the white population (Bennett, 1961 and Campbell, 1991) . Subsequently, whites became anxious and sought more systematic and legislative control. Regulations were established and implemented on interracial contact. Laws were legislated to prohibit bearing arms, and learning to read and write. Slaves were made to acknowledge their inferior status through means of attire, icons and the actual carriage of their bodies—inclined heads, downcast eyes, shuffling gait and so forth.

This psychological enslavement was "coined" *psychic trauma,* "introduced" by Sultan Latif and Naimah Latif (1994). They argue that psychological shock and emotional scars resulted from the treatment endured by blacks and these have been passed from generation to generation. The *psychic trauma* continues to be reinforced in today's society. Accordingly, a sense of inferiority is one of the greatest scars from slavery; this has been used to explain most aspects of African American behavior. Reference to the shrewdness of the slave-makers and their propensity to understand human behavior was a critical component to the "success" of the institution of slavery. As such, slave makers surmised that people who still respected themselves would rather die, as many chose to do, than be subjected to the dehumanizing process of enslavement (Akbar, 1984). Self-hatred and low self-esteem were perpetuated through a deliberate systematic process. Various means were used to "break" the spirit and create a sense of inferiority thereby conserving the "peculiar institution" and fostering exploitation.

Atlanta University, Division of Archives/Special Collections preserves many of the original documents, such as, slave ads, manumission papers, indenture papers, passes for slaves, bills of sales for goods and chattel, guardianship and so forth which served as tools for the system and perpetuated a sense of inferiority. Woodson (1919) addresses the issue in relation to education and outlines the making of a slave. He proposes that there were two periods in the history of slavery. The first extended from the introduction of slavery to the insurrection period of 1835. The second period followed when the industrial revolution changed slavery from a patriarchal to an economic institution and insurrection became a major determinant.

Woodson explains that Africans could not have been brought from their native country to serve as a free laboring class to a pioneering society without specific training to meet the needs of the new environment. In line with the ideology, the new slave masters believed that "the more brutish the bondmen, the more pliant they become for purposes of exploitation." This criterion served as the determining factor to keep the African illiterate in American society, for to enlighten the slave would create a longing for freedom and a drive toward insurrection. Thus, the machination to "chain" the mind and exploit the body was initiated and the "peculiar institution" was launched. This dehumanization was also necessary to justify slavery in "free society."

The enslavement of the physical body and the encapturement of the mind incarcerated ambition, dreams, aspirations, motivation and identity (Akbar, 1984; Douglas, 1968). This psychological "entrapment" was capitalized on by the pro-slavery and segregation propaganda before and after the Civil War which served as a prototype for mass production of black memorabilia that created the distorted "coons," "uncles" and "mammies" as an American phenomenon. It was not until The Civil Rights Act of 1964 that mass production of stereotypical images was found to be illegal. However, the black memorabilia had spawned negative images and dehumanizing stereotypes of blacks in America that refuse to be dislodged even today.

The memorabilia were so prolific and demoralizing that they sparked the attention of many researchers and collectors to study black collectibles as American icons of racial and gender stereotyping (Goings, 1994); Patricia Turner (1994) was funded by the Trotter Institute for Black Culture at the University of Massachusetts to conduct a study on black images and their influence on culture; Jan Lindenberger (1993), an antique collector, published handbooks and price guide on black memorabilia. Ms. Lindenberger "remarks" her favorite being black kitchen items because "the smiling mammies in my kitchen, brighten my day" (p. 7). She defines black memorabilia as anything associated with black people: derogatory items, folk art made by blacks, souvenirs, fine art, slave documents, shackles worn by slaves or anything related to the slave era. The stereotypical items and negative images are the most highly sought after items. Lindenberger maintains that black memorabilia preserves black heritage, educates black children on how things were, and exemplifies the perception that many whites had of blacks.

Nevertheless, these disparaging images constructed and aided the evolvement of subconscious acceptance of inferiority and the stubborn persistence of racism today. Stanley Elkins' (1959) controversial study asserts that slavery created a "Sambo" personality type in the American slave. His discourse on slavery and ideology, further states that the current political, social and philosophical issues are "rooted" in the issue of slavery. Ann Lane (1971) disputes Elkins' polemic study. She argues that the use of force was an indication that the "Sambo" personality was not internalized to the extent that Elkins claimed. She maintains that a viable and self-perpetuating slave culture emerged which competed with the slave owners' authority. Lane argues further that the slave owners were unable to perceive this viable, self-perpetuating slave culture therefore they were incapable of passing down this information to historians as a reality (pp. 10-11). Throughout history, the "inferiority complex" theory has been challenged. Numerous clinical studies have been initiated exploring the psychoanalytic interpretations of the black psyche relating social and economic realities. Frantz Fanon (1967) contends that if an inferiority complex exists within the black psyche it is the direct result of a dual process—economics and "epidermalization." He believes that individuals must eradicate the impact left by childhood defects, acknowledging philosopher Frederich Wilhelm Nietzche's statement, "Man's tragedy is that he was once a child" (p. 10). He further states that "man is what brings society into being" (p. 11) and any unilateral actions would not reach the desired goal—psychological liberation. Reality, according to Fanon requires a total understanding.

Growing up black in America, "the land of the free" from slavery to present, tendered many trials and tribulations of being born into a life of struggle and the development of their ability to cope with the existing hardships. As such they contributed scars that never healed.

Significant, to life in America were the negative images assigned to blacks by white America and that were fostered from generation to generation have created resounding effects of establishing a caste structure based on color. Subsequently, the caste structure has created a system of privilege and oppression within the black community. The color complex is deemed "unmentionable" and the "last taboo" among African Americans. In a study on the politics of skin color Russell et al (1992) examine the devastating prejudices associated with the color complex in varied settings—families, work, and social settings. Referred to as a "dirty little secret," they contend that the majority of whites are unaware of the "secret," but its existence was created and perpetuated by white propaganda during the period of slavery. The value of light over dark skin continues to cause division within the black community today.

The Civil War and the Thirteenth Amendment of 1865 brought to a close the institution of slavery. Notwithstanding passage of the Thirteenth Amendment, the Fourteenth Amendment in 1868, and the Fifthteenth Amendment in 1870, granting citizenship, equal rights and permitting black suffrage, respectively, the effects of slavery still reverberate. They dictate, to a great extent, how 130 years later our youth construct their *common sense* world. That is, black America's national identity and many of the troubling realities of the twentieth century are rooted in a history of racism and oppression (Campbell and Rice, 1991; Branham, 1994: Latif and Latif, 1994; Elkins, 1959; Akbar, 1984; Woodson, 1933; Dubois, 1903).

Although emancipation revitalized the issue of the importance of education for black youth, today we are still confronted with a staggering high dropout rate for black disadvantaged adolescents. What subsequent events cause desire to develop into apathy? In more prosaic words Langston Hughes (1951) asks, *What Happened to a Dream Deferred?*

THE PEDAGOGICAL MACHINERY

The social reality of black disadvantaged children cannot be analyzed without taking into account the "machinery" by which their reality is constructed. Historically, the individual and society have shared an inextricably interwoven dialectical existence. The schools represent a microcosm of society, reflecting the conflicts in the larger social order. Essentially, there are two prevailing theoretical frameworks that debate the function of schools in society: (1) the social mobility theory and (2) the social and cultural reproduction theory. At the turn of the century, schools were thought to be the panaceas for upward social mobility and full participation in American democracy for those lacking in social class and wealth. Lawrence Cremin and John Dewey were major advocates of the social mobility theory and the sustaining myth of American democracy—education and equality for all. Compulsory, free education would level out social and economic differences; by improving life style, the quality of life would also improve. Economic and political power would become accessible. Cremin also believed that schools were the determinant factor for equality.

The social mobility theory, views schools as the means for breaking the cycle which perpetuates social status. Advocates contend that education is the step to upward social mobility.

However, the critics of the social mobility theory argue that education does not level the playing field; rather it is a means of reproducing the social order, the dominant ideology and the work force. The school maintains class structure and takes an active role perpetuating and maintaining the existing social strata.

According to Social reproduction advocates, Pierre Bourdieu and Jean-Claude Passeron (1977) education and its social reproduction role maintain that schools promote false consciousness and hidden curriculums, arguing that education perpetuates and legitimizes the class structure, power and production. According to Bourdieu and Passeron this social structure defines educational reproduction as an:

> extremely sophisticated mechanism by which the school system *contributes* to reproducing the structure of the distribution of cultural capital and, through it, the social structure (and this, only to the extent to which this relational structure itself, as a system of positional differences and distances, depends upon this distribution) to the ahistorical view that society reproduces itself mechanically, identical to itself, without transformation or deformation, and by excluding all individual mobility (p. vii).

They argue that redistribution is maintained under the guise of equity and meritocracy, and that "all pedagogic action is, objectively, symbolic violence, insofar as it is the imposition of a cultural arbitrary by an arbitrary power" (p. 5). Symbolic violence works to impose a veil of legitimate authority upon the de facto powers. Through this means an educational institution can declare an agenda without betraying its true objectives.

Louis Althusser (1971), another social cultural advocate asserts that schools are part of a dominant Ideological State Apparatus, replacing the Church in the primary role as an agent of reproduction. Accordingly, students are the perfect captive audience eight hours a day, five days a week for capitalist social formation; for it is through the schools that students construct their social reality and their position within the social structure. Althusser perceives teachers as unsuspecting agents who contribute to the maintenance and nourishment of the state.

However, the most outspoken advocates of the reproduction theory, Samuel Bowles and Herbert Gintis (1976), recognize the role of the schools within the same framework as Althusser, Bourdieu and Passeron. They challenge the liberal education doctrine and contend that schools are not the democratic institution they claim to be, rather, their clandestine role in capitalist America is to reproduce the social order which includes a hierarchal working genre. In their view books written on education are also about politics and schools reflect the limits and promise of society. They charge that "the people production process in the workplace and in schools is dominated by the imperatives of profit and domination rather than by human need" (p. 53). Problems in schools are rooted in capitalist society and each generation of youth repeats the cycle. According to Bowles and Gintis, the persistence of poverty and inequality is not coincidental but a calculated effort by the dominant order to perpetuate the social strata.

Douglas Glasgow (1980) also argues that society perpetuates the domination of the mainstream. In a study of poverty in black youth, he refutes psychosocial models that contend that the condition of blacks is due to individual deficits and charges that these psychosocial assumptions serve to only justify and perpetuate these conditions that serve to keep blacks jobless, unskilled, entrapped, and on the outside of the mainstream of society. He argues that structural factors are directly or indirectly responsible for the perpetuation of poverty and the development of an underclass. Thus, black youth are earmarked for failure and rendered obsolete before they can gain access to entrance into mainstream society. This rejection and labeling are perceived to be safeguards by the school as a representative of the dominant social order.

In a study of critical pedagogy in cultural, political and ethical terms, Peter McLaren, a former classroom teacher (1989) also examines why disadvantaged children are not successful in school and reasons that false consciousness, hegemony and a hidden curriculum are perpetuated in the school system. He contends that thoughts, ideas and theories within the schools are codified, ideologically loaded and intertextually related to the larger social order. That is, ideas are never autonomous or free floating. Rather, they are tied to specified interests related to the existing power structure. McLaren believes that "absolutely nothing is of unmediated availability to human consciousness-to *know* anything is always an effect of power/knowledge relationships" (p. ix); therefore, society reproduces itself.

Mwalimu Shujaa, et al (1994) also support the cultural hegemony theory of education. In a cooperative effort with many authors and practitioners, Shujaa develops an analysis defining the educational paradox—growing up black in a white society. The paradox is a social fact which African-American students confront on a day to day basis. They maintain that the persistence of social and cultural reproduction has programmed black children for failure and will continue to recur until the hegemonic intent is counteracted. This study suggests that African American communities and black children in urban areas must contribute to their self-definition in order to break the hegemonic cycle.

Jonathan Kozol (1991) also addresses the issue of poverty in urban education which places these children on the outside of the mainstream of society. The study finds that the most consistent outcome for poor children in urban education is the "denial of the means of competition" (p. 83). The hidden curriculum and the physical structure of the institution combine to permeate despair and futility. He perceives the physical appearance of these schools as "garrisons" and "outposts" in foreign war zones—guarded doors, drug-free zone signs, windows covered with steel grates, policed patrolled halls, filth, and streets free of taxi cabs. These concrete images are powerful factors in these children's common sense world. He stresses the importance of bringing the children's perception of their day to day realities in schools to bear on proposed solutions and places the retribution of these inequalities in public education at the doorstep of the government.

In a study on the dialectical relationship of the oppressed and the oppressor, Freire (1970) also alludes to the importance of self definition. Thus, the pedagogy of the oppressed must be developed by the oppressed since implementing and defending a liberal education for the oppressed by the oppressor would constitute a conflict of interest for those who create and maintain a system of domination. In a similar study Memmi (1965) agrees that the colonized must cease to define themselves in terms delineated by the colonizer.

Henry Giroux (1981) focuses on the internal discourse of the curriculum as a source of empowerment via understanding and learning. He perceives the school as "a terrain of contestation rather than an ideology machine and pedagogy as an emancipatory activity" (p. 3). He

achers and students as agents of social change through
ment. In Giroux's (1983) ideological discourse, he anticipates
that his work will be seen as a gateway for change for schools.

Since the first law was established in Missouri in 1817 barring blacks
from schools, epistemological issues surrounding the "pedagogical
machinery"continue to precipitate controversy. The majority of black,
disadvantaged children are unsuccessful in school and in their personal
lives. The following section addresses theoretical frameworks that explore
the impasse.

WHY DISADVANTAGED STUDENTS DO NOT SUCCEED

Kenneth Clark's (1963) historic study of black children's self-esteem was
one of the deciding factors in the Brown vs. Topeka 1954 347 U.S. 483,
74 S.Ct. Clark and his wife employed black and white dolls in this study
with children, ages three to seven, who were asked a series of questions
in relation to the dolls. The study documented the negative psychological
effect of prejudice and discrimination on black children. In the Brown
decision, the Supreme Court reversed the Plessy vs. Ferguson, 163 U.S.
537, 16 S.Ct. 1138 (1896) separate but equal doctrine. Despite the Brown
vs. Topeka decision and the development of numerous programs, schools
still do not meet the needs of disadvantaged children and a
disproportionate number of these children drop out.

Do we as a society believe that " a black child is a white child that
happens to be painted black?"(Wilson, 1978, p. 6). Do we assess the
economical, political, and psycho-social development of impoverished
black children prior to a judgement. Do we understand that many white
children do not encounter these same "struggles?" Are we guilty of
condemnation of the black impoverished child while the jury is still out?
Are we "blaming the victim?" According to Woodson (1933) the problem
is one of self hatred, created by the oppressor. He states that Negroes were
taught to admire other cultures and to despise their own African roots. He
contends that the history of blacks has been deemed to be of little
consequences or a problem. In his terms, the education of blacks can be
considered "miseducation."

Jawanza Kunjufu (1984) and Richard Simmons (1985) concur with
Woodson's theory of "miseducation." Taking Woodson's work a step

further, Kunjufu identifies a system of "de-education," a systemic attempt of exclusion of African-American youths and/or the process of their destruction within the system. He emphasizes the development of positive self-images and discipline as precursors to effective education for African American students. Simmons contends that the value system is the crucial element in children's development and that for black children, the value system adversely effects their development.

John Ogbu (1978) argues that 'ideological blinders' which rationalize societal inequities should be removed, and the reality of a caste system should be acknowledged. He views black and certain other minority children as endangered species. Ogbu explains that society, particularly in the 1960s, saw the failure of black and other minority children as two basic problems: 1) there is something wrong with the schools, or 2) there is something wrong with minority children.

The 1960s propagated numerous statistical reports, such as the massive and controversial Coleman Report, *Equality of Educational Opportunity* (1966) and, the Moynihan Report, *The Negro Family, The Case for National Action* (1965) giving credence to the theories that there was something wrong with the schools or something wrong with the children. Society perceived and accepted as fact that these children arrived at school with cognitive, experiential, linguistic, cultural deficits and inadequate home environments. The curriculum was adjusted accordingly with compensatory education, equalization in school resources and preschool programs. Nevertheless, minority children continued to fail and drop out in high numbers. Ogbu (1978) attributes these inadequacies to structural rather than psychological deficiencies. He argues that structural change can only take place when the caste system that in fact creates the discrepancies among racial groups is eliminated.

A report by The National Alliance of Black School Educators (1984) charges that the "rash" of national reports on school reform do not take into consideration the unique past and present problems of African-American children. The report contends that the major reason for failure to attain excellence among African-American students is "the legacy of racism or belief in white supremacy and superiority and its concomitant imputation of black inferiority" (p. 21). The tools of racist, exploitive practices and social injustices have produced the present level

performances. The report continues to state that educational
quality can only be achieved through justice, fairness, compensation and
retribution.

Nathan Hare and Julia Hare (1991) perceive inclusive in the problem,
black and white middle class America educating black, impoverished
inner city children. They see teachers, guidance counselors, principals and
others in the system as trying to assimilate these children to conform to
their values, views and behavior. This system, they maintain, continues
to categorize, label and miseducate poverty stricken inner city children;
it fails to see what reality is for impoverished children. Children who live
in communities surrounded by failure and poverty experience a sense of
being on the outside and contending with rules that do not apply to them.
They charge that schools need to refocus and deal with issues applicable
to their reality. Again, is a black child a white child that happens to be
painted black?

Some believe that the majority of blacks feel inferior to whites and
that this notion has been perpetuated by the dominant culture. Jawanza
Kunjufu (1985, 1986, 1990) sees society, the black community, educators
and all others who have the responsibility for raising black children as the
perpetrators. He challenges the "conspirators" to develop programs and
organizations to counter the conditions that are destroying black youth. As
such the the African-American child is perceived as an endangered
species.

In his classic study, *Blaming the Victim,* William Ryan (1971) was
one of the first to refute the "myths of poverty," According to one myth,
minority children in poverty areas perform poorly in school because they
are "culturally deprived." Ryan contends that the differences are related
to "style" rather than ability. In his study, he challenges the adage of
"blaming the victim" and critiques the mindsets and assumptions of those
who create the adage.

James Comer (1988) develops a holistic intervention system in
education as a means to save minority students. In a longitudinal
ethnographic study of younger African-American children conducted by
the Yale Child Study Center School Development Program (SDP) and
directed by James Comer, they contend that minority students who live in
poverty do not lack ability but have suffered periods of discrimination,

economic, educational, cultural and social deprivation. Slavery, a state of enforced dependency and inferiority, offered no future, in contrast to the dominant Anglo culture which placed a high value on independence and personal advancement. Thus, the dominant culture devalued the imposed black culture and many blacks in turn developed a negative self image.

Moreover, f we scrutinize the dialectical existence of the schools and the curriculum closely, at what point do we ask: what is actually being taught and learned in the schools? And is the curriculum designed to teach something other than the three R's? And why?

Therefore, the pedagogical machinery and the theoretical frameworks in which black disadvantaged adolescents are educated are critical in the construction of reality. Other crucial mechanisms contribute to reinforce this complex construction.

THE SOCIAL CONSTRUCTION OF REALITY AMONG BLACK DISADVANTAGED ADOLESCENTS

Burger and Luckman's (1966) treatise in the sociology of knowledge maintain that the social construction of reality is the "knowledge that guides conduct in everyday life" (p. 20). They argue that "reality is socially constructed and that the sociology of knowledge must analyze the process in which this occurs" (p. 1). Identities are constructed from a series of social processes. Burger and Luckman theorize that identity is a key element to subjective reality.

Children's reality is subjectively created and personally meaningful. Yet how does the perception of the larger society affect ways in which they *see* their *common sense* world? Do they believe they are on the outside looking in? Do they perceive that they are trapped in a world that does not relate to or understand them? C. Wright Mills (1959) alludes to this fact in that

> Nowadays men often feel that their private lives are a series of traps. They sense that within their everyday worlds, they cannot overcome their troubles, and in this feeling, they are often quite correct: What ordinary men are directly aware of and what they try to do are bounded by the private orbits in which they live; their visions and their powers are limited to the close-up scenes of job, family, neighborhood; in other milieux, they move vicariously and remain specters. And the more

aware they become, however vaguely, of ambitions and of threats
which transcend their immediate locales, the more trapped they seem to
feel (p. 3).

Are children's perceptions any less real? Thus, the theoretical frameworks
attempt to answer the questions: How do black disadvantaged children
socially construct their reality? How are their identities formed? How do
they define themselves? How have social processes impacted on the
construction of their everyday reality?

To answer these questions we must "embark" from Southerners
migrating from one oppressive condition to another gives background
information which brings the freed slaves into the twentieth century. The
southerners gave up sharecroppers shacks in exchange for housing
projects, leaving one type of poverty to encounter another just as dismal
or hopeless as the previous. Nicholas Lemann's (1991) states that the
white mainstream power system used this bleak predicament to their
advantage to exploit the freed slave. Michael Katz (1989) also argues that
the issue of poverty is an American political discourse. He questions
whether family, race and culture are factors and argues that inequality,
power and exploitation are the hidden agendas. Both suggesting that
poverty is not coincidental but is a calculated efforts of hegemony, hidden
agendas and false consciousness created by the system.

Consequently the struggles of minority groups, primarily of inner-city
African-American males, have led to the construction of enterprising
survival strategies. Richard Majors and Janet Mancini (1992) and Elloit
Liebow (1967) examine young black males' creation of self in America
and how they live marginally in the inner-city. *Cool Pose* and *Tally's
Corner* specify the defense and coping mechanisms employed to make
sense of oppression, inequities and indignities in their everyday world.
There is a created sense of "truth" or social reality of ritualized male
posturing, speech, violence and other modes of expressing black male
masculinity, as they construct *their common sense* world.

Wilson (1990) perceives the evolution of inner city violence as a
direct outcome of "institutionized racism," which affects the lower strata
of the social hierarchy. He argues that black-on-black violence is a result
of deliberate socio-psychological and politico-economic factors instituted

by the dominant order. As such, the "psychological, consciousness and behavioral tendencies of individuals and societies are to a significant extent the products of their personal and collective histories" (p. 1). The role of the social structure rationalizes black oppression and develops false consciousness in black America. He proposes that history is the key to psychological freedom and independence. Wilson contends that in order for black children to understand themselves, they must first understand the history and experiences of the African-American people. Once this is accomplished, they can begin to understand and appreciate other people's history and psychology. Until experiential and historical mastery occurs, African-American children will continue to fail in a system that is designed to educate white children. The effect is even more devastating for children reared in poverty. The period of adolescence becomes more critical for these children. They are products of a society that creates and sustains black violence through socioeconomic conditions which typifies the inner city ghetto.

One of the primary reasons children kill themselves and others, is that a culture of violence is nurtured and perpetuated throughout society. They live in a society that perpetuates drug trafficking, child neglect and abuse, teen-age pregnancy, penal institutions and other causative factors relating to the crisis adolescents face in impoverished communities nationwide.

Consequently, black children "nurtured" in poverty experience a burdensome task during this turbulent adolescent phase. They are confronted with negative elements and seemingly unresolvable issues on a day to day basis. These "social facts" are key components to the construction of their *common sense* world and their definition of Self.

In addition, the social oppression of black adolescents reared in poverty offers a penetrating insight into substandard housing, miseducation, police brutality, corrupt politics, deplorable sanitary conditions, inadequate health facilities, damaged self-concepts and institutional racism. They are forced to cope with these oppressive forces and rely on the "Street Institution" for their "support" and "education." Again, the "social facts" have a direct impact on their total development and their construction of reality.

In a similar ethnographic study Alex Kotlowitz's (1991), examined the same issues of politics, poverty, violence, racism and despair in the

United States, recounting the story of two adolescent boys growing up in the "other" America, the Chicago housing projects. He reveals the identity struggle, the school frustrations, the deaths of friends, the drugs and the gang lure which create a world of terror, violence and pain. He cautions that "despite all they have seen and done, they are—and we must constantly remind ourselves of this—still children" (p. xi).

James Garbarino et al (1991) see the situation with terrifying significance. They compare the lives of children who live in poverty to that of a war zone. Black children who suffer from economic deprivation are perceived at greatest risk. War and violence represents major factors in the children's construction of reality. Their day to day existence consists of conflict and turmoil. These children's lives in the inner-city parallel those who live in war torn and poverty-stricken Cambodia, Mozambique, Nicaragua and Palestine. According to the Chicago Tribune (August 9, 1995), the most frightening part of children witnessing and participating in violence is that at some point it becomes part of their consciousness and they begin to enjoy or at least expect it. The children are "poignant victims of war, hapless bystanders caught in raging conflicts beyond their understanding" (Garbarino, 1991). This type of situation tears the social fabric of any country. It creates a legacy of terrorism and these children will perpetuate violence and brutality to the next generation unless something is done to break the continuum.

Violence has become a way of life for many of our children who live in poverty and despair. It ensues and reaps deadly consequences. In addition the reality and behavior of these children are constructed by violence and the behavior of other members in the community. Nevertheless, the development of strategies that teach coping skills for anger and aggression can change the climate of violence for these children.

In a commentary on black street gangs, Perkins (1987) relates the question of poverty and violence to the development of the black street gang phenomenon. The problem originated from institutional and systematic racism upon oppressed black communities. Black youth gangs were viewed as "urban oppressed phenomena" whether in Chicago or Johannesburg, South Africa. Perkins' historical perspective of gangs from 1900 to the present corroborate that black gangs evolved as a positive response to oppression of the black urban communities and now that survival in impoverished neighborhoods depends on recognizing and respecting territorial markings and signs of gangs. The *common sense* world for black, disadvantaged adolescents is constructed from this "culture" of violence and death. Recently, a book entitled, *My Posse Don't Do Homework* by LouAnne Johnson (1992) which later was released as a movie, *Dangerous Minds*, takes this "culture" of violence and despair and restructures it into hope and belief. The classroom teacher successfully works with children in the inner city, children referred to as "the class from Hell," for whom society has given up any prospect of salvation. The actual story of these children takes place in a government funded program to assist students with low grade point averages and poor attendance.

The themes of violence and exclusion for impoverished African-American adolescents who live in the inner-city are devastating paradoxes of the larger society's rejection of these children from the American mainstream and the hope offered by the American dream. The American tradition of violence and ruthless images creates and promotes a moral legitimacy for violence. These forces exclude the children from participation in American economic and social life. They also target poor children for conspicuous consumption (Carl Nightingale, 1993).

The frustrations created from poverty and exclusion cultivate a desire to embrace the American consumer culture. Nightingale asserts that consumption of promotional blitzes—sports apparel, cheap jewelry, cars, gold and other discernibly visual commodities function to compensate feelings of humiliation and frustration and also offer a piteous sense of inclusion. The commodities become representative status symbols to the youth and as such are also related to a growing number of gang killings in the inner city.

The ghetto blemished by poverty and isolated from the nucleus of the inner city is congruent with these adolescent perceptions of space, created by the limitation of their environment. The construction of the city is an important factor to consider in the constructed reality of black disadvantaged children. Familiarization with territories is critical to survival for children reared in poverty.

Representation based on constructed, consumed images and space is critical in the social construction of reality and identity among disadvantaged black adolescents. Perception of self and others' perception of one are decisive factors in black children's creation of self. In addition, popular culture and media present an integral role in the development of constructed images and perception of self.

THE ROLE OF MASS MEDIA AND POPULAR CULTURE IN SHAPING PERCEPTION OF CONSTRUCTED SOCIAL REALITY

The oral tradition of black Americans is rooted both in the African tradition and in the legal prohibition against reading and writing, an offense punishable by death. Consequently, relying only on their resourcefulness, the slaves succeeded in perpetuating their cultural oral tradition. So, when slavery was abolished and legal bans were terminated, a resonant oral tradition continued to transcend a history of oppression and strife reflecting and shaping black cultural expression (Dyson, 1993). The oral tradition includes collections of animal tales, personal "truth tales", legends, poems, raps, sermons, and biographies depicting black language, life styles and a vivid struggle for survival.

However, prior to works such as Richard Wright's *Native Son* (1940), Anne Petry's *The Street* (1946), Ralph Ellison's *Invisible Man* (1952), Lorraine Hansbury's *Raisin in the Sun* (1959), Paul Laurence Dunbar's *Lyrics of Lowly Life* (1896) and Langston Hughes' *Not Without Laughter* (1930), black life was seen through the eyes and rhetoric of white authors (Emanuel and Gross, 1968). Black writers were not allowed a choice since publishers, editors and critics were all part of the white establishment. So, it was the dominant other who defined the roles of blacks, and this, in turn played a significant role in the construction of black stereotypes. Richard Wright (1940) assesses these models in black literature prior to the 1940's in the following statement

> Generally speaking Negro writing in the past has been confined to humble novels, poems, and plays, prim and decorous ambassadors who went a-begging to White America . . . dressed in the knee-pants of

servility . . . For the most part these artistic ambassadors were received as though they were French poodles who do clever tricks (p. xii).

Although Wright's analogy was somewhat harsh, black writers who protested racism or gave an accurate portrayal of black life were rare exceptions. Typically, black characters was personified as an inherently inferior creature.

The characters of Jim Crow, Friday in *Robinson Crusoe* and "Racoon" in *The Disappointment or, The Force of Credulity* in 1767 attributed to the progression of black stereotypical images in early American theater (Ploski and Williams, 1990). The nineteenth century minstrel shows also propagated dehumanizing racist stereotypes, portraying blacks in comic, witless and inferior roles (Hughes and Meltzer 1967; Sacks and Sacks 1993). This representation was a prime example of white perpetuation of black stereotypes. They defined the Negro lifestyle as pathos, tragic, a heritage of superstition and religious fervor and the "Negro" as humorous with whimsical dialects, music and fancies, all which became the "richest material" translating into hilarious stage performances for white minstrels (Paskman, 1928). White actors donned black faces and mimicked their perception of "black life." Blacks were depicted as savages, lazy, ignorant, content with their lot, and compliant in their enslavement (Branham, 1995; Ploski and Williams, 1990).

Film making in the 1920s to the 1940s also depicted blacks as domestics, savages or in objectionable musicals such as *Hallelujah*. The buffoonery of *Stepin Fetchit* and *Amos 'n Andy* serves as a commentary on these stereotypical myths perpetuated and sustained during this period.

Raisin in the Sun (hooks, 1990), was a turning point in black popular culture. It was a counter-hegemonic cultural production, and Lorraine Hansberry was proclaimed as prophetic and possessing visionary foresight. Bell hooks argues that education for critical consciousness is an important task for those in the academy and sees their literary mission as one of liberatory pedagogy through critical intervention. Thus, today, Hansberry's contemporaries, film maker Spike Lee, novelist Toni Morrison, poet Nikki Giovanni, rap artists Snoop Doggy Dogg, Bone, TLC, Ice Cube and numerous others continue the oral tradition by representing and exploring black life through the eyes of African-Americans, revealing poignant, insightful and experiential

accounts and imagery. Throughout history this imagery has been crucial.
Hooks (1992) states:

> The pain of learning that we cannot control our images, how we see
> ourselves (if our vision is not decolonized), or how we are seen is so
> intense that it rends us. It rips and tears at the seams of our efforts to
> construct and identify. Often it leaves us ravaged by repressed rage,
> feeling weary, dispirited, and sometimes just plain brokenhearted.
> These are the gaps in our psyche that are the spaces where mindless
> complicity, self-destructive rage, hatred, and paralyzing despair enter
> (pp. 3-4) .

She maintains that to thoroughly understand how blacks construct their
everyday world it is essential to examine popular culture and the media
experience, which includes literature, music, television, and film. The
ideological disposition of imagery determines not only how we perceive
see ourselves but how we are perceived by others.

In addition, popular culture is an arena where blacks can discover and
"play" with identification. Recently, a comprehensive anthology was
assembled from a black symposium entitled "Discussion in Contemporary
Culture." It is an amalgam of contestation, testament, theory, critique and
cultural consciousness. The authors contend that blacks are imagined and
represented to others (the audience) and themselves through popular
culture. They argue that there is a double consciousness—blackness and
whiteness—which hides the agenda of the privileged class. Popular
culture to which they refer as "black pleasure, black joy" is seen as an
alternative to opposition by representing the hopes, dreams and future for
African-Americans.

According to numerous researchers, black popular culture was
perceived as an element of change—culture in progress (Hughes and
Meltzer, 1967). In the past twenty years, four types of African-American
have evolved since the 1970s: Buppie, ambitious; B-Boys, tragedies of
poverty and molded by Hip-Hop; Bap, enjoys mainstream success; and,
Boho, free spirits. Of the four groups, the B-Boys are the most celebrated
and condemned because of their street knowledge, poverty and anger
(George, 1992). This study attempts to understand the roots and success
of rap and hip-hop, media expression, film makers, athletes, crack dealers,

schoolteachers and others who live in slightly different worlds but who are crucial to the development of African-American contemporary life. Michael Dyson (1993) echoes Langston and George's work, substantiating the complexity and diversity of black popular culture. He speaks of the evolutions and metamorphoses that have transpired from generation to generation. He asserts that black culture has been deliberately distorted and castigated by the dominant culture who view blacks as ugly and savage. He defends African-American popular culture stating that the heart of the growth "has taken the shape in defining interplay of historical contingency and the pursuit of a humane racial identity" (p. 53). Dyson contends that cultural expression must be understood within the confines of the environment and its relationship to economic, political and religious transformations. According to Dyson, black unity and survival continues to persevere because of the narratives of rhetorical strategy by black intellectuals, artists and leaders which imposes provisional order to the perplexing and chaotic politics of racial identity recounting historical and political incidents. He maintains that racial oppression greatly influences black popular culture from literature to Hip-Hop.

Arguing the cultural importance of Rap, Houston Baker (1993) asserts that rap music must be included in Black Studies, stating that Rap reflects the tension and energy of the black urban communities. According to Baker, Black Studies must provide an unbiased audience for the legitimacy of Rap and its contribution to black culture, as a means of black urban expressivity

Tricia Rose's (1994) emphasis on black culture was primarily in Hip-Hop and rap music. She writes a critical expose' on Hip-Hop, rap music and black culture and the debates that surround them. She concurs with Dent and Dyson that black culture has become a new social movement. Exploring the urban politics of the lyrics, music, culture, and themes, she integrates the social context in which Hip-Hop and rap music exist. She examines the ideological, cultural and sexual struggles contained in rap music and how the struggles are experienced by black youth in the music and epics which are, " a cultural expression that prioritizes black voices from the margins of urban America. A form of rhythmic, rhymed storytelling, electronically based music" (p. 2).

According to Kunjufu (1993) Hip-Hop is:

> Music centered, rebellious, the assertive voice of urban youth and is
> shaped by the language, culture, fashions, hairstyles, and world view of
> a generation alienated not only from Eurocentric dominant culture but
> to a surprising degree from its African American heritage. Hip-Hop is
> in many respects a classic youth oppositional subculture rejecting the
> norms and values of the mainstream, measuring success in terms of peer
> approval an equating power with the ability to influence the subculture
> constantly changing insider cues, taste and values (p. II).

Kunjunfu gives a psycho/social analysis of Hip-Hop vs. MAAT (a basis
for the ontological unity between God and humans). However, Robert
Jackson (1994) disagrees with Kunjunfu's negative connotations of
Hip-Hop. He sees it as an extension of be-bop and jazz; a cultural
transmitter, freedom of expression and the "second coming of jazz." He
gives an in-depth examination into hip-hop and rap and its effect on the
African-American community.

Bakari Kitwana (1994) takes rap to the next level, "gangsta rap", a
highly controversial and explosive form of rap music that has been
associated with escalating teen violence. He examines the components of
sexism, racism, gun violence, black culture and male-female relationships
from political, cultural and social perspectives. J.P. Campbell (1994,
N2:10) also perceives hardcore or "gangsta rap" as a powerful cultural
influence. He states that gangsta rap characterizes the conditions of ghetto
life, an existence that the mainstream refuses to acknowledge, "because
recognition would create responsibility for it" (p. 10) . He maintains that
in order to understand hardcore rap, first there must be an understanding
of what it is like to be black living in America and to confront negative
stereotypes on a daily basis such as being conceptualized as" shadows,"
"nightmares" and "numbers." Ralph Ellison's summarizes this sense of
frustration, " I am invisible, understand, simply because people refuse to
see me" (Bell, 1968, p. 23).

The black novel is another important element of the black popular
culture scene, together with Hip-Hop, rap music and films; it is yet an
additional facet in the construction of the black youth's *common sense*
world. Many black authors and their readers have experienced the

violence, discrimination and other factors associated with racist oppression. Fiction writers often give a remarkable resemblance to real life situations. Their personal vignettes voice the social inequities they have endured. Some verbalize their pain in humorous accounts and poetry while others divulge narratives of poverty, violence, and despair. But the common thread is enlightenment. Ralph Ellison (Bell, 1986) once said that "There must be possible a fiction which, leaving sociology and case histories to the scientists, can arrive at the truth about human condition, here and now, with all the bright magic of the fairy tale" (p. 135). Taking the same position, Nikki Giovanni states, "It's not a ladder we're climbing. It's literature we're producing. We cannot possibly leave it to history as a discipline nor to sociology nor science nor economics to tell the story of our people" (bell, 1986, p. 136). This implies that black fiction is complex and relevant to the issue of reality construction. It has varied approaches and different stories to tell, but most relate how black literature informs and communicates the stories of African American people. Some portray how children and police act out the roles of antagonist and protagonist in impoverished and drug torn communities. Others, reveal pain, decay, despair, violence, gang wars, historical events, ritual handed down from generation to generation. Creating a combination of truth and fiction intermingled to give convincing portrayals of black adolescents growing up in America

Black cinema also explores diverse themes in black life. Recently, black film makers: Spike Lee, *Do the Right Thing* (1989), *She Gotta Have It* (1986) , *School Daze* (1988), *Jungle Fever* (1991), *Malcolm X* (1992), *Mo' Better Blues* (1990) and *Clockers* (1995); John Singleton, *Boys N The Hood* (1991) and *Poetic Justice* (1993); The Hughes Brothers, *Menace II Society* (1993); MarioVan Peebles, *New Jack City* (1991) and *Posse* (1993); and Ernest R. Dickerson *Juice* (1992) focus on social conscience issues. And even more recently, films such as Arnon Milchan's *A Time to Kill* (1996) and John Singleton's *Rosewood* (1996) depicting the lives of blacks in south and the social struggles that they confronted.

Poverty is a highly complex social phenomenon and a myriad of factors are identified with it. Adolescence is also multifarious and a critical stage of human development. This analysis of the social construction of reality for these children is crucial in exploring the

complex factors. The diverse literature examined in this chapter provides
a holistic perspective to the study.

CHAPTER 3

Primary Socialization and Construction of Reality

The setting plays a critical role in the social construction of reality. The majority of children who are raised in poverty are victims of negative environments (Comer and Poussaint, 1975). According to Wilson (1978),

> Lack of resources or their proper utilization in the ghetto and the overwhelming abundance of adverse circumstances shapes the minds of the inhabitants, forces them to narrow their perspectives, to concentrate on adapting and surviving in those conditions, spends their cognitive talents on the trivialities of a highly fragmented environment and this forces them to take their pleasures where and when they find them, to take them immediately and to constantly seek escape—most by psychological means such as alcohol, drugs, chronic sexual involvement, to take from their fellow members through crime, whatever amount of scarce resources they may possess (p. 202).

Wilson's account provides insight into the manner by which the physical environment affects an individual's psychological development. These escapist experiences form part of the context in which children in poverty carry out their lives. And their schools also reflect the impact of the oppressive conditions of this environment. Though crime and violence are part of the culture, nevertheless these schools frequently function as sanctuaries for students.

The introduction of the students will provide a historical framework necessary to understand the primary socialization and construction of identity in their everyday world. According to Burger and Luckmann (1966) this, "identity is objectively defined as location in a certain world and can be subjectively appropriated only *along with* that world. The child learns that he is what he is called . . . which in turns implies a designated social location." As such, the children discuss their families, home environment, community and their location within the community.

THE SETTING

School X is in the Englewood district on the south side of Chicago. Ironically, this gang-troubled and crime-ridden community was thought to have derived its name from two ancient outlaws who lived before the days of Robin Hood and his Merry Men. The rogues, Adam Bell, Clym of the Clough, and William of Cloudsley, made their home in the forests of Oakwood, near Carlisle. Centuries later and prophetically, H.B. Lewis suggested that Junction Grove should more appropriately be renamed Englewood because of its luxuriant oak trees and opulent forest (Andreas, 1884).

Today Englewood has grown from a few settlers and railroad laborers to a population of 48,434. Of that number, 48, 027 (99.2%) are African-American and 224 (0.5%) are white. There are 11,067 (73%) single family dwellings and 4,136 (27%) multifamily dwellings. Of this number 4, 626 (27%) homes are owned by community members; 10, 374 (61%) are renter occupied. A full 1, 916 (12%) are vacant (U.S. Census Report [CR], 1994; Woodstock Institute, 1994).

The median household income is $13, 243, 27,183 persons are at or above the poverty status and 20,710 are below (CR, 1990). With a poverty rate of 43.2%, Englewood is one of Chicago's poorest communities, ranking ninth out of twelve. While the nation's poverty rate stands at 13.5%, Chicago's is 21.6% (Putenney and London, 1993). The average household income for Chicago is $26,301 [1990 Census of Population and Housing—selected population and housing characteristics in pending litigation, the City of Chicago is challenging these figures]. The labor force status for persons 16 years and older are listed in Table 1:

Table 1. Englewood Labor Force Status

	Male	Female
Labor Force	8278	8757
In Armed Forces	41	30
Civilian	8237	8727
Employed	5671	6746
Unemployed	2566	1981
*Not in Labor Force	6241	10315

*Students, housewives, retired workers, persons who are not employed and not looking for work, institutionalized persons, and persons doing only incidental unpaid family work (less than 15 hours during the reference week).

Figure 1. Englewood Labor Force Status (U.S. Census Report, 1994)

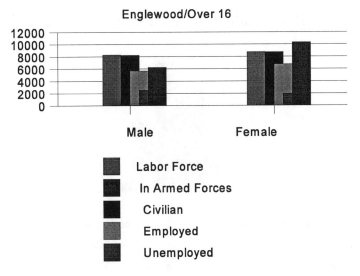

The educational attainment for persons 18 and over in the community are as listed in Table 2.

Table 2: Educational Attainment in Persons 18 and Over

	Total
Elementary (0 to 8 years)	4,303
High School (1 to 4 years) Diploma	8,632
High School (1 to 4 years) No Diploma	10,457
Some College, No Degree	5,645
Bachelor's Degree	850
Graduate or Professional Degree	34

Figure 2. Educational Attainment for Persons 18 and Over (U.S. Census Report, 1994)

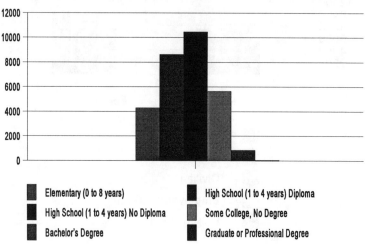

Statistics can provide a synopsis of life in impoverished communities. Although these numbers prove necessary for an analysis of poverty, they do not sufficiently reflect the reality that persists in disadvantaged areas. Gangs are such a reality. They are major cultural and economic forces in poverty areas. Gangs declare territorial dominance, marking their neighborhood turf with graffiti and symbolically advertising the gang's power and status. As such, graffiti warns and challenges rival gangs (Chicago Crime Commission, 1995). Schools in poverty areas are also gang turf and, so, they have major gang affiliations. School X allies primarily with the Gangster Disciples (GD), and to a lesser degree with the Black Disciples (BD) and Black Peacestones (BPS). For children reared in impoverished communities the gang creed is part of their earliest education. During the interviews, two participants explain the reality of being a small child in a gang-ridden area:

Jim: I grew up with the rough life. I didn't grow-up like nobody white. I didn't grow-up like that. I grew-up in the rough life I see things happen and been through things and know how it feels to be in the system and all that.

Q: Tell me about that. How did you grow up rough and knowing the system?

Jim: When I was little I used to see things that . . . people getting shot in the head, people get killed. I was little. I used to live around there an environment like that.

Q: Where were you living when you were little?

Jim: 57th and Wabash, 67th and Marquette, 73rd and Lowe and 71st and Racine and now I live at 71st and Troop. I saw everything that happened. But, I ain't scared, I got use to it. I grew up.

Q: There is a lot of gang activity around here, how does that affect you? Are you involved in a gang?

Sam: Yes.

Q: Which one?

Sam: GD.

Q: How long have you been in GD?

Sam: Three years.

Q: Three years. You are fourteen, so when you were twelve?

Sam: Eleven

Q: Is that the average age when you join?

Sam: No. There are some younger. Some nine or eight years old.
Q: Is this something recent with the young ones?
Sam: It started this year.
Q: So they are recruiting nine and eight-year-olds.
Sam: Yes.

Pooh explains that children as young as six are knowledgeable about gang activity. She describes how children become familiar with gang activity:

Q: Now look at the map, can you tell me which gangs control the schools? Are you familiar with the different gangs in the area? Is everyone in the neighborhood familiar with the area?
Pooh: Yes.
Q: Everyone knows? What about the little kids, six, seven or eight years old? Do they know the area?
Pooh: They smart enough to know
Q: Are they in gangs? Is it just part of growing up, knowing which areas you can and cannot go into? Is that a part of your education in the neighborhood?
Pooh: Yes.
Q: Okay. How do you find out about it? How do you learn where you can and cannot go?
Pooh: Because, if you go up in that area and see they have their hats a different way or the leg thing, if you pull up your leg on your pants, you can tell by that or you can see them doing a handshake or you see them throwing up a gang sign or a bunch of stuff. It's just you know which areas you can and cannot go in. Because people talk about it, they be like, well Stones are over by 74th and all up there.
Q: So it's just something understood in a sense.

The children must be conscious of gang signs, colors, and turfs for survival. When asked how, when, and what age they became aware, they answered, "you just know, it's something you grow up with." The areas surrounding the schools and parks also reflect the extensive influence that gangs have on the community. Children encounter warning signs posted on street corners and neighborhood parks discouraging gang activity. The signs read "Warning, Safe Zone. You have entered a Safe Park Zone: criminal penalties are severely increased for gang recruitment, activity and possessions, use or sale of drugs and weapons" (Chicago Park District, 1995). Around the schools signs read, "Warning, Safe School Zone, increased penalties for gang activities and the use, sale or possession of drugs and weapons in this area" (City of Chicago Project Clear, 1995). Gangs and gang activities are obtrusively pivotal in the construction of reality for adolescents living in the Englewood community. Gang graffiti on buildings, signs, stores, and schools signifies the gangs' hold on the community and its members.

The homes, schools, and residents reflect the futility of the situation. The children live in and develop through an environment of poverty, gangs, death, and decay. On a normal school day the children can walk in and around a sixteen-block radius, with an average of seventeen liquor stores and lounges, and 25.5 churches (mostly storefront churches), drug dealers, drug users, alcoholics, pimps and prostitute of all ages standing along the perimeters of the sidewalks and doorways. Many homes and buildings are in various stages of deterioration. Daily, the children at School X look out on a shelter for the homeless and six vacant six flats. They walk over sidewalks and streets in need of repair, and even their schools are marked by graffiti, boarded-up windows, and unsanitary facilities. This is the reality in which the participants live and through which they construct a common sense of the world.

The children in the community come from diverse living situations. Of 16, 674 children in households: 11, 830 (70.8%) live with parent(s). Of this number 2,830 children live in households headed by two married parents, 604 live with their fathers with no mother present and 8, 396 live with their mothers with no father present while 4,404 (26.4%) live with a relative and 422 (2.5%) live with a non relative.

THE PARTICIPANTS

The twenty participants, in a seventh/eighth grade split class, range in age from twelve to fourteen and are considered incorrigible by the staff. The dual level class was specifically selected to provide a greater range of adolescent age distribution. November 9, 1996 The A male teacher with the reputation as a strong disciplinarian was moved from a 4th grade class to teach the seventh/eighth grade split to accommodate the children's disciplinary needs. Several students have failed and are repeating a class.

Test bands in the IGAP for reading and math are 3.1-6.5 and 4.0-7.1 respectively in the seventh grade; 4.2-6.7 and 3.8-7.2 respectively in the eighth grade (scores are for the study group exclusively). The sixth and seventh grade scores used respectively for the seventh and eighth participants are Iowa Test of Basic Skills (ITBS). The following segments will introduce the members of the seventh/eighth grade split.

THE SEVENTH GRADERS

There are eleven seventh graders in the seventh/eighth grade split class. Although, fewer of the seventh graders than the eighth graders have gang involvement most of the students have one or more family members who are gang involved. The majority of these students live in single parent homes or with a relative.

Pooh

Pooh is an attractive, outspoken thirteen year old, although small in stature, her demeanor demands respect from her peers. Her appearance belies her street smartness and toughness. Her moods range from happy and carefree to belligerent and defiant. Pooh rarely backs down in a confrontation, whether it be with a peer or adult, male or female. Her brother G.T. refers to her as a "gang banger." She has also been accused of being a GD Queen, but she only admits to gang involvement in the Deuces or the 69th Street Girls. During an interview, a classmate discussed Pooh's gang involvement:

Q: Who runs this school?
Shas: Me.
Q: This is GD.
Shas: Oh, GD.
Q: Who from GD runs this school?
Shas: Most of the Boys like Sam, Nate.
Q: Who's in charge? Who is over them?
Shas: Little Boy, Nate and Ray.
Q: That's it?
Shas: That's all I know. Over the girls, see there is such a thing called false flag. Pooh, false flag.

Q: What does that mean?

Shas: Like if you call something that you are not, that's a false flag.

Q: What did she claim?

Shas: She claim she GD off the Dukes. But the First Lady off the Dukes told me she ain't GD over there, she ain't even GD and then you know people ask her, she say now I'm GD from 69th. But if the First Lady find out, they gonna jump on her. Even though they is cool. They real nice.

Q: Is she GD at all?

Shas: No. She just say she is, I ain't do that, cause I know what you will get. You'll get a pumpkin head. They will beat you so bad you head will swell.

Q: Does she do that to keep safe? Because she doesn't really want to be in a gang?

Shas: She do it that just to be doing it. She want to be GD so bad that she just scared to do it. She talk so much, she talk all that dope, she scared because she think she got all them to back her up. But they gonna do exactly what they did to Tina. They put all of us together and Tina went over there to fight this little girl and they stood right there and watched Tina get her butt kicked. And Tina still claiming GD from the Dukes.

Although Pooh's gang involvement is questionable, she is continuously involved in confrontive situations (according to her brother, Shashqua and the principal), and having serious problems at home.

Pooh has a 4.7 reading score and a 5.2 math score; she repeated the second grade. Although her standardized test scores are low, she receives above average to average grades and has excellent attendance.

Pooh has lived with her paternal grandmother for the past three years because of her mother's drug addiction. Her brother, G.T., an eighth grader is in the same classroom. Currently, the family is in court for reunification. During the interview Pooh discussed her family.

Pooh: . . . And now I live with my grandparents . . . I have been living with her for the past three years. Before that I lived with my aunt because my mother is on drugs. Now she went to rehab and now she is gonna to get us back in like, the next time we go to court. My father, he works at Clark and Division.

Q: Can you explain to me why he does not live with you?

Pooh: Because my mother don't like my father. She, me and my brother, my mother had three kids by my daddy but one of them died. My brother's name is Gus. My mom has another boyfriend. Well she had a couple of them since my daddy and her had us and then they broke up. I thought that we was gonna be the only three, G.T., Gus and me. I thought we were gonna to be three but while she was out there (rehab), she had another baby by this man . . . It was a boy . . . When she got through going to rehab, somebody in Peoria is keeping my little brother for her until we get through, until she gets settled and straight. Now we have overnight visits and my little brother . . . live with my mother now, She got her a place so we can move with her and that's when we go to court next.

Q: How many brothers and sisters do you have?

Pooh: About 14 or 15.

Q: Can you explain to me about your 14 or 15 brothers and sisters.

Pooh: See my mother, she got six kids.

Q: Where do your mother's children live?

Pooh: G.T. stays with my auntie. My brother Gus stays with my grandmother and me, and . . . stays in Peoria, and . . . stays with my momma. And my daddy just had two kids that are the same age. One is named . . . and one is . . . And my daddy had another baby which I don't think is his because he says its his around her but he says no because the girl don't even look like him. But we still count her as our sister. And I have a sister . . . and I have a brother . . .

Q: How old are your mother and father?

Pooh. Both of them are the same age, 32. My mom will be 33 next month. And my father will be 33 next year.

Q: How do you feel about living with your grandmother and not your mom?

Pooh: It feels okay.

Q: Where would you rather live?

Pooh: With my mom.

Q: Okay. So you have met with your case worker for reunification?

Pooh: Yea.

Q: When is your next court date?

Pooh: My mother don't know yet. She gonna tell my grandma when. Hopefully, it will be before Christmas.

Q: Now does that include G.T.?

Pooh: Yes.

Q: So that is all six of you?

Pooh: Yes.
Q: Okay. So she has found some place to stay?
Pooh: Yea.

Subsequently, Pooh was reunified with her mother. She had problems with the mother's live-in boyfriend and eventually ran away.

Wolf

Wolf is a thirteen-year-old with homicidal and suicidal tendencies. He is soft-spoken, with a quiet, but lethal, demeanor. Although his maternal grandmother is listed as the legal guardian, he has been moved from residence to residence by DCFS. Currently, he resides with his grandmother. According to Wolf's homeroom teacher, his mother is a drug addict and dying. Wolf claims little knowledge of anything related to his mother. He has lived sporadically with his grandmother since he was a small child. He started school on October 3, 1994 because he had just been released from the hospital. He had been attacked by a rival gang while he was living on the Westside. Wolf is a member of the G.D.s. He explains the incident during the interview:

Q: You were out of school for the first few weeks because of an incident,
           tell me what happened?
Wolf: I got jumped on.
Q: Who jumped on you?
Wolf: Another gang, some Folks
Q: Is that a name of a gang?
Wolf: Yep.
Q: And where were they from?
Wolf: The Westside.
Q: Do you know why they jumped on you?
Wolf: Yep.
Q: Tell me about it.
Wolf: Because I nearly killed one of their boys.
Q: How?
Wolf: By beating him with a sledge hammer.
Q: What prompted you to do that?
Wolf: Cause he tried to stick me up?
Q: When you say "stick me up," do you mean he tried to rob you?

Wolf:	Yep. He tried to shoot me too.
Q:	Did you have a gun?
Wolf:	Yea., I have one. I got two.
Q:	How did you come about getting a gun?
Wolf:	My father.
Q:	Your father what?
Wolf:	When I was a little kid, when we moved and came over here, I snuck two of my father's guns.
Q:	He doesn't know that you have them?
Wolf:	He should by now. He knows now. I told him.
Q:	How old were you when you took the guns?
Wolf:	Five or six.
Q:	Five or six, that's how long you have had the guns? Have you been recruited by a gang?
Wolf:	Yea.
Q:	Is that what happened with the incident?
Wolf:	Cause they jumped on me? Like I had told you, I almost killed one of their boys. And the police didn't do nothing about it. Cause they are scared.
Q:	They are afraid of the gangs?
Wolf:	Yep.
Q:	What gang were you recruited by?
Wolf:	GD.
Q:	Are you a member?
Wolf:	Yea.
Q:	How long have you been a member?
Wolf:	About five years.

Presently, Wolf complains of headaches and experiences some memory loss from the attack. His doctor has prescribed antibiotics for his condition, anticipating some memory recovery. Wolf stated that if he thinks too hard, his head hurts and he becomes agitated. He has the characteristics of a sociopath acting without conscience and no regard for right or wrong. He has been arrested six times in a one year period for the following offenses: car theft, attempted murder, robbery, drugs, and breaking and entering. About the attempted murder, the question asked:

Q:	What happened with the attempted murder charge? Was this the boy you beat with the sledge hammer?

Wolf: No.

Q: What happened this time?

Wolf: This was my little sister.

Q: What happened to her?

Wolf: I nearly stabbed her in the head with a butcher knife.

Q: How old is she?

Wolf: Around three or four years old.

Q: Is she older than you?

Wolf: No, she is four.

Q: She is three or four years old now?

Wolf: On her birthday, I don't even know, she is around six or seven. I don't know. And my little brother, he is around six or seven too. They are both around the same age.

Q: Well, tell me what happened.

Wolf: I don't know. She kept bothering me. I was baby-sitting and she kept making me mad. She sneaking out of the house when I told her not to, then she throw a temper tantrum, then I grabbed a knife and chased her downstairs and I nearly stabbed her in the head

Q: You stabbed her in the head?

Wolf: I nearly.

Q: What stopped you?

Wolf: It hit the wall.

Q: That's the only reason or were you just trying to scare her?

Wolf: I ain't trying to scare her, I was gonna do it.

Q: But you missed. Who found out about it?

Wolf: My stepmother.

Q: And what did she do?

Wolf: Called the police and then I ran. And the next day after that I got caught robbing a gas station.

Wolf has spent time in a residential institution in Peoria for adolescents and teens who are unmanageable and who have emotional problems. He calls the setting a "crazy home for kids." He was given six months but he escaped along with his stepbrother who was also institutionalized. Right now he is under house arrest. Wolf has a 5.4 reading score and 4.4 math score and repeated third grade. The school records validate this history: he receives average grades, is extremely artistic and creative, but the majority of his drawings relate to violence and death (see Wolf's Artwork).

Lee Lee

Lee Lee is a twelve-year-old, small in statue and well-groomed. She is one of the few girls in the group who has no gang involvement, although members of her immediate family are gang members. However, she is totally aware of gang signs, safe and unsafe areas in the community because it is a matter of survival; ignorance could mean death. When asked if she knew the different gang signs, she responded, "Yea, you see it around here." Lee Lee has a 6.5 reading score and a 7.1 math average, testing as high as 8.6 in math computations. Contrary to the rest of the group, Lee Lee receives all As and Bs and does her homework on a regular basis. Altercations with her peers and teachers are infrequent, but still happen on occasion. Like many students, she has moved excessively, having attended four schools in seven years (on occasion returning to a former school). One of her class remarked about her intellect, "She's smart to be black." When the other young woman was questioned about her perception, she insincerely responded she was joking and refuted her previous statement declaring, "all black people are smart." During the interview, Lee Lee talked about her family.

Lee:	I got three sisters, I am the second oldest.
Q:	How old are your sisters?
Lee:	Sixteen, eight and six.
Q:	Is the one sixteen in school?
Lee:	Yes.
Q:	Who else lives in your house?
Lee:	My momma's boyfriend, his daughter and my momma.
Q:	Can you tell me about your father?
Lee:	He lives on 87th. He lives with his girlfriend and my sister (the sixteen-year-old).
Q:	So who exactly lives in your house?
Lee:	My momma, her boyfriend, his daughter and me and my two sisters.
Q:	Are your mom and dad divorced?
Lee:	Yea.
Q:	Or should I ask if they were married first?
Lee:	They were married. My daddy is a construction worker but my mom don't work right now. She doesn't have a job.
Q:	Okay, then how does your mom receive her income?

Lee: I think she is on welfare.
Q: Does her boyfriend work?
Lee: No, but he does odd jobs.

Lee Lee and her three sisters have lived with her grandmother on several different occasions for various reasons. She explains one move, "My momma had trouble with her boyfriend and they were trying to get an apartment." She also stated that her grandmother could not handle her sixteen-year-old sister, who sells drugs, has been arrested and continually runs away. The sister now lives with her father. Since moving with her mother, Lee Lee feels unsafe and threatened.

Joseph

Joseph a thirteen years old who repeated third grade, is the most disruptive student in the class. He is continually and unsuccessfully disciplined by all of his teachers who send him to the principal's office on a regular basis. On April 7, 1995, he was placed in the EBD room for students with emotional and behavioral problems. He was born a "crack-baby." Joseph and his brother were abandoned by their mother at very young ages. Both children live with the paternal grandmother and step-grandfather. Joseph has been arrested four times this year. The step-grandfather often attempted to monitor Joseph's behavior in school, but he was unsuccessful. Conflicts arose at home between the grandparents. His grandmother wanted him to stay, but he had exhausted the patience of his step-grandfather and was told to leave. He moved to the projects with his aunt on February 7, 1995 but was back with his grandparents on March 1, 1995. Since then he has been removed from school in handcuffs twice, once for assaulting another student on the bus. In the second offense, Joseph beat a student from another school so badly that the boy's mother pressed criminal charges.

During the interview Joseph discussed his family situation:

Q: All right Joseph. One of the things I am interested in understanding is your everyday experience. Tell me something about yourself that will help me understand you and your views. The best way to do that is to discuss your family situation. Where you live, who lives in your house and then we will go on from that point.

Jos.:   My grandma, my aunties, my uncle and my brother and my three cousins.

Q: What about your grandfather?

Jos.:   And my grandfather. Well he talking about moving. And we gonna move with him.

Q: Who is we?

Jos: Me, my grandma and little cousins and my brother.

Q: Repeat that again. Who stays in the house?

Jos: My auntie, my other auntie, my uncle and my daddy, my grandma, my little cousin and my other little cousin and my brother and my other little cousin.

Q: How many people is that offhand?

Jos: About six.

Q: That's more than six. Do you live in a house or apartment building?

Jos: A house.

Q: How many bedrooms?

Jos: Five.

Q: You said that you have two aunts and an uncle?

Jos: Yea.

Q: How old are they?

Jos: My auntie she 28, my other auntie 25 and my uncle 22. They all brothers and sisters. And my daddy is 31.

Q: Is your daddy the oldest?

Jos: No, my auntie she 35.

Q: Are those your grandmother's children or your grandmother and grandfather's children?

Jos: My grandma's children.

Q: So your grandmother remarried. Where is your other grandfather?

Jos: He lives in Memphis.

Q: Do you have any contact with him?

Jos: Sometimes he calls us sometimes he don't. Sometimes we drive down there and see him.

Q: How many working adults are in the house?

Jos: My grandma, my grandfather, my daddy, and my auntie and my uncle.

Q: What does your grandmother do?

Jos: She works at AMA. American Medical Association.

Q: What does she do?

Jos: She cooks food for the handicap people and stuff.

Q: What does your grandfather do?

Jos: He works on the railroad tracks.

Q: And your dad?

Jos: He works at Burlington Coat Factory.

Q: Where is your mom?

Jos: My mom is in California.

Q: Do you have any contact with her?

Jos: She called me once.

Q: Once in your life or once this year?

Jos: Once this year. And she told us she was going to send us some stuff by the little brown trucks.

Q: United Parcel.

Jos: Yea. She said she was going to send us some clothes and stuff by those people. And they haven't came yet. My dad just buy me and my brother stuff.

Q: When was the last time you saw your mom? Do you know how it came about that you stay with your grandparents instead of your mother?

Jos: She left us at this house, her husband's house and his grand mamma and his sister live there. Then my grandma came and got us and said that these people were going to come to get me and my brother.

Q: DCFS?

Jos: Yea. So we started living with my grandma and my dad.

Q: How old were you?

Jos: Ten.

Q: You stayed with your mother up until the time you were ten?

Jos: Yes.

Q: Do you know why your mother left you and your brother?

Jos: No.

Q: Was she having some problems? Be honest with me , is she on drugs?

Jos: I saw her do it one time before. She was chopping rock, but I didn't see her do nothing else.

Although Joseph claims no longer to be a member of the GD's, the majority of his classmates identify him as a ranking gang leader and drug dealer in the school. Joseph's grandfather stated that a vital factor to be aware of when relating to Joseph is that he is a con artist. He warned, " you may think you are doing a study on him, but he will be doing a study on you." Adding credibility to the statements made by his classmates and grandfather, Joseph contradicted himself often and consistently, by drawing gang signs on his school folders and papers, periodically carrying large sums of money and repeatedly throwing up gang signs to other members in the class.

Anthony

Anthony is thirteen years old who lives with both parents. He claims no gang affiliation, but admits that his fourteen-year-old brother is a member of the GD's and was recently jailed for alleged robbery. He also stated that his twelve-year-old cousin was killed this summer by a gang. Anthony has three brothers and one sister. He transferred to the school in fifth grade and receives average grades and has average Iowa Tests of Basic Skills (ITBS) for his grade level (with room for improvement). Many classmates perceive Anthony as obnoxious. Some of his behavior can be attributed to immaturity. His homeroom teacher reports that he needs to improve his social skills and habits. He is a member of the band and basketball team. Anthony's home life appears to be more structured than many of his classmates. His mother and the principal attempted to place him in a bordering school to prevent harassment or injury from gangs, but were unsuccessful in their efforts.

R.J.

R.J. is a twelve year old who has attended School X since kindergarten. She has also lived in the same house for twelve years. She resides with her mother and six year old brother. Although her parents were never married, R.J. states that both are college graduates. R.J. is probably the only student attending the school who wears braces on her teeth. At the start of school she wore her hair stylishly braided and cut evenly in a "page boy," her uniform was crisply ironed and neat (a discernable contrast from many of her classmates). She is constantly ridiculed by her classmates and always the "butt of a joke" being called derogatory names such as "metal mouth," "needle mouth" "dog," and many other mocking adjectives. Although R.J. plays the game ascribed to her by her classmates and often by her teachers, she has average ITBS scores and school grades. At times she tires of the insults and lashes out, but the majority of the time she accepts the derision and "plays" the part. She has no gang involvement and no immediate family members in gangs.

Jason

Jason is a twelve year old who entered the school in sixth grade. He has attended three schools since his education began and has moved five times. He lives with his mother, one sister and two brothers. His parents were never married. Jason is consistently ostracized by his classmates. Although R.J. is ridiculed by the students, she is not excluded like Jason. At times his behavior can be described as bizarre. During the interview, he was questioned about his friends, he responded:

Q: Okay, what about your friends? You have not mentioned any friendships.

Jason: I don't have any.

Q: Is there any particular reason that you don't have friends?

Jason: It's hard trying to make friends.

Q: Okay, can you tell me a little more about that?

Jason: See everywhere I move to, every school I go to, somebody always tries to beat me up. See that's why it's hard for me to make friends.

Q: Do you have any idea why they try to beat you up?

Jason: No.

Jason's reality is quite different from the other children's. He stated that he wants to be a priest like his father and grandfather, when the definition of a priest was given, it was suggested that they were possibly ministers. He responded "maybe." Jason has strong religious affiliations. He used to sing in the church choir, but was dismissed because of an unusual incident, ironically by his aunt who is the choir director. He is a member of the school choir and band. During the interview he stated that he wants to be a gospel singer instead of a priest.

Jason has low ITBS scores and receives average to below grades. He rarely does homework and spends most of his time in class daydreaming and fantasizing. At age twelve Jason does not know how to write in cursive. He has no gang affiliation, but one of his brothers seemly is linked to a gang in the neighborhood.

Dan

Dan is also twelve years old and lives with both parents and his brother and sister. He stated both parents were in the army and both completed college. Unlike his peers, Dan and his family set aside one day in the week for family night when they go out for dinner. Dan is the president of the youth club at his church, attends bible class, a member of the Boy Scouts, on a park district football team and works at the police station. He moved from Gary, Indiana at five years old to his present home. He has attended the school since kindergarten.

Dan has resisted gang recruitment through his involvement with the church and family support. He has been approached and threatened by gangs on several different occasions. Subsequently, gang members have been bold enough to knock on his door and ask his parents if he could come out, unknowingly they consented, and when he resisted and went back into the house, they threw eggs at his door. Although Dan has resisted recruitment, he is very much aware of the gang signs, territories and activities.

Academically, Dan has the highest ITBS scores of the seventh graders in the group. His scores are at grade level and above. Classroom grades are above average.

Keisha

Keisha is an attractive, neat, and well groomed young lady. Her appearance contrasts sharply with most of the other girls in the class in demeanor, dress, style and ability. Many girls in the class are jealous of her. The boys however constantly "shower" her with attention.

She transferred to the school on September 12, 1994. After attending for two weeks, she ran away several times, each time she stayed with her father and his family. She stated that none of her friends attended the school and that her mother was having problems with her stepfather. Keisha's mother is also concerned because of Keisha's association with an eighteen-year-old girl who is not in school. Keisha lives with her mother and stepfather. Her mother and biological father were never married. During the interview she commented on the her home situation:

K: I ran away cause my mom and step-dad are always arguing. He always starts that. Like if me and my mom go out somewhere when we come back like at 11:00, he gets mad and starts fussing and other stuff. And I get tired of it. He just ran our phone bill up and don't want to pay and my momma paid it anyway. She said if she don't get her money, she is going to sue him.

Q: Do you get along with him?

K: Sometimes I do, sometimes I don't. Sometimes he know my momma gets paid and she don't want to give him her money and he still ask for it or when my momma give him the money to give to be cause she has to be a work at 5:00 A.M. she'll give him twenty dollars to give to me and he won't even give it to me.

Keisha's records were not available. However, her reading skills are more advanced than those of the children in the room, including the eighth-grade class. She does not interact with the other girls in the class, but will talk to the boys.

Nicki

Nicki is thirteen and repeated the fifth grade. She entered the school in 1990 in fourth grade. Her ITBS scores are almost at grade level. Her classroom grades are average and below. She has encountered personality problems with several of her homeroom teachers, which possibly accounts for the failure in fifth grade. She pouts constantly and is inattentive is class. Nicki is the youngest of six children. During the interview she discussed her family:

N: I got four sisters and one brother and my momma said I have two brothers on my father's side ages thirty-four and thirty.

Q: How old are they?

N: My sister just made twenty-eight yesterday, my older sister is thirty, my older brother just made thirty and my other sisters are twenty-six and twenty-five. Just me and my momma live together.

Q: Were your mom and dad married?

N: They were never married, they just lived together.

Q: Are your sisters and brothers all by the same mother and father?

N: No. My sisters, my momma married my sisters father. I had a different father from my sisters and brothers. My momma was married to their father but they divorced.

Although Nicki claims no gang involvement, she admits other family members have been recruited.

THE EIGHTH GRADERS

The eight-grade section originally consisted of twelve students. One of the twelve students attended twice for the school year and another transferred after two weeks of school. The eighth graders were more mature and more streetwise than most of their seventh grade counterparts. All of the twelve students were gang members, most claiming allegiance to the Gangster Disciples. The students came from single family homes or lived with a relative, typically a grandmother or aunt. Most of the boys had been arrested at least one time for various infractions of the law such as selling drugs, theft, and/or curfew.

Sly

Sly is a fourteen-year-old male. His hair is long, unkempt and braided into five sections. He lives with his grandmother. His total appearance is unclean. Since entering school in 1985, he has attended four schools; he averages 67.5 days' absences a school year and as many as 124 days in a school year. Currently he is truant, attending school only twice since it began. Although upon entering school his test scores were at and above grade level, they decreased at a consistent rate. He repeated first, fifth and sixth grade.

Sly uses profanity constantly. He does not complete a sentence without using expletives. He is an active gang member and has been implicated by the majority of his classmates as a big drug dealer and user.

Tina

Tina is a thirteen-year-old who has transferred seven times since entering school in September of 1986. She entered school X in December 1991 and transferred in September 1994. Her ITBS scores are below grade level; however, she has maintained average grades and has not repeated any levels.

Maykeyla

Maykeyla is thirteen years old. She entered school in September 1986 and has never transferred or repeated a class. She has the highest ITBS scores in the group, slightly above average in math (7.7), and somewhat below grade level in reading (6.2). She receives average to above average grades and has excellent attendance. Maykeyla is the most outspoken member in the class and has an explosive temper. She has artistic ability and is on the boy's basketball team.

Maykela is the youngest of fourteen children. Her mother and father moved from the south, lived together until she was four, but never married. She lived with her mother and stepfather until a recent dispute, and now she resides with her aunt. Maykela claims no gang involvement, but four of her nine brothers are GDs. She stated seven of her nine brothers have been arrested. At the time of the interview, one brother was in jail for a gang related battery incident and another had been shot in face. Her twenty-four year old brother is Chief of Violation (see figure 6, p.183) and her eighteen-year-old brother is a First C (see figure 6, p. 183). According to Maykela her brothers have given her the following advise, "They know they'd be doing wrong. They tell me don't be in no gang. Go to school, go to college and be someone. Don't act like them." Maykela revealed during the interview that she receives pressure from her peers to join GD,

Q: Do the girls try to recruit you?

May: There's a couple of them in my classroom, they be trying to give me the business.

Q: What do you tell them?

May: No.

Q: And they just accept no. Do they ever pressure you?

May: They keep trying and trying and trying. They still try.

Q: What do they say to you?

May: They be like you know_____, I'll be like yeah, they like she's so smart, she's town coordinator. They like don't you want to be GD? I'll be like no. Don't you know Nicole? She's like why don't you want to be GD? I'm like I don't want to be no G.D. Then she told me a whole lot of stuff.

Q: Nicole is GD?

May: Yeah. Then she be telling me how many girls they are going to get and
       how they plan it and kill people and stuff.

Q: That's what Nicole told you?

May: Huh huh. She's doing it for real because she and my brothers are in the
       same gang.

Q: Who else tries to recruit you?

May: That's the only girl. Don't no boys, because they know my brothers and
       my brothers tell them don't being trying to get me into their stuff.

Q: Have you ever talked to them about being in the gang?

May: My brothers ain't going to listen to me. They going to hardly listen. I
       barely see my brothers. Cause most of my brothers don't live with me.
       So I don't see them on a everyday basis.

Q: What do you think the worst part of being in a gang is? What fears do
       you have for your brothers?

May: I fear for them about everything because when they sale drugs they can
       end up in jail for so many years and stuff and then they can end up
       getting shot when they go different place like or be taking me, like
       when I go to Zake's house and stuff. People be there messin with them
       when we get in the car, so I scared to ask them to take me places. I
       don't want nothing to be my fault.

Q: Okay. Are you afraid of them being shot?

May: A couple of them been shot. One of them was in a wheelchair. They
       shot him in the leg, thigh, heart, arm, and shoulder. They shot him
       seven times.

Q: And he is still around? Which one was this?

May: Huh huh. Mark. It was not in his heart, but it went through his chest. It
       was horrible. It went in his chest. My mamma said it must have been
       God. It went in so far and just turned and came out his arm.

Q: Is he still in the wheelchair?

May: Uh uh. He got a rod in his leg because it fractured his bone. And he
       limps.

Q: What about your other two brothers who were shot. What happened to
       them?

May: Well my brother got shot in the face with a Tac nine. He got shot in the
       face by some Vice Lords. He was dropping his friend off and him and
       his friends are G.D., so he got shot from just being there. And they ain't
       seen him, They didn't know he wasn't in no gang because he had on no
       hat, but his friend was in the Vice Lords last year, was taking his baby
       home with his hat turned to the right and they had theirs turned to the
       back so they shot him. They killed him.

Q: So at the same time they shot your brother in the face, they killed his friend?

May: Huh huh.

Q: Were there two friends or just one?

May: There were two friends. They shot one in the stomach and all over the front and stuff. He was coming off the porch and they shot him everywhere and then he ran and jumped. My brother had a foam roof and he jumped in there and then one went up to the car and he shot my brother in the face and then he started shooting at the ones in the back. I don't know, he said he lost control then, he just put his foot on the gas and just kept on going and then when he got to a red light, he just collapsed and he just let it go and that's when the police crashed into him and knocked him into a tree. And that's how his car got totaled.

Q: How long ago was this?

May: Like this summer. It was this summer. He saved the two boys lives and the other one died like five hours later, then the other one lived. The one they shot in the stomach, he lived for almost a month and then he died.

Q: So both of his friends ended up dying?

May: Yeah. He's the only one left alive.

Q: And this is the one that got out of the gang?

May: Huh huh. After school he got out. That's what made him go back to school. Then he said he wished that didn't have to happen to show him. He said that's the only way, because he said if it wasn't for that he probably still be in the gang.

Q: When he dropped his flag, what happened to him? What did they do?

May: They didn't do nothing because he had rank. Once you get rank and you drop your flag because like when you first get in you Boss and then when you get higher and you rank DOC and once you get DOC then you can drop your flag.

Q: What's a DOC?

May: DOC like. I don't know what it means, all I know is that you can get out.

Q: Okay. So they don't have to get what do you call it, go on the wall, when they drop their flag?

May: Violations, because if you still boss then like they get thirty seconds to shoot at you or put your head on a fence where the spokes come out of it and hit it with a bat like that. They can beat you up to fifteen minutes or stuff like that or do a lot. It's whatever they choose. Some of them

have favoritism and they hit some of them soft and let them drop their
flag, but some they hate so they kill them on purpose.

Q: Do they give them opportunity to run? What do they do?

May: They like tell them to come in and they won't drop their flag. So they
will be like on their set where they have their meeting at. And then they
just run so far in the distance where he can hide but they only have
thirty seconds to try to kill him, if they want or they can put his hands
on the fence where they can beat him up or most times they will beat
him up for five or fifteen minutes.

Maykela's brothers' gang involvements have made her more determined
to be successful in school. Because of her brothers many court
appearances, she has become very impressed with the courts and the
lawyers in particular. Her ambition is to become a lawyer. She is very
involved in school activities and has the most potential in the class.

G.T.

G.T. is the fourteen-year-old brother of Pooh. He entered the school on
October 28, 1985, transferred on October 19, 1987, transferred again in
September 1988 and reentered School X on September 21, 1989. His
ITBS scores are at grade level in math (7.2) and below average in reading
(4.5). G.T. receives special services for a learning disability once a day.
During the interview G.T. discussed his family and his gang involvement.

Q: Tell me who lives with you or who you live with?

G.T. I live with my auntie.

Q: Who else lives in the house?

G.T: My cousins.

Q: I need to know all the people that live in your house. So if you live with
your aunt and cousins how many cousins live in the house?

G.T.: 6,7

Q: 7? Do you know their ages?

G.T: Yes. A girl is 18, a girl 12, a boy 14, a little boy 7 and a girl 5.

Q: And then there is you. Is this your mother's sister or your father's
sister?

G.T: My mother's auntie. She is my great auntie.

Q: Okay. Is she married?

G.T: No.

Q: Who do the children belong to?

G.T: To my aunt. My momma's sister's children.

Q: Where is your mother's sister?

G.T: I don't know where she is.

Q: Okay. Why doesn't she have her children?

G.T: She was out on the streets and not doing what she suppose to.

Q: Is she out on the streets because she is on drugs?

G.T: Yes.

Q: And your mom?

G.T: She was doing the same thing.

Q: Where is your mom now?

G.T: My mom got herself settled down and got an apartment . . .

Q: How does that affect you?

G.T: It don't affect me at all and I'm fixin to move back with her . . . in about a month.

Q: You and Pooh?

G.T: Yes . . . in December (1994) or January (1995).

Q: How many brothers and sisters do you have?

G.T: I got ten brothers . . . and about seven or eight sisters . . . my mom has five . . . one of my little brothers live with my mom. The other lives with a foster family in Peoria and one lives with Pooh . . . he is ten and goes to school here . . . my father has about fifteen . . . the oldest is twenty-three or twenty-four . . . I am the youngest of my father's children.

Q: How old is your dad?

G.T: Thirty-five.

Q: So he was about thirteen when he had his first child?

G.T: Fourteen.

Q: How old is your mom?

G.T: Thirty-two

Q: Are you your mom's oldest child?

G.T: Yes.

Q: Did your mom finish high school?

G.T: Nope.

Q: How far did she go?

G.T: Sophomore.

Q: Do you know why she dropped out?

G.T: Nope. She never told me.

Q: Was it because of the drug problem?

G.T:	No. She started that when she had my other little brother . . . he's ten, but she started when he was five . . . the social worker said he could not come to see us.
Q:	Did you ever live with your mom?
G.T:	Yea. Before she got on drugs.
Q:	So all of you lived with your mom?
G.T:	Just three of us at the time . . . She had one when she was still doing it. It got taken away. But when she stopped, she had the other one.
Q:	How did you and Pooh get separated? Did DCFS do that?
G.T:	No. Her grandma took custody of her. She was once living with me. But then she wanted to live with her grandma and her grandma said she would take her.
Q:	What is your mom doing now?
G.T:	She is trying to get herself back together. So she is on general assistance.
Q:	Are you involved in a gang?
G.T:	Yes. I got out and then I got back in because I liked the way they were running the organization.
Q:	How long were you involved in the gang?
G. T:	Ever since I was twelve . . . my cousin got me into it . . . when he started he was about nine.
Q:	Which one are we talking about and what were they doing that you liked?
G.T:	GDs . . . They was keeping the area clean. If you throw paper down, that a fine. That how they was . . . They like help you with you school work and all that . . . They make sure you stay in school. They got laws that you have to go by. That you got to learn. If you break them, one of the laws is stayin' in school. If they catch you out of school, you get a violation.

G.T. also discussed the violence, money and drug dealings associated with being a gang member.

Thomas

Thomas is fourteen years old and one of the most well-groomed boys in the class. His seventh grade reading and math scores are 5.1 and 4.5 respectively. He also receives a resource class for a LD. He is an only child who lives with his father who was twenty-three when Thomas was born. His mother was fifteen years old. His parents were never married and consequently his mother gave up custody when Thomas was four years old. He has not seen or talked to his mother since the court hearing.

Thomas and his father recently moved from Mississippi. He has attended School X for one year. Although, newly returning to the city, he is an admitted Gangster Disciple.

Nate

Nate is a fourteen-year-old gang member with a reddish-blond streak in his hair. He has earned the rank of Chief Enforcer with the group where he is "plugged." Nate talks about his gang affiliation during the interview:

Q: What does plugged mean?
Nate: To join.
Q: Do you belong?
Nate: Yes.
Q: You pay dues? How much do you pay?
Nate: A dollar. Then somebody in the seventh grade he talk about paying a quarter everyday you in school.
Q: Who?
Nate: Joseph.
Q: This is Joseph and the gang? GD? So he told you he ranks over you? What is he?
Nate: First C. He ain't First C in the gang, he First C in the school, cause at a session two weeks ago, they told him that he was the First C in the school and he was giving out spots in the school, like for more positions.
Q: So he can do that? So he has rank?
Nate: Yea. He was giving out more rank at school.
Q: Do you have rank?
Nate: Chief Enforcer.
Q: What does a Chief Enforcer do?
Nate: He give out mouth shots and all that.
Q: What happens with a violation? What do they do?
Nate: A minute on the wall. One of the people will strap you up and the other boy, he punch you, so he has to hit you everywhere he can for a minute.

Nate was initiated by his sixteen-year-old brother who is also a Gangster Disciple. The boys live with their mother, who is a homemaker and father who works for a moving company. Neither parent received a high school diploma. The mother dropped out sophomore year and the father dropped out in his junior year. The boys are allowed to stay out to 10:30 on school nights and 12:00 on the weekends. Consequently, Nate is frequently unable to stay awake in class.

Nate's ITBS scores in reading and math are 5.8 and 5.7 respectively. He has excellent attendance, but his grades range from average to unsatisfactory. His conduct is borderline and needs to improve to "unsatisfactory." Nate feels a need to seek attention from each of his female instructors. His homeroom teacher commented that Nate's mother ignores him.

Jim

Jim, a fourteen-year-old member of the Gangster Disciplines, was recently released from the Audie Home. He returned to school on September 28, 1996. Jim has been arrested six times for various charges ranging from stolen cars to accessory to murder. At the time of the interview he was on "house arrest." The authorities allowed him to go to school, but he had to be at home by three o'clock to check in with his probation officer. He was only able to leave the house for school or when accompanied by his mother. During the interview, he discussed the arrests and his philosophy about his gang affiliation:

Q: . . . What happened the first time you were arrested and how old were you?

Jim: First time I went to jail I was driving a stolen car, I was twelve. Second time, curfew, I went to the station.

Q: How old were you?

Jim: Still twelve. Then I was arrested for criminal trespassing. I was in somebody's car and the other person was driving, I was the passenger and they gave me criminal trespassing. I wasn't suppose to be in the car.

Q: What do you mean you weren't supposed to be in the car? Whose car were you in?

Jim: I don't know.

Q: You don't know whose car you were in Jim?

Jim: I don't know. It was some man's car we had bought it from. And he said we had stole it from him.

Q: And that was the fourth time. What happened next?

Jim: Mob action, walking on the street late at night with more than four people.

Q: And the fifth time.

Jim: Violating probation.

Q: From what?

Jim: Not going to school.

Q: And the sixth time?

Jim: Same thing.

Q: You told me there were some different charges earlier. Didn't you tell me something about attempted murder?

Jim: No, I had accessory to murder.

Q: What happened?

Jim: That was when we was in the car with mob action and one of the guys had a gun, and the gun was supposed to have a murder on it, so they said I had accessory to murder. I beat that case.

Q: What does it mean to you being a GD. How important is it to you?

Jim: It ain't important. You win, you in it to win. Just being whatever. For protection.

Q: So you aren't in it for any other reason, just for protection? Why are you in? Tell me.

Jim: Cause I just want to be in it. I make myself in it.

Q: I understand that, but, what are the reasons that you are in it?

Jim: I want to grow and develop.

Q: Grow and develop. What do you mean?

Jim: GD's are smart. I know a GD right now, today he go to college. GD's go to school. You got to go to school.

Q: How do you get a gun?

Jim: Just from being around the neighborhood for a long time. Like a person like me, everybody know you, give you connections, buy you things for a little protection. I could get you one if you wanted to be protected. If you don't. It is on you.

Q: I asked you before about your six arrests, whether or not it is something you are proud of. I am going to ask you again. How do you feel about the six arrests?

Jim: I ain't proud of it. Just got arrested six times. I'm through with it now, I guess, got to do, that's what I got to do.

Q: Has the judge ever said to you "If I see you in here again I'm going to do such and such to you?

Jim: He try to scare you. He say if I see you again I'm going to hold you in custody. You don't listen to that.

Q: What do you mean you don't listen?

Jim: If you go back in jail you gonna do some time. It's gonna be meant for you. They send you to jail, God sending you a message. Once the man upstairs saids you got to go to jail, get sick, catch cancer, aides, ain't nothing you can do about it, you got to live with it. Maybe if you on the street, you might get kilt.

Jim also commented on his family situation:

Q: Who do you live with?

Jim: My mother and stepfather, my stepfather don't live there, he just be over there.

Q: Who else lives in your house?

Jim: My sister.

Q: How old is she?

Jim: Twenty-one. My little brother who's nine, my little sister that's six, my nephew that's three and my other nephew that's one, my niece that's five months.

Q: Whose children are your niece and nephews?

Jim: My sister, she got three kids.

Q: Is your sister married?

Jim: No.

Q: How old is your mom?

Jim: Thirty-four.

Q: Your sister is twenty-one and your mom is thirty-four?

Jim: No. She is thirty-six. She was just thirty-five, her birthday just pasted so she thirty-six.

Q: So she was fourteen or fifteen when she had your sister.

Jim: Fifteen.

Q: She had to get pregnant at fourteen.

Jim: Right.

Q: Where's your dad?

Jim: He's dead.

Q: What happened to him?

Jim: Caught in a fire with a car. A fire kept coming to his car and it blew up. I guess, that's what they told me.

Q: Was your mom married to your dad?

Jim: No.

Q: Do you and your older sister have the same father?
Jim: Yep.
Q: What about the other two?
Jim: A different father. My stepfather.

Excluding Jim's two stays in the Audie Home, he has attended six different schools. He enrolled in School X on March 3, 1993. Jim's ITBS scores in reading and math are 6.0 and 6.7 respectively. He has received average and above average grades throughout school; until eighth grade his attendance had been very good. Jim wants to be a rapper. He is able to memorize the intricate wording and rhythm of the music, singing and dancing incessively throughout the day. Currently Jim is in the Cook County Juvenile Detention Center awaiting trial on a murder charge.

Shasaqua (Shas)

Shasaqua a fourteen years old, unlike most of the students she has attended School X since kindergarten. However, she moved to New Orleans on November 4, 1987 and returned to Chicago and School X on February 23, 1988. Her standardized test scores have been slightly below average throughout grades one through seven. Shasaqua repeated third grade because of her poor reading skills. Her seventh grade reading and math ITBS scores are 6.7 and 6.4 respectively.

Shasaqua's mother dropped out of high school when she became pregnant with her. She also attended School X. Shasaqua talks freely about her family and her gang involvement during the interview:

Q: We will start with who lives in your house.
Shas: My mother, my auntie, my grandmother, my auntie's two kids, my mother's kids is me, and my little brother and sister and my cousin.
Q: Is your mom married?
Shas: No?
Q: Was she married to your dad?
Shas: No.
Q: Now was your mother in a Gang?
Shas: My momma was in every gang there was. My mother was a OG, a BG, BD. A Blackstone, she was a Black Peace Stone, and she was Folks, a Vice Lord, a RVL. She was like in every gang there was. But my

momma had so much rank that they said she had her first child, the first child was goin to be Folks would live and die as Folks, no matter what. No matter what that child choose to be. But, I don't know how, but see when they said that and then I was GD, or whatever, something happened. See they jumped on me, that's when they did wrong. and then I went back and told my momma, and momma had you know, dropped all that gang stuff when she had me. Cause when My momma was little, my momma used to be devious. She would shoot you in a minute.

Q: Has she ever shot anybody?

Shas: I think so. Not that I know of but I know my momma has shot many a people. Shot at somebody.

Q: Has she ever been arrested?

Shas: Yes. Plenty of times.

Q: Has she served time in jail?

Shas: Yea. They said about two years, something like that. That was before she had me. She was seventeen. It was about two years and then she got out of jail and she got pregnant. Then she dropped everything.

Q: What did they have her in jail for the last time?

Shas: Assault and battery and attempted murder. Three counts of attempted murder.

Q: You said your mother had a high rank in the gang?

Shas: It was like everybody knew her. Didn't nobody bother her, it was like.

Q: What did they call her?

Shas: They called her the Big OG, the First C, Regent, Second C, all that stuff, The First Lady and when you First Lady ain't nobody can say nothing to you. Can't nobody tell you nothing wrong. Everybody respect you. Wrong or you know. If something happens you got to stand there, tell them what to do, when to do it, what time, whatever. In other words, my mother was just oooh! Then when she started doing drugs whatever, her whole life just changed.

Q: Did she sell drugs before then?

Shas: Yea. When she was young she use to sale them.

Q: How do you feel about drugs?

Shas: I don't like it. Tell you the truth I really don't. I can't stand it. The first time I saw my momma do it . . .

Q: What did she use?

Shas: The pipe, it's clear and you inhale (crack). But the first time I saw my momma, I was real little and I just busted in the room, she didn't know

I was standing there and I wanted to slap it out of her hand, then I took my little sister and then I ran.

Q: How old were you then?

Shas: I was six. No eight or nine.

Q: You knew what she was doing?

Shas: Yea. I knew what she was doing.

Q: So she had a pipe. Did she use a needle?

Shas: No.

Q: Just smoke. What crack or rocks?

Shas: Yea, rocks.

Q: Are you in a gang?

Shas: Yes.

Q: Which one?

Shas: Black Peace Stone (BPS).

Q: That's an oddity in this area. Isn't it? How do you get away with being a BPS in a GD area?

Shas: Yea. I don't know., you know everybody know me, everybody around here know me and most of the people around here know I'm a BPS but you know they just say "she cool, that's Shasaqua, that's my girl," cause all of us grew up together. But I don't go around gang bangin or nothin like that, it is just what I am.

Q: Why are you in a gang?

Shas: I don't know . Probably because, see when I was comin up, my mother was on the street. When I was little, my mother was on drugs for about four or five years and during that time my grandmother was taking care of me and my family and also the BPS and GDs. It's like GDs over here are watching my back and I go to my cousins house and they watch my back and then they take care of me, every time I needed something that I don't have to ask, they just give to me.

Q: Now if a boy was in your situation as a BPS, how would it be for him to live in the area? Could a boy do what you are doing?

Shas: Not really.

Shasaqua's BPS gang involvement has led to several physical altercations, even one that included family members. Shasaqua continues to talk about her family and their history of gang affiliation.

Q: How many living brothers and sister does your mother have? Tell me something about them.

Shas: She had five brothers and four sisters?

Q: Were they in gangs?

Shas: I don't about them (speaking of her oldest aunt and uncle, who are 43 and 40 respectively). But they was most likely. Everybody in my whole family has been in a gang.

Q: Where are they now, your uncles and aunts? I know you live with one.

Shas: Yea. My youngest uncle, he's in jail, my next uncle's in jail.

Q: How old is your youngest uncle?

Shas: He twenty-three.

Q: Why is he in jail?

Shas: First they had him for first degree murder. He had twenty-eight years, then they dropped all charges because they had no proof of nothing.

Q: Was that gang related?

Shas: Yea. They said he had beat a little boy to a slow death because he was in a Gang, but he didn't, his friend did. They pinned it on him.

Q: How old is your other uncle?

Shas: He's about twenty-nine now.

Q: What is he in jail for?

Shas: For armed robbery and car theft. All this dumb stuff. He was on drugs too, so then he got off drugs. Now he is in jail.

Q: How long has he been in jail?

Shas: He's been in jail for a year now.

Q: Anybody else in jail?

Shas: My Uncle Jody just got out of jail. He lives in the suburbs.

Q: That's your third uncle. What did he do?

Shas: He stabbed this boy in the neck because he tried to come over to his house to get daughter. His daughter is pregnant by this boy and this boy came over cussing him out and he stabbed him in the neck with a ice pick.

Q: Is that gang related?

Shas: No. Then my other uncle, the police be looking for him. They fixin to take him to jail because he used to do drugs and he stole one thousand dollars from where he used to work at 71st, at a bowling alley.

Q: But they haven't found him?

Shas: No.

Q: Is that all of the boys?

Shas: Yea. None of the females are in jail. The fifth boy just got out of the hospital for a kidney transplant. He walk around here working.

Q: Who gave him the kidney?

Shas: My auntie. The one that comes here for writing class. . . she gave him a kidney.

Q: Was he in a gang?

Shas: Yea. He was a GD.

Q: Okay. That's something. What about your dad? Where is he?

Shas: God knows. The last time I heard from him I was nine and I called my grandmother every day to find out if she heard from him and she say "Yea, I saw him yesterday" or something like that. I tell her if you see him, tell him to call me or see me or something because one day he was across the street from our house and he didn't ever come see me. And that was two days before my birthday. And then when my birthday came around, he called and about a week later he called and I asked him where he was and he said he was at the station on my birthday, coming from out of town.

Q: Does he work?

Shas: Yea.

Q: What about your mom? Does she work?

Shas: She hasn't worked. She stay home and take care of the kids. She looking for a job. She gonna get a job.

Q: So she is on government assistance?

Shas: Yea.

Q: What about your grandmother? Does she work?

Shas: No. My grandmother don't work.

Q: Is she on assistance?

Shas: Yea.

Q: What about your aunt?

Shas: No.

Shasaqua is assertive and is always ready to defend herself.

Sam

Fourteen year old Sam is the largest boy in the class. He could easily be mistaken for a high school student. However, once a conversation has been initiated, it is immediately clear that Sam is merely a large fourteen year old. He has attended School X since kindergarten. Both of his parents also attended the school. Sam's ITBS reading and math scores are 6.5 and 7.1, respectively, and he receives average grades.

He lives with his grandparents and admits to being a GD for the past three years. Sam discusses the reason that he lives with his maternal grandparents instead of his mother and his gang involvement:

Q: Tell me the members of your family. Who lives in your house?
Sam: Me, my grandfather, my gramma, my auntie, both aunties.
Q: Are you the only child in the house?
Sam: Yea.
Q: Where's your mom?
Sam: She probably be on . . .
Q: How long have you lived with your grandparents?
Sam: All of my life.
Q: Can you tell me why you do not live with your mother?
Sam: Cause I live with my grandparents so long and I don't move with my mother.
Q: Why were you living with your grandmother and grandfather initially?
Sam: Cause I guess my grandfather ain't want me to move.
Q: Not when your mother had you as a baby. Why are you living with your grandparents?
Sam: My mother was living with me.
Q: For how long?
Sam: About when I was thirteen years old.
Q: So your mother lived with your grandparents from the time you were a baby until you were thirteen? Then what happened?
Sam: She moved out when she had my little brother and I stayed at home.
Q: How old is your mom?
Sam: Thirty-one.
Q: Were your mom and dad married?
Sam: No.
Q: Does your mom work.
Sam: Not now. She used to work at a restaurant, Wendy's.
Q: So who lives with your mom?
Sam: Nobody now. Me and my grandfather took my brother over to his father's.
Q: Wait a minute. You and your grandfather took your brother from your mother?
Sam: She was acting like she was going to move. She was acting crazy, because she wouldn't call him and we couldn't get in touch with her unless we went over there. We seen my little brother and we took him over his father's house . . . and he still there.

Q: What does your mother do when she is acting up? Is she on drugs?

Sam: Yea. She use to drink a lot.

Q: She's an alcoholic?

Sam: Yea.

Q: That explains why you still stay with your grandparents. Okay. Where is your dad? What does he do?

Sam: He's on . . . and he works at AFF out there past O'Hare. He got two jobs.

Q: Do you have any contact with him and does he help take care of you?

Sam: Yea. I was going over there every weekend. Sometimes. Holidays and stuff like that. Now I call him when I need something.

Q: Okay. There's a lot of gang activity around here, how does that affect you? Are you involved in a gang?

Sam: Yes. GD.

Q: Do you have any rank?

Sam: Once before. Chief of Security.

Q: What does Chief of Security do?

Sam: Secure all the people when we have a meeting. Send people out on security. It is a look out.

Q: A look out to make sure no police or other gangs are coming?

Sam: Yea. But they kicked me off they account.

Q: Why did they kick you off the account?

Sam: They got mad over some incidents and stuff. I wouldn't help them.

Q: What incidents?

Sam: About Jim and stuff like that.

Q: What?

Sam: They talking about he flipped BD. When school first started.

Q: Who flipped BD?

Sam: Jim. They said he flipped BD before he got locked up.

Q: And what happened?

Sam: They told me to get him and I told them I wasn't going to do it. Cause I be known him since I was little when we used to hang out all the time. I told them I wasn't going to do it. They been mad at me since. Then they kicked me off account.

Q: Sam, they didn't do anything to you after you didn't do what they told you to do?

Sam: No. They didn't do a thing to me. Not a single thing. I raised with them, see I know all of 'em. They knew I knew him. I know everybody from 72nd and all that. I know the big fellas and all of 'em.

Although, Sam is a member of the Gangster Disciples, he acts out less then the other children in the class. Many teachers seek him out to assist them in various tasks.

Nicole

Nicole is the most physically mature girl in the class. She wears a jacket everyday, even on ninety degree days. She stated her mother said never to take off her jacket, but she had no understanding why she had made the request or more accurately stated the directive. Nicole transferred to School X from Altgeld which is only several blocks down the street. She has attended six schools since kindergarten. She also repeated grades three and seven.

Nicole has received average grades except grade three when she failed five of her major subjects. Her ITBS scores in reading and math are 5.8 and 6.0 respectively. Nicole's school attendance since kindergarten has been poor. Her grades and attitude had improved a great deal before the class conversion in which all seventh graders remained with their original teacher and the eighth graders went to the other eighth grade room because of a reduction in staff.

At times Nicole seems reserved compared to the other students. Although she does act out when annoyed by certain classmates. She lives with her mother, her mother's boyfriend and her four sisters. Nicole's parents were never married and neither finished high school. Her mother receives general assistance. All of the girls are gang members. Two of the older girls have babies. During the interview Nicole discussed her family and gang involvement.

Q: Can you tell me how old your mom is?
Nic: Thirty-three
Q: And who is the oldest child?
Nic: My sister Rosha. She is seventeen. Tina is sixteen, I'm fifteen, Jas is five and Jamie is two.
Q: Is your older sister in school?
Nic: No. She don't have no babysitter for her baby. When she had her baby my momma say she help out but my momma looking for a job and she

trying to get a babysitter. She trying to get into school, she get in by January.

Q: Is your sixteen-year-old sister in school?

Nic: No. They trying to go to the same school cause she got a baby too.

Q: Now you have four sisters. Do you all have the same father?

Nic: Me, my sister Rosha and Tina got the same father.

Q: And the other two?

Nic: They ain't got the same father. My baby sister Jamie's father died in a car accident. Jas is five. Don't anyone know where her daddy at.

Q: They don't know where he is?

Nic: No. Cause he appear on her birthday then he just disappear.

Q: What about your dad? Where is he?

Nic: In jail.

Q: Can you tell me what happened?

Nic: He was in jail since I was three.

Q: What did he do?

Nic: My momma say he just rob a bank or something.

Q: Okay. So do you ever see your dad? Do you know what prison he's in?

Nic: Yea. He is in Stateville. I go see him every month or two.

Nicole openly discusses both her gang membership and her sisters:

Q: Okay. There are a lot of gangs in the area, one in particular. Have you had any gang involvement?

Nic: Yes. GD.

Q: What does being a gang member mean to you?

Nic: Nothing.

Q: How old were you when you joined?

Nic: Thirteen.

Q: So what did you have to do when you joined?

Nic: Nothing, all I do is go to one of the meetings and they gave me my papers and I had to study fore a week.

Q: What is that? What kind of papers?

Nic: Membership papers. Then I got to study. I had to say my prayers when I get to the meeting.

Q: What are the prayers?

Nic: A whole bunch of stuff. I forget some things.

Q: What does it involve? It's not like a prayer to God is it?

Nic: No. It's like a prayer to Hoover, they say when he get out of jail.

Q: Do you have any rank?

Nic: No. I was First Lady now I'm Second Lady.

Q: Do girls have to go on the wall too? And do they get mouth shots?

Nic: Yes. Violations. But they get big old girls to give you violations. If ain't no big enough girls to give you violations then they let a boy do it.

Q: Are your sisters in a gang?

Nic: Yea. My sister Rosha is GD and Tina is BD.

Q: Does that cause a conflict?

Nic: No.

Q: Do they have rank?

Nic: My sister Rosha, she my First Lady.

Q: How did it happen that your other sister became BD?

Nic: When we was staying on Laflin, she became a BD when she was about ten and she was going to Bunch.

Q: Is the gang important to you?

Nic: Not really.

Q: Then why are you in it?

Nic: I don't know. My sister was asking me. She was like you going to become GD or BD, whatever. Then she was like all right. Then we moved on 81st and I became a GD. My sister Tina's boyfriend, Fish, I think he First C or Second C or something. He in jail now. We have to go see him.

Nicole's sister Tina who is a BD was told to do a 180 (shoot her) on her sister Rosha, but refused. Nicole claimed that's when she got out of the gang on 81st street. It is rumored that she is now a member of the BPS. Nicole insists that she is going all the way through college. She said she does not want to end up like her sisters.

Tamika

Although Nicole is the most physically mature girl in the class, Tamika is chronologically and socially more mature. On the first day of school she appeared with an earring in her nose, numerous holes in her ear, diagonal cuts through her eyebrow and marcelled hair with a blond streak. On any given day her hair color could be purple or another bizarre color or style. During the interview she stated that her older sister was a hairdresser.

Tamika lives with her mother, two sisters and her grandfather. During the interview she discussed her family situation.

Q: How old are your two sisters?

Tam: One is thirteen, one nineteen.

Q: Does your mom work?

Tam: No.

Q: How do you get your income?

Tam: By SSI and aid check. We get like two SSI checks and one half an aid check?

Q: Is your mom ill? Is there a reason she doesn't work?

Tam: No. She just don't. She be wanting to work but she don't be like getting up and going to work. She want to work but some people don't hire her. She don't know what she want to do really. She really want to house keep, because that what she do better and she used to work at a hospital. She don't work there no more 'cause she had to take care of us.

Q: Are there any other things that would keep her from working?

Tam: No.

Q: Did your mom finish high school?

Tam: She went to Dusable. She didn't finish all the way.

Q: Where is your dad?

Tam: My mom married my stepfather and he has been with us since I was little. I saw my father but I don't get along with him. I saw him at the bus stop but he started calling us and he say he was looking for us. Nevertheless, I didn't believe him.

Q: So your mom and dad were not married?

Tam: No. My stepfather and mom were married.

Q: Now, you have a younger and older sister, who is their father?

Tam: We all have different fathers.

Q: Whose father is your stepfather?

Tam: Nobody.

Q: How long has you mom been married to him?

Tam: For about two years but they lived together since I was three.

Q: But, when I asked you who lived there, you didn't mention him.

Tam: He don't live there no more. They ain't divorced either. But my momma go see him. They had problems at the house. They had problems where we used to live at but they still see each other but they ain't divorced.

There is some question about the identity of Tamika's father. She related an incident that occurred when she was at a restaurant with her older sister.

Q: Let's get back to your dad. Does he live around here? Your real dad.

Tam: He live around my house, but, I don't know where he live and my cousin say they saw him around this street from us. He live on that block but I don't be seeing him on that block. Okay, when I first saw him one time when like a couple of months ago. I didn't believe he was my real dad. I was in a restaurant and my sister say there go your daddy, she often lies to us and say that. There go your daddy Tyrone the one that claims me and Randy claims me too.

Q: What does your mother say?

Tam: My mother didn't say. She said that he keep on calling just to get back with her.

Q: Which one?

Tam: Randy. The one who claims me.

Q: So who is your father? Randy or Tyrone? Do you know?

Tam: No (laughter). They confuse me.

Q: Does your mother know?

Tam: Yea, she know. She told me but I forgot. Cause I don't be thinking about them. I don't really care about them no more. I am really used to think who my father so I don't really care. My stepfather was with me so I call him father.

Q: So when you were in the restaurant and your sister was teasing you, what happened?

Tam: I looked out the door, and I say you better not be laughing at me cause I be doing stuff, asking, so I went up to him and said, "Is your name Randy?" and my sister came up and said "Do you know your name Randy?" and he said "Yea." I said "Do you know a lady named Rochelle," he said, "Yea. I had a baby by her. And I am looking for my daughter right now. But they ran off." My sister came out and say, this is your daughter. Then he said "What, you got big." I look at him like he stupid and he said, give me your phone number so I can call you up and buy you stuff. I don't really care because I don't really believe he was going to buy me stuff. And he didn't. So he kept calling but when his check day came, I didn't know where is was, my mother said, I bet when his check comes, he don't buy you nothing. And he didn't.

Tamika has only seen her father the one time, but she has talked to him on the telephone.

Gangs are pivotal factors in disadvantaged areas, many entire families claiming allegiance to one gang. However, Tamika's family has several different factions. She talks about her family's gang involvement:

Q: Are you involved in a gang?

Tam: Where I lived in the projects I was a GD. So I got out.

Q: Are you out now?

Tam: I don't know why I out. I ain't in no gang no more.

Q: You dropped your flag? What happened when you dropped your flag?

Tam: Nothing. They didn't do nothing to me.

Q: Isn't that unusual?

Tam: My auntie was the gang leader of that gang over there but she left so my cousin took over. And I don't know what happened then.

Q: You stopped at thirteen?

Tam: Yes.

Q: And no one has approached you about it?

Tam: No. They knew I was in it but they don't do nothing to me. Like the Stones around my house don't do nothing to me cause I be with them so much, they do nothing to me. They knew I was in a gang.

Q: They knew you were in GDs? Did you ever join the Stones?

Tam: No. They wanted me to but I didn't. Cause I said I wasn't going to be like that. I ain't going to join no gangs. I ain't gonna get myself in that situation.

Q: Do people think you in a gang?

Tam: Probably the way I be looking, how I be behaving, they don't do nothing to me. I be having my blue scarves on my head walking around.

Q: Do people in this school think you are in a gang?

Tam: They know I used to be in one. But they still think I in one, but I just tell them I ain't.

Q: Blue is who's color?

Tam: Blue and black is GD and red and black is Stone's color.

Q: Do you wear a lot of blue and black?

Tam: I wear all types of colors. It don't really matter for me, they don't do nothing to me no way. My momma just don't want me to wear red. Cause it Stone colors.

Q: Okay, was your mother ever involved in a gang?

Tam: No. Wait a minute, I know my auntie was, they called theyselves Stones and my uncle was in a gang. My cousin was a BD, my uncle was Brother, I think they BD too, and my uncle was a GD and my other cousin was a GD and my two other girl cousins was a GD and my auntie used to be a Stone. She go to church now. She ain't about them now. My cousin had rank, but, my auntie didn't. My mother and them first cousins.

Q: Is it unusual for families to be in all different type of gangs?

Tam: Then my cousin he used to be BD, he changed to a GD, then he started stealing they money and they after him.

Tamika has difficulty keeping up with the rest of the class. She has a learning disability (LD) and receives resource once a day. Tamika repeated first grade. She attributes this failure to her poor attendance, averaging twenty-nine days of absence each school year, while in first grade she was absent sixty-four days. Tamika stated her mother kept her at home because, "They transferred me to Healy and I couldn't catch on at Healy so they kept on transferring back to that school and transferring back to Coleman. My momma just kept me at home." Although Tamika's grades are poor, she has managed to pass each year, with the exception of first grade. Tamika's ITBS scores in reading and math are 4.8 and 3.8, respectively.

Mary

Mary is an attractive, precocious thirteen year old who is impressed with her own appearance. According to Mary she considers herself extremely appealing. She made the statement, "I think of myself that I am so fine and all I do is go home and look in the mirror or do my hair . . ." However, her perception of self does not have a negative affect on her behavior in class. On the contrary, she is the only student that does not act out in class. She received an A in conduct, whereas her counterparts received Fs and Ds. Presently, Mary lives with her grandmother and great-grandmother. The essence of guardianship remains somewhat nebulous. Mary contends that her mother gave up guardianship, to her knowledge, for unknown reasons. Although, during the interview alcohol, drugs, abandonment and abusive relationships came up repeatedly. Mary discusses her home situation in some detail.

Q: Who lives with you?

Mary: My grandmother and great-grandmother. And my mom stays sometimes but she really lives with my aunt, because she pays her rent. And my grandmother doesn't work. She gets a check for me and her mother. Cause my Great-grandmother used to stay in Indiana and she stayed in a nursing home until my grandmother took her out so they give her a check for taking care of her. And she gets a check for me from welfare.

Q: Okay, tell me something about your mom. Why aren't you staying with her?

Mary: Because her and my grandmother went to court over me and they gave me to my grandmother. And since then I have been living with my grandmother.

Q: What was happening in your mother's life that would make the courts give you to your grandmother? They don't just do that.

Mary: She had told me that they had given custody to my grandmother. But when I moved down south, she wanted full custody of me so they asked for my mother's address and phone number so they could call her and ask her to come to the hearing to try to defend herself or anything. And she didn't come. They couldn't get in contact with her, so my grandmother went to court and got full custody.

Q: Okay but they had to prove your mother unfit. What's mom involved in? Is she on drugs?

Mary: There ain't nothing wrong with her. She got a job, got a house, well she's in an apartment, and my sister stay with her.

Q: How old is your sister?

Mary: Four. And then she had just got through like two weeks ago, she just moved away from her apartment because of her boyfriend. He kept hitting on her and beating and hollering at her. And whatever he tell her to do, she better do it or she gonna get hit or something going to happen to her. She got tired of it. And this happened before and she went back. But this time she moved all her furniture out, what she bought and everything . . . And she only had one hundred dollars and something left and that was supposed to be for my TV, cause she was trying to get stuff for my room since I got a room now . . . But she couldn't cause she had to use the money to pay my auntie and get her some money to put down on her apartment.

Q: Now, what about your dad?

Mary: I don't know him. I seen him. He came to my house one time when I was ten years old. He came and rang the doorbell and he was like, "Hello, is your name Mary?" and I said yeah my name is Mary. I had seen his face and already knew who he was. He was like "I'm your

Dad." So he was telling me what happened, how he got out of touch with me, saying that if he had played my birthday numbers that something would happen and we would lose distance, be far apart and he did anyway and that's how we got far apart. I was like okay and I was just sitting there listening . . . Then they called my momma to tell her he was in town but they couldn't get in touch with her. She go away for a long time, two weeks or something, and then she probably call or we will call her.

Q: Now to your knowledge is your mom on drugs or alcohol?

Mary: No, she drinks and smokes sometimes.

Q: What do you mean smokes sometimes?

Mary: Cigarettes. But when she be with her brothers, around my uncles and stuff then they go get some weed or something.

Q: Do you and your sister have the same father?

Mary: No.

Q: Was your mother married to either of them?

Mary: No.

Q: Did your dad ever get you the things he said he was going to get you?

Mary: No, because after the first day I seen him, I didn't see him no more. They finally got in touch with my momma and told her and she was like, well don't be around him. If he come up to your school run away. Because my uncle, he was there too, and he was judging by the way he was sitting and talking and he was like he was sitting like a sissy because his legs was all funny. He told my momma well he a pervert, don't be around him and all this stuff. If he comes to you, run away or go get an adult or something . . . And since that day, I don't see him no more. He ain't never come back no more or nothing.

Mary has a confusing history of moving from place to place, she relates her transient life style:

Q: Did you ever live with your mother?

Mary: Yea. I stayed with her and my grandma.

Q: Tell me who you lived with if you can remember. Go back as far as you can and tell me who you lived with and where you lived. When you were born, who did you live with?

Mary: My mother because we stayed in Chicago but I forgot where. And I stayed with her, we had this one bedroom apartment and I was staying with my grandma and my momma worked in a candy store.

Q: So your mother and grandmother were staying together when you were first born?

Mary: Yea. And after I got older, my mom just left, I don't know where she went.

Q: How old were you?

Mary: I was like, when I was three, they still together but we moved to Indiana.

Q: When you say together, you mean your mother and grandmother?

Mary: Yea. At this time, my auntie started staying with us. Just my auntie and then all of us moved to Indiana where my grandma's husband stayed. So we started staying with my grandma's sister. But my granddaddy he ain't stay with us, he stayed back in Chicago, here, so it was just me, my grandma, my auntie and my momma and my other auntie and her kids. She had two kids. We lived in a house and it only had two bedrooms. And I was like three and everybody was staying together. But the family was acting funny because they go buy food and have in they room and so we stayed there for a couple of months and had to move from there and move somewhere up there by Parnell. I was seven.

Q: Where did you go from the time you were three to seven?

Mary: We kept moving back and forth from Chicago to Indiana. Let's see. From when I was seven, I stopped seeing my momma. She come around every once in a while and that was it. And then we kept moving back and forth and I was staying with my grandma and my auntie was staying with us too. But not my momma. Then her brother started staying with us . . . And then we was staying in this apartment on Peoria and we was staying in there and had to share a room with my auntie. All the girls would be in one room and the boys were in the front room. My grandma and her husband be in they room. And we stayed there for a couple of months and then we had to move again and that's when we moved to 63rd and Peoria. And we lived there for a while. Now it was me, my grandma and her husband, my auntie and her brother and her other brother and her brother's girlfriend. So seven of us staying in this two bedroom apartment. Mostly everybody slept in the front room. And my auntie had her own room because she had a baby.

Q: How old is your auntie now?

Mary: She is twenty-four.

Q: So if you were seven, that's six years ago, she was about sixteen or seventeen.

Mary: Yea. Then there was me, her baby and her husband sleeping in one room and everybody else was in the front room. We stayed there for a

> couple of months and had to move again. Then that's when we stayed on 63rd or 64th. There wasn't nobody in the house than but just me, my grandma and my great grandma. Just us three. My momma was out of the picture for a while.

Q: How old were you then?

Mary: From ten to now. Then we had to move out of there because one day my cousin came over and everybody was sleeping and he decided to play with matches.

Q: When did the fire happen?

Mary: August . . . last year . . . And then my auntie took us down south and then we stayed down there for eight months . . . and I was going to school. The electricity went down, we couldn't go to school or nothing. . . . so she decided we was going to move again and stay with her son who stayed in Milwaukee, so we packed all of out things up, this was in February after Valentines Day of this year. I couldn't go to school, I had been out for five or six months. From February all the way through June 1st.

During the stay in Milwaukee, Mary was molested several times by her twenty-four-year-old, pregnant aunt's boyfriend. She would commute from Chicago to Milwaukee on the weekends. She did not tell her aunt until last month. She was also molested by her uncle—her mother's brother after the incidents with her aunt's boyfriend.

Mary's school records are somewhat disjointed because of her family's transient nature. Her attendance records show large blocks of time missing from school since second grade. Her experiences in sixth and seventh grades prevented her taking the ITBS, but the records indicate eighth grade scores in reading and math, 8.8 and 7.3 respectively. Thus, even though with numerous moves and transfers, she managed to receive average to above average grades throughout school.

SUMMARY

The introduction of the participants is essential to our gaining an understanding and exploring their everyday world and the multi-faceted components that are critical to their construction of reality. Realities are consistent within their social context. Consequently, the children revealed situations that most people only read about. These situations are analogous to the essence of Elizabeth Keckley's poem in 1868 which is still meaningful for today's disadvantaged youth:

The bright joyous dreams of freedom
To the slave faded—were sadly altered,
In the presence of that stern,
Practical mother, reality (Bell, 1986, p. 54).

Children raised in poverty are consigned to a reality of ignorance, gangs, violence, drugs, sex, and dysfunctional families. These characteristics are relative to their ways of "seeing" and construction of their *commonsense* world. The questions and situations that will be explored in chapter four will propose the social constructivist view of their reality and offer insight into their experiences. How do the children perceive the reality of schooling and its relationship to their lives? How do they define self? What are some of the psychological/social-psychological factors that relate to social-reality construction? And does the media function as "culture-bearers" in shaping perceptions of their social reality? The children will define their social space and contributing factors that are critical to the development of this definition.

CHAPTER 4

Listen: Do You Hear What I Hear?

Silent Survival

> This Child Has Always Lost
> Lost Her Childhood, Her Mother, Her Happiness.
> This Child Has Lost Her mother's Affection, Trust, And Love
> Mother of Mine, What have I Done?
> Did I Speak Too Much?
> Didn't I Say The Truth?
>
> Mother Of Mine, Why Love This Vile Bastard Filled Inside
> With A Black Soul?
>
> Why Have I Lost This battle?
> Though All I Did Was To Tattle.
> Tattled Truth, Tattled Fear.
>
> Couldn't Anyone See, Couldn't Anyone Hear?
> Hear My Crying Heart. My Bleeding Life.
>
> Though I'll Survive
>
> Survive For Myself,
> No More Covering
> No More Silence,
> No More Suffering
> No More Reliance

Reliance On My Mother's Blind Eyes To Be There.
There To Cover Me With Her Protecting Arms,
From That Vile Bastard Who Took Her from Me.

I Fought For Her,
Fought For Myself.
Though The Devil Was Behind This Vile Bastard,
God, Why Did I Lose?
Why Did I Walk?
Walk So Far That Now,
I'm Alone, Alone Inside.
Alone Again Without Arms To Run To.
To Console My pain, My Weakness.

All Those Who Hurt Me More,
Crumbling My Heart, Stomping My Soul.

I Survived, I Did Before.

What Makes Them Think They've Won Now?
Now That I See What I Have To Gain.
I've Won
I'm Here With God On My Side Showing I'm Worth My Pain

(Alejandra Fuentes, 1996)

"Silent Survival" provides significant insight into the common sense world of its fifteen-year-old author who lives in a disadvantaged urban area. For her and all other children like her, socialization, which serves as a determining element in the development of self and the social construction of reality, is objectively and subjectively created. A sense of abandonment permeates each line of the poem, underscoring the fact that the definition of self and the construction of individual reality in children is in large measure based on their interactions with others.

For Burger and Luckmann socialization is the ontogenetic process by which an individual becomes a member of society. Before the process of socialization is fully accomplished, children must undergo primary socialization, the most important component in this process. All subsequent socialization is considered secondary, receiving its basic structure from the former. Burger and Luckmann (1966) define primary socialization as "the comprehensive and consistent induction of an individual into the objective world of a society or a sector of it" (p. 130) Thus, they contend that a child raised in poverty

> not only absorbs a lower class perspective on the social world, he absorbs it in the idiosyncratic coloration given it by his parents (or whatever other individuals are in charge of his primary socialization). The same lower-class perspective may induce a mood of contentment, resignation, bitter resentment, or seething rebelliousness. Consequently, the lower class child will not only come to inhabit a world greatly different from that of an upper-class child, but may do so in a manner quite different from the lower class child next door (p. 131).

Paulo Freire (1993) agrees with Burger and Luckmann but stresses the severity of poverty's impact on individuals' worldview in that, "their perception of themselves as oppressed is impaired by their submersion in the reality of oppression . . . that oppressive reality absorbs those within it and thereby acts to submerge human beings' consciousness" (pp. 27-33).

For children the school experience is one of the primary components in the construction of their reality and in their attempts to make sense of their everyday world. In addition, children's actions and others' perceptions of those actions help lay the foundation for the educational experience. Berger and Luckmann observe that, "All human activity is subject to habitualization. Any action that is repeated frequently becomes cast into a pattern, which can then be reproduced . . ." (p. 53). In addition to the individual's repetitive patterns, actions are also built from a course of shared history—that is, they are not created instantaneously but received in a process that is a function of the group and of its development across time. Freire expresses this idea of objective social reality as a product of human action with a historical basis; it is not chance.

In other words, not only do these children develop their identity in and through the school experience—which includes but is not limited to their interactions with each other, their administrators, teachers and others in the milieu—but also the subsequent reflection back to them of themselves as worthy, teachable, educable, etc., or not, becomes one of the greatest determining factors in their success or failure in the process of education. How do these children, then, view their school experience? How do their actions abet the social construction of their identity? Do these children perceive school as necessary for their needs? Is it sufficient to meet them?

PERCEPTION OF THE PURPOSE OF SCHOOLING

On September 8, 1994, the halls are filled with children returning from the long summer vacation. The school building is old, but it is clean for the new school year: floors polished, bulletin boards brightly decorated with Afrocentric themes of self-empowerment. Teachers bustle, anticipating their new students. By the group, they are led into their homerooms. Classroom 130 is decorated in the school's colors—orange and green; the chairs and desks, old and marked with graffiti, have been overhauled for the beginning of school. A handwritten message, "Welcome Students, " greets students and another admonishes, "Use Your Time Wisely." The shades are drawn to camouflage the windows, boarded up to conceal the decaying neighborhood. The students in room 130 enter the room anticipating, speculating what the 1994-1995 school year will "yield."

Typically, the new school year affords students the opportunity to discuss and compare summer experiences—travel, camps, special programs, and more, but the students in room 130 discuss radically different events in their lives: gang activities, thefts, arrests, shootings, killings . . . The school's new administration has already reviewed the summer events and their possible effects on the current school year. Thus, determined to make the school a neutral and safe zone, they initiate measures to implement new safeguards. To be sure, the administrators and staff are fully aware that this still pristine school year faces the challenges of the old year—the school's affiliation with the Gangster Disciples, an alliance known to every student and adult and *understood* and *accepted* by the youngest to the oldest child in the building.

The reality of the circumstance precipitates the adoption of the current, "no nonsense" stance to diffuse some of the compelling influence of the gangs. Rules are to be strictly enforced; no student is allowed in the hall without an adult; the main office is to be informed of any student infraction. Uniforms—white or blue shirts and blouses and navy or black pants and skirts—are part of the reformation. In adopting uniforms the administration is attempting to eliminate the "flagging" of gang colors.

In this setting and the climate that arises from it, the school children construct their perception of the elements and factors that connect and shape the reality between schooling and their lives. They are eager to respond to questions that focus on their perception of the "purpose"of schooling.

THE MEANING OF SCHOOLING

Q: What does school mean to you? Is it important?

Jim: A place I come to learn things I don't know. A couple months ago when I was about to forget school, I talk to one of my older gang members and he told me I should go to school because he in the gang and went to school and got a good job. He work at the post office makin' fifteen dollars a hour, driving a fork lif'. He's like boy you goin' need that school diploma. That's important because all these other gang members that drop outta school, they goin need that job an' without a high school diploma you can't get it. That's why I got out of high school. Those four years are goin to go real quick . . . People end up with all type of knowledge. Because some of the stuff you learn in school help you on the street. Make you street smart.

Q: What are some of the reasons you stopped going to school?

Jim: I just stopped going. It got boring. Like every time I come I have problems with one of the teachers. They say something to me and I snap. Like one day, I came to my homeroom and I told the teacher she had wrote a T on the board, but it was suppose to be a F. She like said it's a F and we got to arguing about it. I was like forget it . She said get out. So I said why are you goin put me out because you wrote the wrong letter on the board for? We got into it, because she had made a mistake. We use to get into it everyday. Anybody say something to her would get into it. I was like, I don't want to come to school because I don't want to hear their mouth. So my probation officer start catching up with me, she caught me and I went to jail. She was like a year or two, a couple of years. I was like no. I like cry and I was like no, I don't want to go. Then my probation officer came and she was like, didn't I tell you I was going to get you? She was like, I give you one more chance, everybody make a mistake.

Six-times-arrested and as of this writing convicted of manslaughter, Jim makes a perfunctory link between schooling and his "future," while his "reason" for not going to school seems even more arbitrary. But the Honorable Judy I. Mitchell-Davis, who presides in the Juvenile, Domestic Violence, and Eviction Courts, provides a basis on which to more fully understand Jim's narrative and the point at issue. In a speech delivered to the members of Trinity Resources Unlimited in 1994 she explains:

> The parties appearing before me have been overwhelming minority persons, represented for the most part by white lawyers—whether private or court appointed. In addition, whether poor or middle class, many of the respondents or defendants has shown little, if any, understanding of what was his or her individual responsibility or involvement in the case before me or why the consequences. It is as if his or her behavior was outside or apart from the person standing before me. It is as if the party did not understand that all behavior, including his or hers has personal consequences.

> That the parties had not realized or accepted the sometimes harsh legal consequences of their behavior is apparent from the pitiful sobs and repeated appeals for reconsideration by mothers when I have ordered "14 days to move" in eviction cases; by the shocked-into-awareness of adjudged juvenile delinquents when, after repeated warnings and chances, I have announced "Commitment to the Illinois Department of Corrections" . . . or when I looked into the eyes of a young defender and observed bewilderment upon being told, "Find a job or keep a job diary or go to jail." (n.p.)

Jim's repeated infractions of the law and some of the complex reasons for these were the essence of Judge Mitchell-Davis' discourse.

Q: They caught up with you because you were not in school?

Jim:	Yep. She caught me and say I give you one more chance and I was crying and everything. My momma say she trying to give me a gift and I got to crying. Momma, tell her I want one more chance.
Q:	What are some other reasons you stopped going to school? You said you were always getting in trouble.
Jim:	I tired of it. I was like tired when I woke up in the morning because I was kicking it late. When my momma go to work, I came out like I'm goin' to school but I go to the East side, makin' me some money. You know
Q:	Doing what?
Jim:	I be selling a couple of bags, you know sacks.
Q:	Where do you get them from? I not talking about people.
Jim:	From whoever, you know. I'm cool with this dude, I ain't goin' say his name, he give us a sack, twenty-five or thirty dollar sack. We get paid one hundred dollars off of it.
Q:	What does "sack" mean?
Jim:	Sack, like twenty-five, thirty rocks.
Q:	When you say rocks, do you mean crack?
Jim:	Yep. You get paid one hundred dollars and turn the rest of the money in. They move real fast. And I won't come in till eleven o'clock at night and my momma be "like where have you been?" I be like lying or somethin'. Then I just wake up every morning and do the same thing. I just don't feel like goin' to school.
Q:	Is school important to you?
Jim:	It is important for me now cause, I know if I don't go to school, I go to jail. I know if I don't be in school everyday I go to jail. So it's important for me to be there. It's like, I wash up every morning and I be there. And she call and check on me every morning and say were you there today? Is Jim in school? Yes, he is.
Q:	Is that your probation officer?
Jim:	She be like were you in school today? Why not? And I say because I have a rash and she be like let me talk to your momma. And my momma said yea I had a rash and she be like okay. I had to make sure you were in school. She thought she had me boy!
Q:	So what I hear you saying Jim, is that if it wasn't for the fact that you would get locked up, you wouldn't come to school.
Jim:	I go now. Now you know if I don't come to school I get locked up. I talked to people that have been through the same thing. You need school.

Thomas' answer is concise:

Q: You spend a lot of time in school. What does it mean to you?
Tom: Get an education and get out of here.
Q: Is that important to you?
Tom: Yea.
Q: When you say get out of here what do you mean?
A: Get out of school and get a good job. Get out of the ghetto Shashqua
          reflects a similar perspective for the meaning and value of schooling
          expressed without enthusiasm or interest.
Q: What does school mean to you?
Shas: Oh. School? An education.
Q: And what else?
Shas: And it's important. Without an education you can't get nowhere in life,
          without a diploma.
Q: Do you believe that or are you just saying it?
Shas: Well, I believe it cause I see it. But, it just that sometime school can
          become real, real boring and real, real irritating.
Q: If school wasn't mandatory would you still go?
Shas: I don't think so. I would be at home asleep or over my cousin or
          friends' house having fun.

Mary, more explicit than her classmates in her perception of the purpose
of schooling and its relationship to her future, still expresses the same
ideology.

Q: Okay, Mary, what does school mean to you? Important, unimportant,
          what is it?
Mary: It's important because you go there to learn how to read and do stuff.
          So you can get a good job. I am trying to be good because I want to be
          a RN and to me eighth grade is hard and all the other grades haven't
          been too hard. Yea. My momma wants me to be a RN. Mostly, my
          family, all the women have something to do with medical. They are
          either nursing assistance or nurses aide, what's that when they go to
          different homes watching the people, they do that. I want to do
          something like that too. I wanted to be a doctor but if I made a mistake,
          you know I mess up my whole medical career and all that, so I said I
          would be a RN.

Common threads link the children's philosophy: low expectations, unrealistic, and unassuming goals, wants and needs that are simplistic and that often are not related to each other. Their voices all echo the defeat and poverty that pervade the ghetto. For Madhubuti (1994) these children have descended into deprivation: "most children are born into the world at the top of their game, genius level. The culture that receives them will either nurture and develop the genius in them or silence their minds before they reach the age of six " (p. 6). The culture of poverty in which these children are developing precludes them from attaining even an adequate measure of their intellectual and social capacity. In Mary's discussion of her future, demonstrating her lack of basic information and conceptual knowledge, the point is clearly illustrated.

Nicole has been held back twice—in third and seventh grades—because of poor attendance. During the discussion about the relevance of schooling, she also discloses reasons for her absences. Nicole's reality conflicts with her stated career goals, which would be realized as a result of a productive, successful education.

Q: You spend a lot of time at school, Nicole, what meaning does school have for you?

Nic: It means a lot. I am going to get an education. And when I graduate, I want to finish college and stuff and get me a job.

Q: You are absent quite a bit. Why?

Nic: Cause of my momma and a couple of times I was absent because my momma so she could do something.

Q: And when you stay home what do you do?

Nic: I got to watch my little sister.

Q: What about the some of the other times? The five year old is in school, isn't she?

Nic: Yea, but, the two year old don't go to school.

Q: What about your sisters' babies? Who watches them?

Nic: I watch them when they ask. They have to pay me to watch them though.

Q: Do they ever ask you to stay home to watch them?

Nic: No.

Q: And the other times you are out, what happened?

Nic: I got to see my grandma.

Q: On a school day?

Nic: Yea.

Q: Why would you see her on a school day?

Nic: I don't know. Cause my momma told me to go down there, in Gary to ask her something.

Q: Why couldn't you just call her on the phone to ask?

Nic: They ain't got no phone.

Q: So, how do you get to Gary?

Nic: I get one of my friends to take me there.

Q: So the only way you communicate with you grandmother is to hop in a car and go to Gary?

Nic: Yea.

Q: Couldn't you do that after school?

Nic: No, cause then my grandma be gone. She leave around two-thirty or three o'clock.

Q: Where does she go?

Nic: I don't know.

Q: She just leaves?

Nic: Yea.

Q: So the time you have been out of school, your mom basically has caused the absences because she wanted you to do something or babysit?

Nic: Yep.

Nicole related the experience she had to endure at her previous school.

Q: How does this school compare with your old school?

Nic: These teachers are smarter.

Q: In what ways?

Nic: At my old school, we watched T.V. and tapes. And we talked. We had math at one-forty-five and sometimes social studies. Our teacher in the seventh grade would come in and put her head down on the desk. We played games. When she woke up she would call the girls b_ _ _ _ _ s. She had a fight with practically every girl in the class.

Q: Who started the fights?

Nic: She did. When she woke-up, she called the girls b _ _ _ _ _ s. And she always got beat-up.

Q: Didn't anyone complain?

Nic: No.

Q: Did you think that was the way school was suppose to be?

Nic: No. I had gone to another school for sixth grade.

Fear, intimidation, and ignorance are factors that shape the social reality of disadvantaged adolescents. The gangs' influence extends into the school and determines if and where a student attends high school. During a class visitation, Officer Don Lewis from the Bureau of Staff Services, Preventive Programs Division of the Chicago Police Department, asked the students whether they had made decisions about high school selection. Throughout the classroom, the eighth graders spoke out their "choices": Robeson, Simeon, Kenwood, CVS, Englewood, Bogan, Academy of Our Lady, Julian, Curie, Simeon, Harlan. However, the reality of their situation dictates the "choice": Robeson, the home high school and more significantly, Gangster Disciple territory (with smaller factions of Black Disciples). Eight of the ten eighth graders attend Robeson after graduation; Shashqua goes to Calumet because of her affiliation with the Black Peacestones; Thomas and his father move to the suburbs.

Officer Lewis then outlines a scene that is repeated in many schools. He first asks how many girls are not in gangs. Several girls raise their hands; murmurs of "liars" go through the room. He describes the approach and how the "decision" is made. A girl is approached by other girls if boys "look" at her. This "look" designates that she is to be approached. The girls ask who she "belongs with." If she says "no-one," they say she does not have "back-up." Then, they brush up against her and jam her into a locker, or some other intimidation that forces a conflict. So, when she goes to her brothers, sisters, cousins, or friends for back-up, she is, in fact, coerced into gang affiliation. These types of confrontations permeate the students' lives at school. They construct the school milieu, the children's very identities, and dictate the boundaries of their inner and outer lives.

The social and cultural reproduction theory most clearly "explains" the nature and quality of the adolescents' lives in the study. They perceive schooling as a means to social and economic advancement in the vaguest sense; however, they do not connect schooling with social empowerment and civic responsibilities. Out of twenty students, eleven state that schooling provides education and ultimately, career preparation. Nine of the students see school as a passageway to college and a job; however, in keeping with Freire's position cited earlier, while the students can articulate the "correct" cultural ideology about the value of education, they appear to be oblivious to their oppressed state. Only one acknowledges and expresses the desire to leave the impoverished conditions of the ghetto.

PERCEPTION OF AUTHORITY FIGURES AS EXTERNAL "SHAPERS" OF SOCIALLY CONSTRUCTED REALITY

In poetic symbols, Toni Morrison alludes to Madhubutti's notion of the promise within when the child receives the proper environment and appropriate adult attitudes:

> Had she paints, or clay, or knew the
> discipline of dance, or strings; had
> she anything to engage her
> tremendous curiosity and her gift for
> metaphor, she might have exchanged
> the restlessness and preoccupation
> with whim for activity that
> provided her with all she yearned for,
> And like any artist with no art form,
> she became dangerous (Bell, 1986, p. 22)

Another factor contributing to the students' construction of reality is their perception of authority figures as "shapers" of that reality. Some aspects that have a powerful impact on the behaviors and attitudes of these children within the classroom (Stevens, 1993) include their teachers' attitudes and the beliefs and assumptions under which they function (Bourdieu and Passeron, 1977; Bowles and Gintis, 1976; Giroux, 1981; Johnson, 1992; McLaren, 1989). How do the students perceive these aspects of those in authority over them? What impact do they have on the students' choices? To what extent do children internalize the attitudes, beliefs and assumptions held by the figures in authority over them? Maykela is clear in her perceptions of her teachers and their relationship to her education. She describes an incident from the previous school year that had negative carry-overs to the following year.

May: I use to read but I usually get a book and sat and read but then I got there and the teacher, she like show you that you need to read a lot to be a lawyer and to bring up my reading scores up. And then when I had to go to Ms. K, I use to hate to because we never liked each other . . . I believe deep in my heart she use to do it on purpose like out of everybody's paper, every time my paper use to always have a F on it and then my mamma come up here and show her then she'd correct it. But every time it use to be my paper coming up messed up. I'd be like she'd be doing this on purpose. Sometimes I use to tell my mother. So I'd be like I'm not going to keep having my mother up here, she's going to keep on doing it over and over and then my mother said she was going to talk to the principal and after we showed her, it stopped happening for awhile until the end of the year and then it started back.

Q: You had her for class last year? So that's why you behaved the way you did when you first started in her class. You gave her a hard time.

May: Because like she use to do stuff to me on purpose cause like when I first came to this department they use to be like cause my brothers been bad and everything when they use to go to school and her and Ms.S when I was in the sixth grade, she use to always say I'm going to be like my brothers and stuff. She use to tell me what I'd be like.

Q: Who would say that to you?

May: Those two teachers. They would say I'm just like my brothers and I'd be like them.

Mary is one of the few students that received an A in conduct. She conforms to the "norm"; she is quiet in class, seldom talking or acting out; however, it is important to note when speaking of the "norm," that the ghetto in which these children live does not represent a microcosm of the larger society . Rather, it is a special population , an entity unto itself in its impoverishment. Mary's relationships with her teachers have been better then her classmates'. Mary discusses some of the problems she has encountered in school.

Mary: Ms. K is my favorite teacher. She okay. She ain't never hollered at me cause I don't do nothing wrong. I don't back talk or nothing. When she teaches us math, sometimes I don't hardly listen to her because I don't understand it. And so I just write or do something else.

Q: You don't raise your hand and tell her you don't understand?

Mary: No.

Q: Is there a reason why? If you don't understand, how is she going to know that you don't understand and how are you going to correct that?

Mary: Cause when she teach, she teach right and the kids raise their hand and all that and they like be doing prime factoring, we be doing that, yea. Like we go on with that. I didn't understand it and she called me to the board and I was like, well what did I do? Can you help me? And she showed me how to do it and walked away. Then there was this girl who sit in front of me and I was asking her to help me cause I don't go to lunch, I stay in the classroom. . . and ask her to help me with my math. And she help me understand it and all that and when the teacher come in she be saying we going to do this, do that and do it another way and then that's when I get off track.

Q: Do you tell her then that you don't understand because it's just a small group?

Mary: No.

Q: Why don't you tell her?

Mary: I don't know. Cause if I say I don't understand, like if I raise my hand and say I don't understand, I don't want everybody looking at me like, you don't understand this is easy and all that junk. I don't want to hear that. If I don't understand, you know I just want it between me and her and she just help me and it just me and her.

Q: That's why you stay after school?

Mary: Yea.

Q: What about Mr. S?

Mary: I liked Mr. S. It was nice in his classroom . . . except for math, I didn't understand math.

Q: Would you tell Mr. S. You didn't understand math?

Mary: Yea. I told him one time I didn't understand, he went over it on the board and everything. Then other kids got the hang of it too. I did, I understand part of it, I didn't all of it. But I did it.

Q: What else did you like about Mr. S.?

Mary: Um, he was nice, not mean. He didn't holler a lot. Had the class under control.

Q: What about Ms. S?

Mary: She okay.

Q: What's okay about Ms. S?

Mary: She don't holler at you.

Q: So if they don't holler at you they are okay?

Mary: Yea.

Q: What did you think about Mr. U?

Mary: He okay, he was nice.

Q: What did you think about the room when you were in there?

Mary: It was a total mess. Everyone move there seats around, hollering, cussing.

Q: And that was okay for you?

A: Yea, cause as long as I stayed away from those people that was cussing, I was okay. Along as they don't say anything to me.

Q: How about a school situation and learning in that particular room? Like you said it was chaotic. So how can you learn in a situation like that?

A: Well if I sit in a place were other kids are sitting there wanting to learn, then we would call him over there and would teach that group right there. And the other people that are too busy talking, I don't know about them.

Q: What did you think about that particular method? The room was in chaos and only a couple of kids in the class was doing work. Do you think it is a good learning situation?

Mary: No. Because they are not getting anything out of it. And other kids try to do it.

The situation which Mary discusses at the end of her interview takes place on an average day in her English class; the entire spectacle is one of total disorder and upheaval. In this classroom, the students are particularly disruptive. As they enter the room, the teacher routinely passes out a conventional worksheet without any instructions. The majority of the students have their own agendas and the work sheet is not part of it. Joseph yells out of the window. Practically the entire class is walking around and talking. Jason plays with the shades. Sam swears. Shasaqua passes around a sheet for the class to sign for the locker of the seventh grader who drowned at Navy Pier over the weekend. Nate harasses Nicole who, in turn, jumps out of her seat. G.T. swears from his desk. Nate and Pooh stand and do the "butterfly."

Mr. U steps out of the room with Maykeyla. G.T. gets up and throws a book on the floor. R.J. hunts a bee. Pooh jumps over the desk. Joseph and Nate wrestle on the floor in the front of the classroom, while the teacher stands there, oblivious to the turmoil. The students have not been taught a single lesson since school started, except during the period when the principal came to observe. The students do whatever they choose without reprimand—even Nicole becomes animated. Pooh screams as she wrestles with Joseph. Jason screams imitating the actions of Pooh. Pooh, Mary, and Nicki slap at each other. Paper flies around the room. Shasaqua locks Anthony and Joseph outside the room. Mary punches Sam. Someone yells that the principal is coming. Silence. After the "false alarm" the students get up and walk out of class. This has been a typical day in room 127.

The majority of the students do not seem to grasp the profound consequences of the teacher's ineffectiveness. They think he is "nice" because "he does not holler" at them. Although the room is in total anarchy, neither consideration enters into their calculation of him: his being "nice" makes him "okay," almost without exception. Maykela is the only student who disagrees with the general consensus on Mr. U's "affable" personality. She articulates more critical reasoning:

May: I don't think he was a very good teacher. Cause he let kids run over him and do what they want to do and stuff. He gives you work and say here do this and don't explain it and gives out homework and collects if. Don't go into detail or show how it should be done. And then he just get the day over with and just like this piece of paper, I want you to finish this and do this. And then when you ask for help, he just hurry up and gives you a look.

Subsequently, the students are asked to identify certain aspects of a teacher's behavior that makes a "good" teacher. They are able to discern many attributes; however, being "nice" and not "hollering" at them are major, determining components for these children.

Q: What do you think makes a good teacher? What would they need?
Mary: It would have to be not strict. Well not all the time, they can teach us. They don't have to put the class together. Let them know when they playing and when they not playing and teach them a way they can understand it and laugh and have fun with the kids sometimes. Not all the time. And don't let them back talk them or let them get carried away.
L.Lee: Teaching kids, Mr. S is a good teacher. Some teachers don't care as long as they get paid. They just let you run over them, but he teaches. I like the way he disciplines and stuff. The teachers who discipline you,

who teach your, and make sure you get an education and who don't have attitudes.

Nic: When they want the students to learn. When they care.

May: What makes a good teacher? Just don't give you no work and just expect you to do it, one that explains it and help you and then one that don't expect you to get everything right and some teachers like if you get stuff wrong they explain to you how to get it right and stuff. They give you chances and stuff. Figure it out or help you figure it out. And not always help you. Sometimes you'll be thinking they mean because they make you do it on your own, but, most of the time I look back and it be the best for me cause every time I need something the teacher will do it. But now I can do it on my own and then when I learn how to do it on my own, I learn better than them explaining it to me and doing it their way. If I do it my way I can do it better.

Dan: Teachers who have respect for the kids, don't curse them out or make fun of them. Don't put they hands on them. Get involved with the kids parents. And make sure they do all they work and get an education.

Keis: They teach, they give you but not pile you with homework, but you learn something in the classroom. They teach you stuff, they not, you know, accusing kids and just . . . not mean, they don't have attitudes all the time. The kind that if you treat them wrong, they treat you wrong, but if you treat them right, they treat you with respect and you give respect back.

Sam: To qualify for the job you'd have to have a nice attitude and teach the students whatever they can. You have to have a attitude where you want to teach or she gonna make you learn, not just gonna sit there. One that makes your try to do you best, to make you learn And she not just getting paid.

R.J.   They teach you good. They be more nice instead of hollering and cussing and fussing.

These students are absolutely clear on what makes a good teacher; their perceptions are rich and complete, for they require that their ideal teacher not only educate the mind, but also the human spirit. The children speak of qualities such as understanding, tolerance, and discipline tempered with affability, humor, connectedness, and solicitude. Their ideal teacher wants to teach, understands methodology, and requires that the kids "do all the work." That is, school is not a "holding operation" for neither teacher ("She's not just getting paid") nor student ("make you try to do you best"). These children also understand that teaching and learning require a community orientation—"get the parents involved." Interestingly and against expectations, such issues of current focus as race and gender do not surface in this conversation.

The students are also asked to discuss whether or not they consider the knowledge received in school useful in their everyday lives. The answers are immediate and short range. There is no significant understanding of the correlation between what is learned now and its relationship to their futures. The majority of the students indicate that math is useful at the grocery stores, "counting change to make sure that the store owners don't cheat you." Several others declare that school has no use in relationship to their lives.

Q: Are the things you learn in school useful to you in your everyday life? If so give me some examples.

Tom: Social Studies, well, I don't listen to their social studies. I'll just . . . well I'll say Black History, about Malcolm X and stuff like that. That mostly it. Well, math helps when you go to the store, and you have five-hundred dollars, if you don't know how to count, you going to be through. Reading, cause if you going to be a basketball player, you can't read your contract.

L.Lee: Not really, just English.

Keis: I use math everyday, when I go to the store everyday. To ride the bus and get the correct change.

Nic: Like math if I buy something.

Pooh: Telling people stuff. Like tell people about they self. Like if they ain't talking right, proper, proper way or something like that. Math. Sometimes my friends they count their money wrong up in the restaurant.

Mary: Yea. Math. Uh, money. I went into the store and I had gave this man five dollars cause I had bought two bags of chips, cost one dollar. He only gave me two dollars back. I didn't think nothing of it, I just went straight home and then counted my money and went back to the store and said they owed me a dollar and showed him a receipt and everything. And he was nice, he gave me my money. But, I know next time, I have to start counting my money in the stores because most people don't want to give you your money back.

Sam: Yea. A lot. I go to the store, I need math to count and add up stuff in the store.

Nate: Yea. In the store, math and stuff when you buy stuff. English. So you
          can talk right.

Sam's response is more applicable to his lifestyle. The majority of the
children are admitted gang members and many have sold drugs for the
organizations. Sam's first reply deals with his common sense, everyday
world, a world in which drugs are an integral component:

Sam: Yea. Something I can use it in my rap. I can rap about arithmetic. I can
          make some stuff up. Reading and arithmetic. Learn about history,
          Martin Luther King, stuff like that. Like math, people that move drugs.
          Drug dealers they ain't stupid in school. They use their math they
          learned in school, to weigh the drugs and all that, to bag'em up and all
          that stuff. They learn how to weigh those big old kilos and all that stuff.

Anthony's answer conforms more to the "norm" for the larger social order

Ant: Well take for instance if you're doing some work with your dad,
          carpentry. You need to know how to do inches, meters, centimeters, and
          stuff like that. I need to know when someone is hurt, how to put
          pressure on their finger or something. English, for your grammar.

Finally, there is Joseph who believes that nothing he learns in school is of
any value.

PERCEIVED FUTURE OF SCHOOLING IN RELATION TO THE COMMON SENSE WORLD

The students are given an opportunity to imagine and create a school that
will meet their unique needs. Their answers represent a range and type of
personally constructed realities for their age and stage of development in
relation to their perceived social reality. Asked what type of school would
they plan, they provide a rich a range of responses.

Q: If you plan a school the way you wanted it to be, what would it look
          like? I mean inside and out, what would it have? Would it be just like
          this school? Or would it be completely different? How would your
          school be?

Shas: My school would be completely different. My school would be rebuilt. I would have marble and just nice desks. I would have everything, the walls would be redone. The windows would be tinted. The inside would be able to see outside but they couldn't see in. I would get some new wardrobes for the dance class, new cap and gowns, new choir gowns, new pianos, new desk, tables, chairs, books, cabinets. Everything. Get them a lunch lady who can cook, somebody to clean the school right. Mop the floor every night. I would find some teachers that would teach, make teaching fun, not sit there boring. Tired of them asking you to read this, read that, answer the questions

L.Lee: It won't have all this graffiti and stuff on it, written on the wall and stuff. And to pass you have to be in your right level because they just pass them because they want to get rid of them. I know you can't stop the rats and roaches. It won't have no windows like this, broken and written all over.

Jason: It would be big. I have a big teachers parking lot and big playground for the kids and a playground for the pre-school and kindergarten. And for the upper grades they would have a tall building and for first to fifth grade there would be a small part of the building. First of all I would not have any mean teachers. I would pick-out every teacher. I would see what is teacher is doing. I try to find out what is their background. And then if they can do it perfect, I pick'em. I have a swimming pool. A place where kids can go to learn more, like on the weekends. On the weekends the kids can come to school and do some more work, extra work. The principal would not be mean. They would be rules. They would have educational videos. And they would be draw art, culture club, dance, a lot of stuff. A lot of activity things. There would be south part of the building where the doors would be sound proof, so nobody can hears but the people that are in the dance room.

Keis: First we'd have good food in the cafeteria. Plenty of books, desks. Make sure walls had no rats and roaches, no writing. Like if we had broken windows, we get them fixed right away. Heat would be working. Walls won't have holes in them and stuff. I'd let the kids talk in the lunchroom. But they couldn't get rowdy.

Jos: I get it rebuilt. Make it look nicer, decent. And make some new teachers come in here that feel good about the students.

G.T.: It would be like this school here, but, you know it would be cleaner and nobody in a gang. I would just throw them out. They can't come to this school. Who ever I catch fighting, no matter who right or wrong, they be thrown out too. We would have twenty-four hour security. That way nobody could write on the school.

Nic: It would be good. I would take out all the gangs. Good teachers, clean it up a little bit. It would be no gang bangers writing on the walls, there names or nothing.

Sam: I probably have it in the suburbs and stuff. Cause city kids more wild and more gangs out here. They have some in the suburbs but not many. Have better inspection and stuff. Try to keep it up, clean and all. Have nice teachers, nice attitudes.

Mary: It would be a better paying job, it wouldn't have no roaches in the lunchroom or classroom and it would be clean. It would be big enough and have all the equipment it need for science, social studies and all that. The teachers would be strict. Cause some of these kids they don't care. They just plain bad. They would be nice sometimes but they would be strict when it's learning time. The curriculum would be the same.

May: It would have a lot of activities. It would have blacks and whites and then it would give a good education. And I would support my school. I would try to get the teachers to teach more about our school and gangs and stuff. And don't start they when they get in eighth, like when they in first grade. Try to talk about them and try to talk to them about gangs and stuff and show them how people end up. And I use most of my brothers for examples.

Thom: I wouldn't want all black teachers. You be around a whole lot of black people, be a whole lot of arguments. A special place for disabled and handicapped kids, they have a special side of the school and then have K through eighth on the other side. Social studies would be different. Because it would be about black people.

Again, the students' remarks are insightful and rich. Their sense of need and want do not diverge: each of these children would escape the decay and degradation of their environment if they could. They would each design a place and a set of adults who could help them accomplish this extraordinary dream. The dream school stands in stark contrast to their environment: it is "rebuilt," "marble," "walls that are redone," and "tinted windows" so that they can "see out." This school has "no graffitti;" it has materials, equipment, "a lunch lady who can cook," and "somebody who can "mop the floor every night." Here, the kids can come "on the weekends to do extra work," but "there would be rules." Mostly, "new teachers would feel good about the students." When these children speak of their reality—the omnipresent gangs, violence, and decay—they are tough in a world of constant conflict, a "war zone" populated by unfeeling and uncaring adults. But given the chance to dream, they know with certainty what kind of people and environment they need to realize themselves through education The pilot study (see appendix A), shows children who focus on curriculum and excelling—with no mention of gangs, physical plant or teacher behavior.

PSYCHOLOGICAL AND SOCIAL FACTORS RELATED TO SOCIAL REALITY CONSTRUCTION

Of Courage

> It takes so much courage to survive, really survive.
> For although you want to rest and rest and rest,
> It is only rest that will slay.
> You must, first of all. Flow with the pain.
> Don't fight it.
> Acknowledge it.
> Don't welcome it.
> An invited guest it may or may not be.
> Don't feed it.
> The cost too high, the visit too long.
> Don't delay it, but do admit it.
> This feels like what?
> Humiliation? I burn.
> Guilt? I am ashamed.
> Loss? I am empty.
> Hate? I am too angry-with me.
> So, when I strike out—with bullet, knife or words.
> Understand.
> It is not courage you see.

(Mitchell-Davis, 1993)

Many factors are involved in the psychological and social reality construction for children raised in poverty. Self-preservation is foremost, as presented in Judge Mitchell-Davis' poem. " These children are not only exposed to violence, they are also increasingly the perpetrators of violence" (Zinsmeister, 1990, pp. 50-51). Thus, black, disadvantaged children in the inner city are adept at developing survival techniques, for walking or driving into the wrong "set" could mean injury or death. Whether "plugged" with a particular gang or not, these children must be on the alert for gang activities—colors, boundaries, signs, etc.—since the decision to wear a hat to the right or to the left is crucial for survival.

Many of them have to assume adult responsibilities at an early age. Unlike their middle-class counter-parts, disadvantaged children are confronted much earlier by sex (fifteen of the twenty students are sexually active), violence, death, drugs, etc. (White, 1984). Consequently, they seek gang affiliation even if the "safety" that they get is illusory, for it is security, belonging, power, discipline, identity and family that these children want (Perkins, 1987). They become cunning, resilient, and resourceful (Comer and Poussaint, 1975). These traits must develop to counteract the feelings of insecurity, powerlessness, and negative self-concept—feelings of lower "caste" status—that develop in black children and their parents almost from infancy (Hopson and Hopson, 1990).

PERCEPTIONS OF SELF IN RELATION TO THE ENVIRONMENT

The children discuss a series of questions and issues which reveal facets of their everyday lives and ways of "seeing." Several of the questions reflect their social psychological perceptions of "self" within the context of the specific environment which makes up their realities. They are asked to color code a map of Englewood which indicates the safe and unsafe areas in the community according to their gang affiliation. Figure 3 is a composite of the children's diagrams. The map includes the predominant gangs in the area's elementary and high schools. Jim begins the narrative with a litany of his experiences, which includes his periods in Juvenile Detention Centers.

Q: How long were you in placement?
Jim: About two weeks, eleven days. About that long. I didn't even count. I
       knew I'd be out of there.

Q: Now when you are in placement, you said you were in Skokie, do you
        go in for consultation. Do they give you counseling?

Jim: Nope. You do your time. You watch T.V., eat, sleep, go to school.

Q: Do they have group counseling? Any other corrective procedures?

Jim: Nope. You sleep, wake-up and go to school. That's all. If you do
        something bad they put you in confinement.

Q: What's confinement?

Figure 3. Gang Territories Chart

A composite which outlines gang territories in the Englewood community. Each
school is designated by a major gang affiliation.

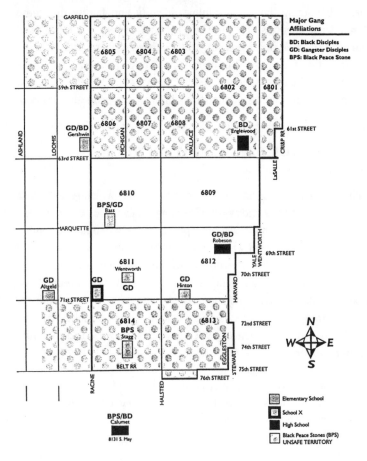

Jim: When you get into trouble, they put you in a room, lock you in there for a couple days. You still eat and everything. There's a bed, toilet, a sink and a window.

Q: Have you ever been in confinement?

Jim: Yep. For kickin' it off. A riot. That's when everybody in a session. One gang gets together and beats up the other gang. I started it.

Q: So most of the people in there are in different gangs?

Jim: Yea. That's what I was in confinement for. The second day, cause I was mad and I told myself that if I ever got locked up, I was going in and kickin' it off. That's what I did. My word is my bond.

Q: Your word is your bond?

Jim: Yep. I kicked it off.

Q: Were there a lot of GD's in there?

Jim: It's more GDs' then anything.

Q: Then who were you Fighting?

Jim: BDs, Stones, whatever. Anybody that wasn't GD.

Q: Okay, how did they know that you started it?

Jim: Because I stole on a boy?

Q: What had you done?

Jim: He had said something, and I stole on him. His friends tried to help. Me and my friends we whipped them. And we all went in confinement for a couple days. It's nothing though. It was like sitting in a room, you can't do nothing, so there nothing you can do.

Q: Anybody get hurt?

Jim: Somebody got hit in the head with a chair. It wasn't me.

Q: Did they have to take him to the hospital?

Jim: They took him to medical. They don't take you to the hospital. Once you in that place, you ain't going out of there for no reason. They got doctors in there. So I don't know why people try to hurt themselves to think they go to the hospital. You staying right up there. You ain't going no where. You staying right there. Ain't no use trying to get hurt or hurt yourself, that's on you. They don't care about you in there. That's what's wrong with the system.. Some of them do but some don't, some, do. I grew up in this system. The only counseling is for smoking weed. That's the only thing they got. A little program you want to stop smoking weed, you come there. But no one talk you to stop. If you don't stop the first time you get out. That's on you. They don't have no counseling. They don't care about counseling you. If you go there and get out of there, you do the same thing, you stupid.

Q: When is you time in placement up?

Jim: I thought I was staying but they let me out. My probation officer and my lawyer made a negotiation that I stay in the house for thirty days to January twelfth, which I'm on now, and they let me out. I don't care. I don't care if I get out or not. There wasn't nothing to do anyway. I'm like I did my time, I'm out of here. You be in school, the hours been going quick. As long as I was out for the summer.

Q: Do you think being in a gang will help you to be successful?

Jim: I know a lot of GDs that are successful. I had a cousin, he successful, he got a good job. He don't gang bang. He works at the post office making about twenty- one dollars a hour. He got a good job. He GD. You can be in a gang and don't have to gang bang.

Q: But you gang bang.

Jim: I don't gang bang. Somebody gonna gang bang on me and I'm gonna gang bang. But if you don't say nothing to me, I don't say nothing to you. We ain't in a gang anyway, we in an organization. Ain't no gang. A gang is people who go around beating up people. We don't beat up people who don't mess with us. Or will hurt us or try to do something bad to us. We the organization.

Q: Do you see yourself "dropping your flag?"

Jim: One of these days I am. I ain't gonna be in this stuff forever. Once I get a lot of money, I gonna sit back and laugh.

Q: How do you plan on getting a lot of money?

Jim: Get me a job like my cousin.

Q: Have you ever been locked behind bars?

Jim: I never been behind bars, I be behind doors.

Q: But you told me you were in the same place with the two boys that killed the eleven year old.

Jim: Right, but they are not behind bars. I be in a door just like this. You just can't get out. That's all.

Q: Where were you at that time?

Jim: In the Audie Home at twelfth and Hamilton.

Q: How do you feel about being in the Audie home? Is it any different than being in placement?

Jim: Same thing to me. That's cool. Same thing. You just out of town.

Q: When you were in the Audie Home do they have counseling or group sessions for corrections in behavior?

Jim: Nope. Same thing, the drug rehab. That's all. We have no counseling. Nobody cares. The correction is when you are locked up. That lock you up trying to teach you, That's your counseling right there. People come there to be drug rehab and stuff. Nobody come talk to you one on one. People maybe come from church and talk to you. But no counseling. Don't have a special day, nobody come and talk to you. . . If they had group sessions, a fight will break out before anything. Ain't nobody going to have a group session, somebody will mess around and have a fight, have a group and this boy in another gang, he will say something smart and they will fight. Ain't going to have no group session. People be scared. . . The counselor people in there. They don't want all the different gangs that come together. Somebody say something, kick it off right there in counseling.

Q: So you are telling me that the adults are basically afraid of the kids?

Jim: No, some of them will beat you down.

Q: Has that happened to you?

Jim: No.

Q: Do you know why they haven't beat you and they have beat some of the others?

Jim: Cause people be talking smart to them. If they don't get smart with me I don't get smart with them, but they ain't going hit me. I hit'em back. They can't kill you. That's one thing they can't do. Just put a couple of bruises on you and you do the same thing to them. So, I ain't scared of them. They try to beat you, but if you fight them back they won't mess with you anymore. The only thing they can do is to put some bruises on you but you can do the same thing to them. They can't hit no harder. So you just take it.

Q: So that's the way you look at it?

Jim: Right. My momma and my father taught me that. Can't nobody hurt you and you can't hurt them worser. Somebody hit me in my eye, you hit them even harder.

Q: Have you ever been shot at?

Jim: Got shot in the leg about two weeks ago. I'm straight though. I'm okay. It didn't hurt, it just burn. I was out the hospital in the next two hours, then I be outside chillin'.

Q: Who shot you?

Jim: I don't know, some Stone.

Q: Where were you?

Jim: On 71st and Morgan.

Q: Is that Stone territory?

Jim: Naw, they just be up there every now and then ridin through there or walking through there after school.

Q: So you have no idea who shot you?

Jim: I know he is a Stone, I saw his face and everything but I don't know his name. . . I told the GDs not to do anything. I see him one of these days by himself. Wait and see. If I don't, I don't. Maybe it was a message, I don't know. . . But if I see him again, I'm gonna hit him with something. He don't shoot me and get away with it. If I don't see him, I don't see him. I ain't gonna look for nobody and go back to jail. I ain;t stupid to go to jail for no murder. I don't want to be in jail that long. I don't want to be in jail period. That stupid to go to jail for murder. Why would you kill somebody when you could just beat them up.

Q: Have you ever shot at anybody?

Jim: Nope. Yea, I shot at somebody one time, a couple times rather.

Q: For what? Different gang?

Jim: (Pause) Shoot at me, I shoot at'em back. You ain't going to shoot at me and get away with it. . . Did the shooting first, they shot at me first. Or I had to go take care of some business and shoot first.

Q: When you say take care of some business, what do you mean?

Jim: They did something to one of our Folks, and the older Folks sent one of us out to care of our business.

Q: So the people that have rank are the older people in the gang?

Jim: It maybe somebody young but not too young.

Q: Okay they tell you to go take care of business?

Jim: Yea. They going get with them first and they tell us what to do and we go take care of business.

Q: So when they tell you to do something, you go do it?

Jim: Naw, I don't do like that. If you want to do that, They ask you if you want to volunteer and do it, it ain't like everybody think it is. Like the authority said go shoot somebody in the head. They ask if you want to go do it. No, I don't want to do it, I got too many cases. O.K. you don't have to do it. But if you want to do it on your own you go do it. If they did something to you. I know if they did something to me, I going back for them. I won't try to kill them, just try to hurt them, but, if they die, they die. I know if they shoot me they would feel the same way about me, forget him, he dead.

Q: How would you feel if they did die and it was somebody you shot?

Jim: I don't know. I ain't never shot nobody and killed them.

Q: Where do you get the guns?

Jim: Buy them. Anything, twelve gauge, 9mm, anything, get'em all.

Q: You are telling me at fourteen and eleven you were in the gang when you started

Jim: I started shooting when I was thirteen, I thought the gun was too big for me to shoot and somebody told me you can shoot any gun. So I started shooting any gun, twelve gauge, anything.

Q: So you are telling me at thirteen, if you want to buy a gun you can just go get one?

Jim: You buy you one when you are eleven.

Q: Is it that easy Jim?

Jim: Yea, you got connections, you like me, if you been in this thang for a long time, you know all about it, you get the gun like this. A little bit of nothing and go get it.

Q: So you know where to go?

Jim: Well, I call and get some connections. Get some info. You learn just from being around the neighborhood for a long time. A person like me, everybody know you, you know, they give you connections, you know can buy you a thang, a little something. This for protection.

Q: Okay, tell me this. Where, when and what makes you feel safe?

Jim: I feel safe all the time. Unless I going somewhere another gang territory at. Other than that I feel safe. . . I don't be scared. I go to other gang neighborhoods. Ain't nobody do nothing to you unless you disrespect them. Just disrespect their Nation and they be like, we know you in this gang but just don't disrespect any of our Nations or do anything to our People. And it's over.

Q: What do they call disrespect?

Jim: If you say throw down their Nation or something. Or throw down a five or throw down BD or something like that (see appendix).

Q: Any other time you feel unsafe?

Jim: No. I feel safe at school and when I walk home. I don't worry about nobody.

Q: Is there any reason to feel unsafe in school? Isn't this a GD school?

Jim: I don't care about that.

Q: Yes you do.

Jim: GDs up in here!

Q: Anything else up in here?

Jim: I heard a couple other people in other gangs, but, I don't know about that. I don't worry about it.

Q: Black Peace Stones. Is that what you heard?

Jim: I guess. Yea. They don't do nothing to me. I don't care about this territory right here, this is 69 territory. I'm East Side Circa Con City.

Jim's narrative is a "slice-of-life" about real people and real events. It reflects his commonsense understanding of his world and what is meaningful within that world.

The students respond to the questions regarding safety and how some of the experiences in their lives affect their emotional and physical well-being.

Q: Shashqua, tell me something about when you feel good. What happens in your life that makes you feel good?

Shas: When my momma can talk to me without arguing or everybody can be happy once in awhile or I get good grades, some money. Just seeing everybody happy makes me feel good. But I don't want my momma arguing everyday, or having problems everyday, that makes me feel good.

Q: Is she arguing with you or your grandmother?

Shas: Everybody. When my momma has certain days and certain moods, she get real grouchy. My momma change. She used to be sweet and everything, then when she started doing drugs, she lost half of her memory, she totally changed. The only thing she do now is smoke and drink cranberry juice.

Q: Does she go for rehab?

Shas: Yea, she did. She stopped. She went there for like three or four years.

Q: When did she completely stop?

Shas: Three years and four months ago.

Q: Give me an example of what makes you feel bad?

Shas: When my momma and grandmother feel bad, they argue with everybody and that makes me feel bad. When my momma wake up in the morning grouchy and cursing, that makes me feel bad. Problems, when stuff be going on in the house, when people need money, and I be pressing to do something, to go get some money, so I can just give it to them, that makes me feel bad. You know, I feel useless.

Q: Where can you get money?

Shas: I can get money anywhere. I can go to my cousins, I could get money from people out here. Yea, I can go to the Nation. I have to tell them and they'll say do you have a problem about something? And I'll say yea and they'll say what you need, I say I need a hundred dollars or something like that and they'll say what for? I say I am having problems at home, you know we need some money. And everybody take money out their pocket to give to me, that's called Nation Finance or when we just give money to the Nation, that's called Nation Finance.

Q: Do you have to pay it back?

Shas: Yea.

Q: What happens if you don't pay it back?

Shas: If you don't pay it back they like, you have to sell drugs to pay it back.

Q: How long do you think you will be in a gang?

Shas: I don't know.

Q: O.K., when, where and what makes you feel safe?

Shas: Nowhere makes me feel safe. When I am outside, don't nobody like me, most females do not like me. I could care less about what somebody else think of me but all I know, all I hear when I walk around is "they gonna beat you up. . . " They don't like me because I am in a different gang then they. That's because I just ask them "all you want to do is fight and jump on somebody because they in a different gang then you or doing something different then you. You want them to be just like you so you want to jump them and fight then and kill them or something?" I be like just look, " I ain't sitting around waiting for somebody to come jump on me to kill me-I'm gonna come get you first." That's my attitude towards them. I ain't gonna sit around and wait for somebody to jump on me and kill me. I ain't waiting on nothing like that. I just have to do what I have to do. They say you act like a gang banger and all that. You should try to act like a young lady, not a gang banger. I do act like a young lady.

Q: Who says that to you?

Shas: My mother say that everyday. Because that what her momma said to her. I do act like a young lady. When I'm outside, I consider myself as a young lady. A young black lady, that's me. I don't walk around "GD." I don't do that outside, no, I don't do that. That's not me. I try to tell my momma that's not me. I used to do that a long time ago. I use to walk around, "GD, all that." I don't do that anymore

Q: What makes you feel unsafe?

Shas: Okay, when I am walking outside with somebody and I feel a whole bunch of people behind us or in front of us and stuff. I see the people that I know don't like me and they be looking at you, I say, "Look, I know something gonna happen," I know when something gonna happen, the palm of my hands start itching and burning and turning red. I just be, man, I know something is gonna to happen. It's like last summer when I was in Elgin, there was these girls, I used to go out there four years straight. I use to hang with these girls, That's when I was GD, and then I went out there recently, I said I don't hang with you anymore, you doing too much bad stuff. I had heard about the stuff that they had did.

Q: So the gangs go that far?

Shas: Yes. Like I cannot handle this. I can't hang with you all. So I would be with this girl named Fanny. I was fixin to go back to Elgin to start working for her grandmother, and I started hanging with her. I did not know they jump her and they say anybody that be with her will get jumped on too. They gonna have to get taken care of. So me and Fanny was outside one night and we see her cousins with'em. Those girls that jumped her, and then my palms of my hands were coming blood red and they started burning, then I started doing this, "Come on, let's go" and I be saying like this and looked like I had blood coming from my hands and I was like this ain't me, I ain't fixin to do nothin "I'm not going to do anything, come on Fanny, let's go home before something happens." So they walked up behind us. They was like "Come here. Come here." I turned like this and kept on walking and they ran up behind me and I'm thinking they about to grab me and they grabbed Fanny. They was like what you doing with her Shashqua? What you doing with her? And I said, look I hang with whoever I want to hang with. Ain't nobody gonna tell me who I can hang with. You are not my mother, I left my mother in Chicago and my father in the projects.

Q: Would you say that gang activity pretty much takes up a great portion of your time and life and influences you?

Shas: Yea. It do, but it all depends on how you take it. How you control it. It influence you, you know if you walk around gang banging and all that and come in school and just don't do nothing, that influence you. But the gang I'm in make you come to school. If you miss school and go around the people that you know around the gang, they be like, why are you not in school? I ditch. No you gotta go to school to get into college. They there for you. Once you in the gang, you must go to school. You go to school, you can' be stinky, funky or looking bummy or nothing.

Q: Would you say the majority of the people in the gangs have not finished school?

Shas: Yea, but that how come they want you to. They don't want you to end up like they do. Not going to school, not knowing nothing. The new ones tell you to go to school.

Q: How do they feel about members doing drugs? Do they talk about that?

Shas: Yea. They say just like Scarface. You can't get high on your own supply.

Q: Who is Scarface?

Shas: You know the gangster pencil they have, Al Pacino. It was like, if you be selling drugs, you cannot use drugs. If you use them drugs, that you buy yourself to sell to somebody else, you can't be using them.

Q: But they do, don't they?

Shas: Yea, some of them. When they catch you, if you get caught using drugs, you gotta to. You get your body beaten, you gone.

Sam's perception of feeling good, bad, safe and unsafe parallels Shashqua's. His answers are also associated with gang activity.

Q: What are some of are some of things that make you feel good about yourself?

Sam: Seeing my little brother once in awhile, playing with my cousins and playing when I go outside and sit and talk. Me, Butch, Hank and Pooh.

Q: Okay, what makes you feel bad?

Sam: I feel bad when something happen to somebody close to me or something.

Q: What kind of things can happen to make you feel bad?

Sam: A person die or get shot, or be in the hospital.

Q: What about the situation with your mother? How does that make you feel?

Sam: That make me feel bad too. I don't go over there cause I got a feeling that she was doing what she wasn't supposed to be doing. I don't want to have that feeling. And I'll be mad and stuff. That's why I don't go over there, cause I find out.

Q: Has she ever been in rehab?

Sam: Nope. She only do, she get high with her friends and stuff. So when she spend the weekend with me she don't do it, but then she get with her friends, when she come around here, when she been over my grandmother's house, she get with her friends and all that stuff. Most of the times she will do it with her friends.

Q: Have you ever gone to stay with her for the weekend or something?

Sam: Yea. If she be there, she be gone all the time.

Q: Where, when and what makes you feel safe? When do you feel the safest?

Sam: In the house. With my grandfather.

Q: What makes you feel unsafe?

Sam: When I don't know where I am at or something, when I'm lost. When I am out of the neighborhood. I feel safe in the neighborhood cause I know everybody. They all know me.

Q: What I hear you saying is, you don't have a problem because everyone knows you?

Sam: Yea.

Q: How do you know which gangs are in what area? No one seems to have a problem drawing these maps (see appendix) of where they can go and which gangs are in which area. They are basically all the same. All the kids know which gangs are in which area. How do you know that?

Sam: I don't know how. You see different things and throwing up stuff.

Q: So when you are riding around they throw up their signs?

Sam: Yea. And you know you got people who came to you or you got somebody, your friend or something, they might live over there.

Q: But it's like a universal language. Everybody understands who's in what area.

Sam: Yea. Everybody knows not to come to different parts. You go where you want to go but it's difficult.

Q: You might get beat up or shot?

Sam: Yea (laughter).

Q: Well, of course you can go wherever you want but you will not be safe.

Sam: Yea.

Q: Now how old were you when you realized there were certain areas you could not go to or should not go in?

Sam: I was about, young.

Q: How young?

Sam: About nine or ten years old.

Q: And the other kids know? Don't they?

Sam: Yea. Older kids taught you. That's how you know. I have older cousins.

Nicole provides a startling narrative that underscores the issue of peril in the lives of these children.

Q: Explain how you were involved in the gun situation to me. How do you feel about guns?

Nic: Yea. Because my ex-boyfriend hit me.

Q: How old were you?

Nic: I was eleven and he was nineteen. When he smacked me, I ran upstairs to his house. His friend was looking at me and I ran up to the house and got the gun and came down and shot him in the arm. He was like what you gonna leave me alone now? Then I looked at him and said, I ain't got no time for you no more. Then my sister asked if we break up again and I was like, "I ain't got time for him" and I told her that he hit me and she was like, do you want me to beat him up? And I said no. Then she said I'm sorry. I said what do you have to be sorry for? Then she was like, I was the one that got you to go with him. I said that's okay.

Q: Did you have any more gun involvement after that?

Nic: Naw, other when they play "It."

Q: What is "It?" Who plays "It?" GDs?

Nic: No my aunties. One is twenty-three and one is going on forty.

Q: Are these your mother's sisters?

Nic: Yea.

Q: Now what is "It?" Explain it to me.

Nic: See they got they boyfriends and since my auntie got a gun in her house. Her kids don't know and she will put it . . .

Q: Is this the one that is twenty-three. How many kids does she have?

Nic: Yea. She got five. Then she was like, Do you'all want to play "It?" Because usually it will be me, my auntie and my other auntie. Then they said they were going to play couples and I sat down. Then they was, do you want to play "It?" And I was looking at them. They sat there, because then if they play "It" they shoot at each other, other then tag, they shoot at each other.

Q: They shoot at each other? What do you mean?

Nic: Okay when me and my aunties was just like, we go out and separate.

Q: You play too?

Nic: Yea. We go our separate ways. And then one of us count, then we got to say ten out loud, then we start running and stuff. You start running and if you get into, if you bump into one of each other, you can shoot at each other if you want to. So when I play, they play like, they get those play guns, because, I don't know why.

Q: When you play they use play guns?

Nic: Yea. Cause they say I might shoot one of them for real, because I have a real gun. I ain't though. But when they play with their boyfriends, they play with each other with real guns.

Q: Are they actually trying to hit each other?

Nic: My aunt is actually trying to hit her boyfriend.

Q: Does your mother play this game too?

Nic: No. My momma say they are crazy.

Q: Do your two sisters play?

Nic: No. They afraid.

Q: But you are not afraid to play "It?"

Nic: Naw.

Q: Do they play this often?

Nic: They play it like every Friday or Saturday. Like on the week-end.

Q: Are they high? Do they do drugs?

Nic: (Laughing) No.

Q: They just play "It?' How do you feel when you play?

Nic: Yea. It's fun.

Q: It's fun having somebody shooting at you and trying to dodge bullets?

Nic: No. But you know, it's like, if you getting into a real fight and then you end up walking off and the girl end up pulling a gun out. It's seeing how fast you can run between you and the girl who pulled the gun on you and trying to shoot you. They try to shoot you, then you can run fast.

Q: So it's like training?

Nic: Yea. Something like that. Since my auntie don't like her boyfriend, so she try to shoot him for real. But they supposed to be a couple. They suppose to help each other. (Maykela commented about the game of "IT" that Nicole plays "Nicole be telling me um how many girls they are going to get—how they play "IT" and kill people and stuff.")

Q: And she is trying to hit him playing "It" huh? Tell me, Nicole, since we are discussing "fun" what makes you feel good? Good about yourself?

Nic: That I am in school and I ain't got no kids. If I have a baby I don't know what to do. I ain't gonna quit school for nobody.

Q: What else makes you feel good?

Nic: That I am alive right now today.

Q: What makes you feel bad?

Nic: I don't know.

Q: When do you feel bad?

Nic: When I do something to my momma.

Q: like what?

Nic: Try to beat up her boyfriend.

Q: You have jumped on your mother's boyfriend? What happened to bring that about?

Nic: He called one of my sisters a "b" and I just hit him.

Q: What did your sister do?

Nic: She started hitting him too. I was the first one to hit him. And my momma got mad.

Q: What did your momma say?

Nic: She was just looking at us, cause he ain't have no reason to call her no "b." Every time we get into it with him, you know, it's involving her and she get mad.

Q: How does your mother feel about all of you being in gangs?

Nic: That's why I'm getting out, cause she don't like me being in gangs.

Q: Was she in one?

Nic: When she was young. She was sixteen when she got out, cause she got pregnant with my sister. She was GD but first she was BD. Then she "flipped" and became GD. And my daddy a BD.

Q: When, where and what makes you feel safe?

Nic: When I am up in the house.

Q: Okay. What makes you feel unsafe? When, where and what makes you feel unsafe?

Nic: When I'm outside because a whole bunch of girls since they don't like me. They pulled out a gun on me, around two or three girls. And I was like if you gonna shoot, why is you scared to shoot me?

Q: Has that happened more than once? Have they pulled guns on you before?

Nic: Yea. It was around two ro three times. And it was the same girls.

Q: Was she GDs?

Nic: No, I don't think so, I think she BD. Cause she don't like my sister, so she got to be with them or something.

G.T. also needs cunning and wit to survive. Originally he states that he is "dropping his flag", but later he recants, claiming that the situation within the gang has improved. He continues to express concern about his safety and survival in the "war zone."

Q: G.T. what are some of the things that makes you feel good?

G.T.:   Seeing my father, seeing my grandmother and playing ball (G.T. is on the school basketball team).

Q: What makes you feel bad?

G.T.:   When people get to yelling at me like I did something wrong. If I don't do nothing wrong, when people blame me for something I didn't do. Like somebody say I didn't do something. I did something to somebody or they say I took something and I wasn't nowhere around that spot. Or something like my cousin said I took some money, and I wasn't even in the house. I left that morning and I didn't come back till that night and he said I took some money. But, I don't have any money. So my auntie thought I had spent it. But, I wasn't nowhere around that day. I was with my father all day, but, then she call up my father and he wasn't at home, then she thought I was lying.

Q: When do you feel safe?

G.T.:   I feel safe when I am with my father, my mother or when I am in the house or when I am at the park playing football.

Q: When don't you feel safe?

G.T.:   When I am hanging around my cousin when he is gang banging.

Q: Your cousin that said he didn't like the gang anymore either?

G.T.:   Yea. But he can't get out because he lives on the set.

Q: What is the set?

G.T.:   That's like your territory.

Q: So if he decided he wanted out and tried to get out, what would happen?

G.T.:   He just get a violation.

Q: But you said he couldn't get out.

G.T.:   If he really wanted to get out, he don't have to except the violation which I know he ain't gonna take it because it going to be a five minute violation. NO cover.

Q: That's little rough. Okay why do you feel unsafe around your cousin?

G.T.:   Because a car with another gang members probably drive pass and throw up the same gang sign he throw up. But they ain't in the same gang. And they come out shooting.

Q: Have you ever been involved in something like that?

G.T.:   Yes. Some Blackstones came through and they was throwing GDs and they was throwing it down (disrespect). Then the boys I was with they didn't have no guns. So the Blackstones got out the car and started shooting.

Q: Did anyone get hurt?

G.T.:   Nope. There was a lot of us too. We was standing on my corner when they rode up.

Q: They rode through your neighborhood. That takes a lot of nerve, doesn't it?

G.T.:   Yea. That's what they do. Like drive-byes. When they started shooting everybody started to run. But I was by a car, so I got under the car and then they just pulled around the corner and got out and then I got up and ran through the lot on my block and into the house.

Q: Have any of your friends been shot or hurt?

G.T.:   No.

Q: Have they been shot at?

G.T.:   Yea, they been shot at.

Q: Have they shot or hurt anybody?

G.T.:   My cousin, he killed somebody. He was in another gang. The boy, he was a Blackstone and he walked on my block. Because on my block, if you in the same gang they is or they don't like you, they gonna beat you up. So he was a Blackstone and he walked through and everybody who was in a gang on my block they beat him up and my cousin came around with a .22 mm rifle and shot him in the leg and in the head and killed him.

After school one day, Pooh, witnesses a similar gang related incident that involves her cousin. Seemingly, from the similarity to G.T's statements, it is likely the same incident. Pooh says that she observed a shooting. A man was shot in the arm and then in the leg. After he was shot, he was kicked and suffered lacerations to the back of the head. He was bleeding profusely and it took fifteen minutes for the ambulance to arrive. She confided that her cousin was told to "bust him" and he did, which coincides with G.T.'s account.

Q: How did you feel about that?
G.T.:   I ain't see it, my cousin told me about it. I was at basketball practice.
        When I got there, there was a lot of blood.
Q: You use to be BD?
G.T.:   Yea. Last year. They wanted me to flip again, they wanted me to be BD
        again. My brother he like the minister of the BDs.
Q: How old is he?
G.T.:   Seventeen.
Q: He is a minister. What does a minister do?
G.T.:   That's just like a head teacher. Tell you what to do.
Q: So Englewood would be safe for you because of your brother?
G.T.:   Yes.

Nate hopes to be a basketball player, but like the other students he fears for his safety and life. One of the few students who envisions college and a professional career, his affiliation with the Gangster Disciples make his ambition unlikely to be accomplished.

Q: What are some of the things you do that make you feel good?
Nate: Basketball. I want to play basketball in high school and college. Then
        I'm going to be a professional.
Q: Are you that good?
Nate: Yea. I get better as the years go by.
Q: Okay. What makes you feel bad?

Nate: Only time I feel is like when I get mad. That would be it. When people mess with me, but I know how to handle myself though. So people don't mess with me.

Q: And when people mess with you, what do you do?

Nate: I go find something, knock their head off with.

Q: Do you go to your Folks?

Nate: First I try to handle it by myself. If I can't handle it, I'm going to get my brother. I don't have to go to them.

Q: What are some of the things that happen around the are, in your neighborhood?

Nate: Shootings and stuff. They be jumping, killing Brothers on 74th.

Q: Are you ever involved in that?

Nate: One time I got chased on 74th by them.

Q: Who is on 74th?

Nate: Stones, Blackstones.

Q: Do you and your brother stay around there?

Nate: No. We stay around 72nd and Racine. But my brother he be over there most of the time but he stay at home, he a house person. He's bad but he still be in the house. Everybody look up to him. Like he a big shot.

Q: Okay, Nate. Where, when and what makes you feel safe?

Nate: When I am in the house.

Q: Is that the only time you feel safe?

Nate: Yea. Because when you leave out of the house, that's like a risk on your life. Anything can happen. You can get hit by a car, bit by a dog, anything.

Q: What is your greatest fear? When do you feel unsafe?

Nate: When you go in the wrong neighborhood. You get chased and you could get killed.

Q: How can you tell?

Nate: GDs have their hats to the right. You know how they have those coats and throw up five, Stones wear their hats to the left.

Q: BDs wear their hats which way?

Nate: To the right.

Q: BDs and GDs wear their hats to the right? Doesn't that get confusing? How can you tell one from the other?

Nate: By the neighborhood.

Pooh understands that safety is contingent upon her knowing the "Lit," which each initiate has to study and be able to recite. Pooh states that she learned her "Lit" by observing her cousin, brother, and uncle, all active members of the Gangster Disciples. Recitation of the "Lit" includes a prayer-like homage to "Hoover" in anticipation of his release from jail. Larry Hoover, the forty-four year old leader hailed as "King Hoover" and "Chairman" of the Gangster Disciples, is serving time for murder (Chicago Tribune, 1995). Although Pooh professes that she recently "dropped her flag," her friendship and loyalty to gang members and the GD Nation remain unbroken. Like the other children, her safe and unsafe spheres depend on gang activity. During her discussion she speaks of the rapist who stalked the Englewood Community, strangling ten women since the beginning of the year in abandoned houses and alleys (Chicago Tribune, 1995). Fear is often visible in the children's eyes.

Q: What are some of the things that make you feel good about yourself? Or what are some of the things that make you feel good. What are some of the things that make you happy?

Pooh: Being on 72nd Street, hanging around with my friends, which my mother don't want me to hang around them. And when I am with my mother or when my daddy buy me stuff or something like that.

Q: When do you feel bad? What makes you feel bad? It can be related to anything. What makes you feel sad or want to cry?

Pooh: When I think about my mother and what she been through and what we been through. When I think about my father's situation, he got to pay child support and all that.

Q: What makes you feel safe? You say you go around your neighborhood a lot. Now this area has a lot of gang activity, doesn't it or does it? I am assuming. In the news and media, you hear about all the shooting and stuff.

Pooh: Staying in the house.

Q: How do the gang members relate to you?

Pooh: I get along with all of them. Because they know my uncle. My uncle, he a gang member. He is twenty-three. Joseph is over all them little boys. My uncle is over everyone around here. They know if they do something wrong or do something to me, they know my uncle will . . . One time this man, he was trying to touch on me and my uncle came over with his friends and beat the man up.

Q: Tell me, when don't you feel safe?

Pooh: When I am around this area, period. Or when I am walking by myself or walking somewhere where I don't suppose to be at. Like in alleys and being up in abandoned houses and playing "it." It be me, My friends and cousins play "it" up in the abandoned house next door to my house. It's rapist and all that around here, so you can't feel safe wherever you go cause it's still bad. It ain't no better.

Although Anthony has no apparent gang affiliation, his three brothers are gang members. Thus, safety is still a major factor in his everyday existence.

Q: What are some things that make you feel good?
Anth: Listening to music and when me and my dad talk and stuff. Or chill. And when I accomplish something like making the basketball team or something.
Q: What makes you feel bad?
Anth: When a close friend of mine or person in my family gets shot or killed.
Q: Is that a constant concern?
Anth: Yea. It is cause I be around a lot of violence.
Q: What makes you feel safe?
Anth: When I am at home with my mom and dad.
Q: What makes you feel unsafe?
Anth: When it be dark and I see a lot of people outside. When there used to be big groups around, you know police think there be mob action and one time I was at my grandmothers house and some people from down there from another gang came down there. And was driving a whole bunch of cars and I don't know what's up. At four o'clock at night, when my brother got shot at Harold's Chicken, got shot in the back and one of his close friends was shot and was in critical condition and died.
Q: Was that your fourteen year old brother?
Anth: No, that's my brother who is twenty-four. The one fourteen is in jail. My nineteen and twenty year old brothers sell drugs and stuff like that.

Thomas also, has some legitimate concerns about safety and longevity because of his lifestyle.

Q: Tell me some of the things that make you feel good?
Tom: That I'm living. Cause all the trouble I do. And I like myself.
Q: What makes you feel bad?
Tom: Cause all the trouble I was getting in and giving my dad problems. And I ain't seen my momma.
Q: When do you feel safe?

Tom: In the house. And that's it. I don't feel safe in school. Anybody can come up in there. Because people be getting raped, I talking about women. Plus when I used to go to Hale, this boy came in school and shot this boy.

Q: So you feel unsafe because of the gangs in the area?

Tom: Yes. Last year a BD came in here and then he ask some more people and they started transferring in. There was a fight everyday. He was sent to Montefiore. And the rest of the people were transferred.

Q: Well they just can't transfer in here unless their parents do it.

Tom: Some people come in here, I don't know how they got up in here. He wasn't suppose to be up in here. I don't know if he lived around here. Just like people think I'm soft.

Q: Why do people think you're soft?

Tom: Cause you won't fight, you got to push me to the limit. See ain't nobody push me to the limit yet. I go off. Start fighting. I don't hit the stomach or arms, I go straight for the head, bust their head.

Q: You said Nate and the rest of them had a fight yesterday. Were you involved?

Tom: No.

Q: Anybody get hurt other than his brother.

Tom: Nope. He just had a bloody nose.

Q: Have you ever seen anybody get shot?

Tom: In the projects, on the Westside. My cousin had a gun and was going like this (waving gun) and shot his momma in the foot.

Q: But with the number of gang fights, did you ever see anybody get shot? What do they do a lot of threatening?

Tom: Yes.

Q: What about drive-bys?

Tom: My father was in one.

Q: He was in a gang?

Tom: Yes. GD.

Q: Is he still one?

Tom: No. He got out when he had me.

Tom and his classmates live in constant fear for their safety. Their identities, their sense of self, of their peers, of those in authority, of the systems in which they live are all forged in and through these inner and outer experiences. This, for Kotlowitz (1991), is the persistent reality historically thrust upon them by resolute facets of society:

> By the time they enter adolescence, they have contended with more
> terror than most of us confront in a lifetime. They have made choices
> that most experienced adults would find difficult. They have lived with
> fear and witnessed death. Some of them have lashed out. They have
> joined gangs, sold drugs, and in some cases inflicted pain on others. But
> they have also played basketball and gone on dates and shot marbles
> and kept diaries. For despite all they have done and seen, they are—and
> we must constantly remind ourselves of this—still children (p. I).

The happiness, sadness, fears, and apprehensions of safety
experienced by the children are created by social processes. This identity
constructed from these social processes for each child and once
crystallized, is maintained, modified, or even shaped by social relations
(Burger and Luckmann, 1966). For black, disadvantaged adolescents this
identity and perception of self becomes melded within an environment
restricted by poverty and violence, and their very survival depends upon
adaptability. The behavioral patterns they must develop in this
environment are usually so confined and inflexible that the children find
it almost impossible to expand their limited concept of the larger social
order (Wilson, 1978).

Clearly, in addition to the difficult questions of research framework
and definition, other important questions are whether and how these
children's conceptual systems can be expanded, and if and how they can
be taught to sustain themselves, i.e., function—outside of their
environment. One important facet in the process is that we must
understand how these children perceive themselves in relation to the
larger social order.

They are asked to respond to questions relating to the physical space
which makes up their environment. The twenty students are presented
with the following list of sites in the greater metropolitan area of Chicago,
identified by Chicago In a Box (Late for the Sky Production Company)
as major city sites. They are to state whether they have "visited," "heard
of but never visited," or "never heard of" these sites. Table 3 contains the
children's responses. Many well known areas of the city can be deemed
to be "another world" for these children, attesting to the commonsense
world of these children who are, in a curious paradox, isolated in the inner
city. The museums are the sites visited more frequently through

school-sponsored field trips, but many of the students are unfamiliar with Wacker Drive, a major thoroughfare in the city. Places of entertainment and cultural centers—even ones as common as Wrigley Field and McCormick Place—have not been heard of by six of the twenty students.

The children were asked a series of questions related to identification of the sites.

Table 3. Chicago Sites and Landmarks

	VISITED	HEARD OF	NEVER HEARD OF
The Water Tower	08	10	2
Second City	0	06	14
The Goodman Theater	0	06	14
Orchestra Hall	0	06	14
Board of Trade	01	03	16
Navy Pier	03	08	09
Wacker Drive	04	04	12
United Center	03	16	01
Oak Street Beach	01	07	12
Grant Park	09	10	01
Museum of Science & Industry	18	02	0
Comiskey Park	10	09	01
Michigan Avenue	12	06	02
De Paul University	01	15	04
Sears Tower	13	05	02
Rosemont Horizon	06	12	02
Soldier Field	08	09	03
Wrigley Field	07	07	06
McCormick Place	10	05	05
O'Hare Airport	12	06	02
City Hall	08	10	02
The "EL"	16	04	0
University of Chicago	08	12	0
State Street	15	04	01
Shedd Aquarium	13	06	01
Art Institute	11	07	02
Field Museum	17	02	01
Lake Shore Drive	18	01	01

Q: Where have you traveled, other than your own neighborhood? What areas of the city are you familiar with? Where don't you go? Where can't you go?

On a map of their community (see figure 3), the children are asked to outline safe and unsafe areas. The map is extended to include a small section of West Englewood. The illustrations profile the restricted environment, delineated according to gang affiliation. Englewood encompasses an area 6.537 squares miles. The northern perimeter is Garfield Boulevard, the southern boundary is 76th Street; west by Racine and east by LaSalle. The area elementary and high schools are also included. The children designate the major gang affiliations in each school. Although, there is no collaboration among the students—each map is outlined in an individual sitting—all the boundaries drawn on these maps are astonishingly similar: all of the children know their parameters.

EXPOSURE TO OTHER PEOPLE'S REALITY

Isolation has a resounding effect on the social construction of reality for black disadvantaged adolescents. Wilson contends that the residents of ghetto neighborhoods have become increasingly isolated socially from the mainstream patterns and norms of behavior (1987). These children have been isolated residentially and socially, and in addition, they have extremely limited interaction with students of different ethnic and racial backgrounds. During the interview the students discuss their multicultural experiences.

Q: Practically everyone in your neighborhood and school is black with the exception of a few white teachers. Have you been around other ethnic groups? How often? Have you developed a friendship(s)? Tell me some of your experiences, if any.

Nate: No.

Q: Never?

Nate: My cousin white?

Q: Your cousin's white? Can you explain that situation to me?

Nate: He's probably not. I don't believe he's white, he just light skin. If you light skin you white.

Q: So you believe if you are light, you are white. You know that doesn't make you white. The black race goes from shades of ebony to ivory.

Nate: You light, you white. Like Nicki, she white. She ain't black.

Nicole does distinguish between light-skinned African-American and Caucasians: "Yea, I got one friend. She light, real light. She black though. She just look white." Mary, like Nate and Nicole states she has never had any contact with any other ethnic groups. Sam comments that his aunt had two white friends who used to come by and visit. But when asked if he knew anyone his own age he stated, "Yea. I got one. He's black and white. Demonstrating again the inability to understand the full extent of their historical background. Nevertheless, Jason's only experience was centered around his contact with next door neighbors, though none of the children were his age. Jim and Wolf's experiences are beset with negative connotations. Jim had formed a comraderie with a young Puerto Rican youth and together they created fear. Wolf, however, created his own terror.

Q: Have you had any contact with other ethnic groups?

Jim: (laughing) In the Audie Home. Spanish, Muslims, everything.

Q: Did you develop any friendships there?

Jim: Yea. I know a couple of them. I had one friend named Josh, he was a Puerto Rican and was cool, that was my homie. He was in a different gang. He got out, he a Latin King. But he was cool with me.

Q: Do you keep in touch with him?

Jim: No, I never got his phone number. He was cool in there though. He keep me underwear and deodorant in his room so somebody don't steal it, because I don't have a room. We use to whip peoples butts. Ain't nobody beat us! They use to call us the Spade Kings. Because everybody that played us never won. That's all we played is spades, card games and chess and all that.

Q: Have you had any experiences other than that?

Jim: No.

Q: You have lived on the westside and in the Englewood area. Have you been around any other ethnic groups?

Wolf : Puerto Ricans, no not Puerto Ricans, what's that name? White people.

Q: Where have you been around white people?

Wolf: Oak Park.

Q: I thought you said you hadn't been to any suburbs?

Wolf: Oak Park ain't no suburb. It is on the westside.

Q: No, it's part of the suburbs. Let me show you on the map. What dealings did you have with the white people in Oak Park?

Wolf: They think I be trying to steal they cars. And they called the police on
          me for nothing.

Q: So what you are saying is that it hasn't been good experiences? What
          about when you were in Peoria?

Wolf: Yea. A whole bunch of white people. There was only three blacks that
          were there.

Q: Did you develop any friendships?

Wolf: No. Because there was one retarded boy that was crazy. He pretended
          like he was superman. And I was asleep one time and he got off the
          bottom bed and jumped on me, my face. And I beat him nearly to death.

Wolf's encounters with other ethnic groups are negative, and in addition,
he does not mention that his step-grandmother is Chinese and that the
grandparents have children. Wolf lived with his uncle for five or six years.
Keisha, Lee Lee and Shashqua also have family members who are of
mixed race. Lee Lee and Dan spent time at camp where they interacted
with people of other cultural and racial backgrounds, and Maykela speaks
of a pleasant, positive multicultural experience at a basketball camp.

May: Many times my school be selecting us to go places and then—one time
          we went to this basketball thing. They sent me—I was the only person
          selected to go. And I was the only black person there. Everybody else
          was white, but, they weren't treating me like I was the only black
          person. They were helping me like they were regular people in my
          classroom and stuff. They weren't acting like oh, let me get away from
          her. They be acting like people be acting towards me and stuff. They
          were friendly like.

Q: Were you surprised?

May: Huh huh. I thought may it be like, I want her to be my partner over here
          or there.

Q: So you enjoyed it?

May: Huh huh. And I have a white friend who lives on the next block.

Thomas, the only student who had a romantic involvement, soon
terminated his interest when the young Puerto Rican girl's mother
threatened to castrate him or in his words "be[sic.] like Lorena Bobbitt."
Two of the other students' multicultural exposure came from church
experience. The children's limited exposure to people of other cultures

caused by the isolation of their environment and their exclusion from the larger culture creates feelings of negativism and suspicion about other races in these children. The overwhelming limits of these children's exposure—to the physical, cultural, and ethnic diversity found in the city—speaks of profound isolation and marginality.

THE COLOR COMPLEX ENIGMA

Dr. Charles Brahnam (1994), historian at the DuSable Museum, explains how historical stereotypes, traceable to slavery, when lighter skinned women and men brought a higher market value, underlie many current perceptions of ethnic minorities today. These stereotypes augmented the division and established a color hierarchy which is still viable. Such as this newspaper ad in New Orleans publicizing an auction on the corner of St. Louis and Chartes Street at twelve o'clock on May 16, 1835. A common spectacle during the slavery period. The following are excepts from the advertisement.

1. Sarah, a mulatress, aged 45 years, a good cook and accustomed to house work, is an excellent and faithful nurse for sick persons, and in every respect a first rate character.

2. Chole, a multress, aged 36 years, she is, without exception, one of the most competent servants in the country, a first rate washer and ironer, does up lace, a good cook, and for a bachelor who wishes a house-keeper she would be invaluable: she is also a good ladies maid, having traveled to the North in that capacity.

3. Frank, a mulatto, aged about 32 speaks French and English, is a first rate hostler and coachmen, understands perfectly well the management of horses, and is, every respect, a first rate character, with the exception that he will occasionally drink, though not an habitual drunkard.

4. Mary Ann, her child *(daughter of Nancy)*, a Creole, aged 7 years, speaks French and English, is smart, active and intelligent. (Atlanta University Center Woodruff Library, Division of Archives/Special Collections).

This exhibition demonstrates how skin color of African-Americans was marketed and promoted. Today African-Americans must continue to struggle with the results of this categorization.

Brahnam (1994) contends that the preoccupations with and perceptions of beauty and status also have to do with living in "white" America. Expressions such as "coffee will make you black" or "I don't want nothing black but a Cadillac," handed down from generation to generation (Sinclair, 1994), are also part of the African-American heritage, following the same normal process of other linguistic expressions. What is unusual about both the norms of beauty and its languaging is the devastating effects they have had on an entire segment of the American population. The negative effects are apparent and far-reaching in the construction of individual identity, for these single, powerful ideas, norms, and even linguistic cliches do not occur singly. Instead, one attribute or another is magnified, and this attracts other possible, defining, fanciful, and likely nonexistent "markers" which blind us to the finer discriminations we would otherwise make in an individual. Russell and others (1992) argue that the politics of skin color has had a profound impact on black identity in complex and unpredictable ways. In black children this awareness occurs between the ages of three and five. Recent research attests to the unconscious self-hatred which these norms of beauty and language (Seymour, 1992) generate in black children.

In one major study that served as an essential factor in the ruling in the 1954 landmark court decision, *Brown vs. Board of Education Topeka Kansas*, Dr. Kenneth and Mamie Clark (1963) indicated that the majority of black children preferred the white doll over the brown doll. Clark argued that "identification . . . involves a knowledge of the status assigned to the group with which he identifies, himself, in relation to the status of other groups" (p. 23). In the novel, *Coffee Will Make You Black,* a female character typifies the black perception of beauty still prevalent in the majority of the students in this study:

> Mama says she wishes I'd gotten more of Daddy's lighter color and especially his curly hair. She says she prayed that if I was a girl I'd have good hair that didn't need to be straightened. Mama says one reason she married him was cause she was looking out for her children. She says

it was almost unheard of for a colored [sic] man to marry a woman darker than himself. Mama says she was lucky . . . Anyway, Mama says she doesn't know where I was when they were handing out color and hair . . . But at Least I got nice features, she's thankful for that . . . she says she glad I don't have a wide nose and big lips (Sinclair, 1994, pp. 7-8).

Mary articulates a similar perception about what makes up "nice features." She expresses her embarrassment about the size of her lips, which she considers an imperfection. "It's just my lips you know, cause they big and all that and when they say something about that, I feel bad and cover my lips. But now I don't let it bother me, since I been growing up with it. So now it only makes me feel bad every once in a while."

Manifestations of the unspoken "caste" system continue in the black community where value of light over dark skin and a perception of beauty based on Caucasian features still dominate as evident in hair styling and coloring practices—hair weaves, microwavable extensions, and so forth.. The children are asked to focus on this aspect of the creation of their identity. They are asked to tell what physical characteristic constitute an attractive male or female and to state their preferences in a boyfriend or girlfriend. Not unlike the Clark study, the majority of the children preferred mates with lighter skin complexions, lighter eyes and, for girls, long hair. Thomas was clear in his perception of female beauty:

Q: I want you to describe what you think is an attractive female. What makes a girl attractive?

Tom: Take care of theyself. Take baths, fix they hair. Intelligent. Look good, like a movie star. They have to look like somebody, like Halle Berry. I like light skinned girls.

Q: Why did you say you like light skinned girls?

Tom: Because I am dark.

Q: Because you are dark? Is there something wrong with being dark? In order to say that—you said it like something is wrong with it. What wrong with being dark?

Tom: Oh, ain't nothing wrong with it, I just like them lighter then me. Not real, real dark. Like Nate is real, real dark, can't have no girls dark like Nate. Because you can't see.

Q: What can't you see? Are you saying there are no pretty girls that are dark? To you?

Tom: Some ain't. I ain't see no pretty dark girls yet.

Q: What about hair?

Tom: Long. I like it long. Not that kinky stuff either. No weaves. No gerry curls.

Q: Can you deal with someone with a gerry curl?

Tom: Yea, as long as they don't have hair as short as me. I got more hair than any girl in the classroom. That's a shame. Except for Dee and Sally.

Anthony has similar preferences:

Tony: Long hair, nice personality, stay fit, well-dressed, church going. That don't mean I go to church you know. Wear nice clothes. Light skinned.

Q: Is there any reason you like light-skinned girls?

Tony: Just like it. Somewhere like my complexion.

Sam's perception of beauty parallels Tom and Tony's.

Sam: Be nice. She don't have to be pretty and stuff. Just be nice. A nice attitude. She has to have hair. Long hair. Not that long. Light skinned. Keep herself dressed nice.

Q: Why does she have to be light skinned?

Sam: I don't like dark skinned girls.

Q: Why? And why long hair?

Sam: I don't know. I just do. Habit I guess. If she have short hair she look like a boy. It just look crazy to me.

Jim expresses a love-hate relationship with the politics of color.

Jim: Pretty things.

Q: What makes them pretty?

Jim: The way they be looking. Light skin, pretty eyes, long hair, big boobs. Not skinny like Ethiopians. They look pretty.

Q: Any particular reason for your choice. You said light skin,

Jim: No brown, black, dark. I don't like light skinned girls. They think they too good. I prefer light skinned girls but most light skinned girls they have attitudes. I want to tell them they ain't all that. You ain't the "bomb." You act so stuck up. I like them but some of them be so, like they can't be ugly or something. Just because you light skin. Like they the most beautiful person in the world. I don't know, they have they nose all crunched up. Boy you too young and you have to tell them, who do you think you is? You ain't found no *Jet* magazine. Who does she think she talking to?

Joseph attempts to be diplomatic in his preference, but the stereotype is still present.

Jos: Long hair. Pretty eyes. Light brown or green. Nice body. Know what she be doing in school. Dark skin and light skin.

Mary shares the same perspective as the five boys:

Q: Okay, Mary give me your description of an attractive black male. Let me put it this way, give me your description of a typical black male. And then one that is attractive. What's a typical black man?

Mary: Dark skinned, tall, rough.

Q: And what would an attractive black male look like?

Mary: I am color struck. I am going to say light skinned but I like dark skinned too, sometimes. Light skinned, pretty brown eyes, tall, have a nice haircut. Nice clothes, probably have a job.

Q: What makes your color struck?

Mary: I just like light skinned people.

Keisha, like the students before her, perpetuates the age-old stereotype.

Keis: A brain. Not dark, medium complexion, cut hair, keep their body clean.

Q: Why not dark?

Keis: I don't know, they just don't look right too dark, medium complexion. They can be dark but not like they stayed in the sun all the time, not too, you know.

R.J. states that her preference is for someone "probably" her color, which is a paper bag tan. Only two of the students say that they prefer someone of a dark complexion—one, a girl who insists that he has to have pretty eyes "with a little touch of brown." The other student is a male who adds, "she must have hair." However, of the entire group only three of the students states that physical appearance is insignificant.

Dr. Alvin Poussaint argues that the development of the negative self-concept of African-American children is a reflection of their environment and color caste system.

It is well recognized that Negroes' self-concept is partly determined by factors associated with poverty and low economic class status. However, being a Negro has many implications for the ego development of young children that are not inherent in lower-class membership. The Afro-American child develops in a color caste system and inevitably acquires the negative self-esteem that is the natural outcome of such a system (Perkins, 1975, p. 157).

With few exceptions the students continue in the grip of the self-fulfilling, racist adage:

If you're white, you're all right
If you're yellow, you're mellow
If you're brown, stick around
But if you're black, step back
(Anonymous)

THE EFFECTS OF SOCIALLY CONSTRUCTED REALITY IN RELATION TO A PERCEIVED FUTURE

Figure 4. "Alive" Cartoon (Courtesy of *The Chicago Defender*)

Poverty, violence, isolation and drugs are characteristic of Chicago's poorest communities. Are children from these impoverished areas permitted to hope? "What happens to a dream deferred?" Nightingale (1993) contends that children raised in poverty "become more avid dreamers than other Americans, because in the dehumanizing experiences of poverty and racism, mainstream ideals promise a desperately needed sense of belonging and personhood" (p. 2). The students' responses to the interview questions reflect how they construct their perceived future from all the factors that make up their reality. The students are asked their career goals. How and where do they see themselves ten years from now? Who do they admire the most? If allowed three wishes, what would they be?

Q: Based on your experiences so far in your life, what do you want to be when you grow-up? What or who influenced your decision? How do you see yourself in the future, possibly five? Ten years from now?

Joseph

Jos: A football player.
Q: Who influenced your decision?
Jos: No one, when I play, it feels fun.
Q: Where do you think you will be ten years from now? All things considered. You said you were arrested four times this year.
Jos: I might be in jail or dead. Because most people be in jail or dead ten years from now. But, I don't want to die.
Q: Who do you admire most?
Jos: My dad. He accomplished something in his life. And I want to accomplish something in my life. He works at the Burlington Coat Factory. He sells suits and coats and stuff.
Q: If you were allowed three wishes, anything in the world, what would they be?
Jos: One, stop the killing. I wish we would stop killing people. Second, my family would be in a safer place than around gangs and stuff. And third, my family was rich.

Sam

Sam: I want to mess with computers and stuff, probably a computer technician. Ten years from now hopefully have a decent job. Work somewhere. I never thought about what I'd be doing. I don't want to be sitting in jail or nothing.

Q: Who do you admire?

Sam: I don't admire nobody. I just admire myself.

Q: What would your three wishes be?

Sam: Probably a car. See my little brother grow up.

Q: Are you concerned about him growing up?

Sam: Yes. Cause he doing what I'm doing. Acting crazy.

Q: You mean being in gangs?

Sam: Yes. I hope he has better hopes and dreams than I have.

Nicole

Nic: I want to be a lawyer. I like arguing. Nobody influenced my decision.

Q: Who do you admire the most? You don't have to?

Nic: My daddy. Cause he always take care of us even when he in jail. I guess he got somebody outside of jail that can help my daddy. He be having a lot of business. He might get out in February. But he had thirty years. But they said they might send him out on good behavior. My three wishes would be—My sister would get a good life. My daddy to get out of jail. Have a good life.

Nate

Nate: Pro-basketball player. Me and superstars I watch on T.V. Michael Jordan, Patrick Ewing, Shaquille O'Neal, Reggy Miller (influenced). All you got to do is try hard. You can get it. I'm going to get it. Ten years from now, I will be in the NBA. I'm going to play for the Dallas Mavericks. If you go to an elite team, you'll get known better. Three wishes: money, a big old house, and live forever.

Tamika

Tam: I want to be a surgeon. Like you work on peoples bodies and stuff like that. I don't know what you call it. I like helping people.

Q: Is there any one you look up to?

Tam: No.

Q: Where do you see your self, ten or twenty years from now?

Tam: In college. I go like years to be a doctor though. So I be working and getting my doctors degree.

Q: What would your three wishes be?

Tam: To have a lot of clothes and shoes and stuff and to have a lot of money. And to stay alive. I don't really want to die cause I don't know how it feel to die. I am afraid of dying. They say you are not supposed to be afraid to die but I am afraid to die though. Cause I probably be shot. Someone probably come up behind me and just stab me and I never be stabbed before, so I don't know how none of that feel. It will happen one day. And I won't go out partying. Because it be too late. That's when the party starts, at night time. . . the gangs be shooting at the skating rink. When you go outside, they be shooting.

Maykela

May: I want to be a lawyer. I think really why I want to be a lawyer cause through my life, my mother and father been going to court with my brothers. It seems like the lawyer be helping my brothers getting out cause when I was little I use to think my brothers will be going to jail and never come back. And they get a lawyer and it seems like it helps them and I use to like lawyers because they always make my brothers come back. And then the way they be talking and doing stuff. I just like that. And I like when they be in court, how they be working and drawing diagrams like that. I like that. And how they be solving those problems, they be like if this happened, where were you at? I look up to lawyers. And if I had three wishes, my first wish, I wish to be a lawyer. My second wish will be that all my brothers get out of gangs and my third and final wish is for my sister Lea, who had been seriously burned in a fire and remains in a coma.

Dan

Dan: I want to be a doctor. Pediatrician, something to do with kids. Ten years from now I'll be in med school. I admire my parents. They always make sure I do all my work and get good grades. They push me to do all my reading and that I don't join a gang. They always back me 100%. If I had three wishes, I would stop violence and the gangs. Second wish, get the drugs out of the world except for what you need when a doctor prescribes for you. A lot of people die from overdoses, people lose their kids to overdoses. I know someone that got their kids. And when they

know DCFS comes, they shut up they house and try to they feed their
kids (drugs) before they come. And God watch over everybody. I see
people shooting up.

The students have various career goals. Some want to be LPNs, several
boys want to be president, entertainers, martial arts teachers, school
teachers, lawyers, architects, and professional athletes. Others express a
wish to graduate and go to college, marry a faithful man, to be happy,
move to a safer neighborhood, rid the community of gangs and violence
be rich, have a large home and live long, healthy lives. Lee Lee
re-assessed her wishes and changed them: she wants to stop the violence,
the killings and the shootings in the black community.

SUMMARY

The students of Room 130 view the world from a particular perspective.
Their perceptions and ways of seeing undergird the construction of their
social reality. All of these children nod their heads in agreement to
fragments of sentences and phrases that pin-point their perceptions: "Bad
conditions"; "Schools in the Black Community, growing-up in the Hood";
"They ain't half-way learning nothing"; "Holes in the walls and
windows"; "A black male student at school is bad, sells drugs, etc." Again
they all nod in agreement, "A Jewish kid living in the suburbs would
probably be smarter than . . ." "We are the roughest class that has ever
been in School X. They were rough last year, but we are rougher now."
There is no comfort in this thought; there is no bravado.

Children rely on the perceptions of others to construct their personal
realities. The voices of the children define them in negative and marginal
terms, but if their perceptions are influenced by the judgments of others,
whose definition are the children reproducing? Is it a definition ascribed
to black Americans, specifically for those who live in impoverished
communities? To what extent do we still act upon preconceived,
damaging, dehumanizing convictions of these children? How are these
still being perpetuated? There is a message in the voice of the children.
The social and environmental factors are essential to an adequate
interpretation of this phenomenon.

Although many schools, particularly elementary schools, are perceived as sanctuaries, the students question the significance of schooling in relation to their lives.

They believe that many of the teachers lack the solicitude and desire necessary for their educational success. Or is " blaming the victim" the answer?

Chapter five will explore the role of the mass media in how the children socially construct their everyday, common sense world. Does the media function as "culture-bearers" in shaping their social reality, and if so, in what ways? The children's voices will explain their interpretation of this commonly-debated theory.

CHAPTER 5

"Showdown": Impact of Mass Media and Popular Culture

Showdown

A motherfucka told me it was gonna be a
Showdown
When I came around
I was up for breakin motherfucka down
Fuck it nigga wit it
Let's rock the town
Flee on the scene
Now what's up baby
Car full of niggas straight lookin shady
Came to loot
Better have what you gonna shoot
Cause we straight lookin crazy
C-o-n-flict, nigga
That's what it is when you tote them triggers
Gangangalistic father figure
Daddy to the nigga that think they slicker
Yeah,
It's a showdown
Not just in my hood, but town from town
Making motherfuckas recognize the flavor
Coming from Chi-town
Be quick to draw

Pick a nigga meat up out a chain saw
We don't play around
Motherfuckas gone die
We gonna kill em up pal
Kill em up in the showdown
    (Dallas Records, 1996)

Hay

Sittin on a quarter 'P of hay
 Thangs is feelin good today
I'm tore up, from the floor up
Sippin on some Crown Royal
Trippin, in a circle of wood
Where everybody smoke they own bud
    (Dallas Records, 1996)

Lyrics such as those of *Showdown* and *Hay* by The Final Tic, are explosive and a highly controversial aspect of current popular culture. Many common people as well as professionals in education, the arts, psychology and social commentators believe that rap music, explicitly gangsta and hard-core rap, have a bizarre grasp and influence on youngsters inciting them to acts of violence, the use of drugs, early sexuality, and other social ills. However, rap, with its origins in black music and oral expression, is not new to the black community (Kitwana, 1994). Rather, it is rooted in African history, slavery, minstrel shows, black music (Du-Wop) of the late forties and fifties and more recently, shows up in the work of controversial artists such as 2 Live Crew, the late Tupac, N.W.A (Niggaz With Attitude), Snoop-Doggy-Dogg, the late Notorious Big aka Biggy Small, Dog-Pound and others. Does rap music in fact, affect the behavior, thoughts, and actions of adolescents and teens, creating a mystical power over them? Is it responsible for the decline in morality or is it a scapegoat for a variety of social ills? Another aspect of this contemporary debate is seen in black films such as, The Hughes Brothers' *Dead Presidents (1995)*; F. Gary Gray, *Friday (1995)* and Spike Lee's *Clockers* (1995).

The critical question here is, what role, if any, does the mass media and "popular culture" have in shaping the social reality in black, disadvantaged adolescents? Or is the issue more properly an opinion perpetuated by the news media and mainstream society? The children voice their answers to this on-going controversy of the power of Hip-Hop culture to shape their own reality. The students are responded to the following question:

Q: Today there is a wide selection of movies, television programs and music. What standard (rule) do you use to choose a movie? A television program? Read a book or magazine? Or listen to music? What meaning does it have for you?

Lee Lee starts the narrative.

L.L.:   *I like* scary *movies.* I like them all, scary and funny. *I seen Menace to Society, Friday,* and *Bad Boys.*

Q: What did you like about *Menace to Society?*

LL: It taught me a lesson. It teach you what goes around comes around. Because if you beat up people then he died in the end. He got shot up. *Jurassic Park* was scary and funny too. And Mrs. Doubtfire, that was funny.

Q: What kind of music do you like?

LL: Rap.

Q: What kind of rap? Who are some of your favorite artist?

LL: Bone, Janet Jackson, doesn't rap, but, she has some rap people in her video.

Q: What do you like about rap. Do you like the beat or the message(s) they have? There are a lot of derogatory things they say about women.

LL: I don't like it, but, Queen Latifah she have a song, telling the boys to stop hollering the names and stuff. She be telling the boys that they shouldn't be calling the girls names.

Q: Do you listen to the message?

LL: Yea. Sometime, I like it because I don't be knowing what they are saying and it be sounding good. I just like the beat.

Q: Do you think kids are influenced by the music? They say some of the rap songs, like gangsta rap have a lot of violence and stuff and influence kids to do things.

LL: No. Not really. They do what they want to do.

Wolf

Q: Okay, Wolf, today there is a wide selection of movies, television programs, books, magazines, video games and music. What kind of movies do you like?

Wolf: Any kind (laughing).

Q: What are the last three movies you have been to see?

Wolf: I can't remember. I went to the show twice.

Q: You have only been to the show twice in your life? Can you remember the last time you were at the show? Since you were a teen-ager or was it before? Who took you to the show?

Wolf: Before. My cousin and his brother.

Q: Is there any reason you don't go on your own?

Wolf: Yea. Because I don't want to do nothing bad. You know because if I go to the show by myself, I be around by the cash register instead of the movie, and I'll wait until they go on their break and I go around to the cash station. Like I did last time.

Q: What did you do last time?

Wolf: That's why I don't never go no more. I went to the cash register and took money. That why they don't let me go anymore.

Q: How old were you?

Wolf: Twelve.

Q: Did you get caught?

Wolf: Nope.

Q: When do they ever go and leave the cash register unattended?

Wolf: When they go on their break. The only time they come when they get off they break, when they see people coming out and get some popcorn.

Q: What kind of television programs do you like?

Wolf: Scary stuff.

Q: Do you read any books?

Wolf: Yea. Adventure stories, gang stories, (laughing) sometimes I read those nasty books.

Q: When you read the gang stories, who do you hope will win. The police or the gangs?

Wolf: The gangs, I don't like the police.

Q: Which video games do you like?

Wolf: Street fighter and Mortal Kombat.

Q: What kind of music do you like?

Wolf: Rap. Cursing.

Q: Which rap? The sex and violence rap.

Wolf: Yea. It's fresh.

Q: Does the music incite you to do anything.

Wolf: Nope.

Joseph

Jos: I saw *Baby's Day Out*, Brooklyn. I like gang movies. Like *Menace to Society, Boyz 'N the Hood, New Jack City*. I like how they fight and stuff and how they make it sound. I wonder how they make it sound.

Q: Who do you identify with in the movies? Who do you cheer on to win?

Jos: The person who be losing all the time. That's the way I be. *I cheer* the gangs. I hate the police.

Q: Why do you hate the police?

Jos: Cause they supposed to be helping the community, they destroying it. *They be* beating up the people. They supposed to be doing something to stop the people from doing stuff and they just beating up the people and making the people worse.

Q: What about books? Do you ever sit down and read books outside of school?

Jos: Sometimes. Sometimes, I don't. But, I really don't.

Q: Which video games do you play?

Jos: Street fighter, F-Zero, Mortal Combat. They fun to play and NBA basketball games. And Karate games.

Q: What about music? What kind of music do you like?

Jos: I like the rappers, they got a lot of experiences. They talk and rap at the same time. They talk about everything they do.

Q: Is that the hard-core rap and gangsta rap?

Jos: I'm not into gangsta rap. They cuss a lot on the tapes.. When they cuss a lot, I can't understand what they talking about.

Q: So, what do you listen to?

Jos: The beat, the words.

Nicole

Q: Today's there is a wide selection of movies, television programs, books, magazines, music and video games. Which ones are you interested in? Let's start with the movies. You said your boyfriend always takes you. What type of movies do you like?

Nic: Any movie.

Q: What about books?

Nic: I like to read the poems out of books.

Q: What type of music?

Nic: House music. Rap.

Q: Do you like the hard-core rap? Gangsta rap?

Nic: Rap, gangsta rap.

Q: What do you like about the gangsta rap. That's all the sex and violence
        and put down of women and stuff. What do you like about it?

Nic: Sounds good. They don't put down women they just , I don't know.
        That's what my momma said, that they put down women and stuff, but
        they don't. They just saying what they mean and stuff.

Q: So you don't think it's a put down?

Nic: No. It's just the way it is.

Q: So as far as obscenities, sex and violence in the lyrics, how do you feel
        about those. Like cop killer and things like that. How do you feel about
        those?

Nic: I don't like those raps. I don't like it. I don't need to be hearing about
        nobody killing a cop.

Q: Do you think with the sex and violence in the videos that it has an
        influence on what happens with teen-agers today?

Nic: No.

Q: Because, a lot of that is in the media. That's what some of them claim.
        You believe that.

Nic: Ain't no music going to make you do nothing. You got a mind of your
        own and can't nobody sit there and say I was listening to this type of
        music, and that's what made me do such and such.

Sam

Q: Tell me what type of movies you like and give the names of the last
        three movies you have been to.

Sam: *Lethal Weapon, Batman*, and *Last Action Hero*. Action movies.

Q: Do you identify with the good guys of bad guys? Who do you like?

Sam: The good guys.

Q: When you see movies like *Above the Rim*, or *Menace to Society II*, who
        do you identify with? Who do you want to win in those situations?

Sam: I probably say gang members.

Q: Why?

Sam: Cause some movies are about us, me and somebody else.

Q: So you relate the movie to you?

Sam: Yea.

Q: And music?

Sam: Rap.

Q: Do you like the hard-core or gangsta rap? What do you like?

Sam: Gangsta rap. I like all that. I don't like hard-core.

Q: You don't like the ones that have all the obscenity, sex and violence?

Sam: Yea. (Laughing) A few of them.

Q: The ones that call women b's and stuff.

Sam: Some of them, not all of them.

Q: Do you listen to the music, the beat or the words?

Sam: The beat.

Q: Now, television always tries to say that sex, violence and bad words in the music influence teen-agers to do bad things. Do you agree with that?

Sam: No. It influence to do nothing, cause it don't tell you to go out there and do it. You have your own mind. If you go out there and do it, you want to do it.

Nate's discussion transcends the violence in music to a scene of domestic violence.

Nate: *I have seen Malcolm X, Mrs. Doubtfire*, and that movie *Man's Best Friend.* That's the last time I been to the show. *I like* scary ones.

Q: What type of television programs do you like?

Nate: Wild Discovery on channel 11. I like them eating each other up. All the violence.

Q: What about books. Do you read outside of school?

Nate: Nope. I read, I don't know. I haven't read outside school in a long time.

Q: What about music?

Nate: Rap. I like a little dusty's. Sam Cook and Jackie Wilson. Blackstreet, Brandy.

Q: When you listen to the rap song, do you listen to the words, music, or beat?

Nate: Beat and the words.

Q: What do you like about the words? There is a lot of sex and violence.

Nate: The violence.

Q: What about the way they talk about women?

Nate: I don't care. I don't care what they talk about. If they want to, they can.

Q: Do you talk about women like that?

Nate: Yep. When they make me mad.

Q: Does your father talk about women like that?

Nate: Yea. That all he do?

Q: Does he talk to your mother like that?

Nate: No he don't talk to my mother like that. She dangerous.

Q: What would she do?

Nate: She be riding, something like that.

Q: They'll be riding?

Nate: They be fighting cause of that.

Q: Have you ever seen them fight?

Nate: Yea. All the time. I'm used to it. They been fighting since I was little.

Q: What do you do when they fight?

Nate: Nothing. Watch T.V.

Q: You don't ever get involved? Does your brother or sister?

Nate: No.

Q: Well how do you feel about them fighting?

Nate: I don't care. They gonna fight anyway. Everything they say, it ain't gonna work out. So they have to do something, fight, to make a decision.

Jim

Jim: I see *Drop Zone*. The last three movies I've seen is *Drop-Zone, Low Down Dirty Shame* and *Menace to Society*.

Q: Now Menace to Society, when you watch a movie like that, who do identify with? The good guys or the people in the gangs.

Jim: There no good guys in there, everybody bad.

Q: How do you feel about that particular movie?

Jim: It was good.

Q: Who did you identify with or did you? Would you say I'm like that person or I would like to be like that person. Or I like what he's doing.

Jim: Yea. O'Dog and Kane. They was cool. The was they acted. You know that was in a movie so you know how that was. You can't do like that on the street, gonna next door and killing somebody and get a video tape and sell it to people for $9.99. All like that.

Q: So what you are saying is the movie wasn't realistic?

Jim: It doesn't happin like that for real. Kinda like that. It was good. I like the way he went out. It was good. When he got shot. He got shot like eight times and give his little boy, he was talking to the little boy's mother. You know they had a good relationship. And they shoot his stomach all up and he ran and jumped over the little boy so he wouldn't be shot. I like how he went out. He saved the little boy. They would have shot the little boy too, it was a drive-by.

Q: Were they rival gangs?

Jim: Well they weren't gang bangin but . . . They wasn't like GD and all that stuff, it was like different groups of people. This group hang with that and other hang with that side of town. Drive-by, reason it was a drive-by, because Kane had got one dude cousin's pregnant and he said it wasn't his baby, so his cousin had came and asked Kane, did you get my cousin pregnant and Kane beat him up. So he came back with his bad guys and did a drive-by. For beating him up real bad. He beat him bad. He stole, kicking him and kick him like eight times and then his old friend kick him in his mouth and he was bleeding and, everything. He came back and killed Cane. Movies like that. Excitement. *Passenger 57, Low Down Dirty Shame, Street fighter.* As long as it has some excitement in it. I don't watch no boring stuff like *Driving Miss Daisy.* I don't like nothin like that. It can't be boring like animals having babies and all that. Some kind of action.

Q: How do you feel about guns?

Jim: I don't know how I feel about guns. I ain't gonna say I don't like them cause, I used them, I saw'em, I shot'em before. But I ain't gonna say I don't like them. In a way they good, a way they not. You protect yourself, cause without them . . . If you in a situation in an area that you don't know, you got to protect yourself twenty-four hours a day. They can hurt you. They good in a way but they hurt your body. That's the bad way, hurt your body, or kill you. So I say on of scale of zero to one hundred, about fifty-fifty. See I don't live in an area, I don't have to worry about protecting myself. The area I live in I know mostly everybody. *When* I go out of the area, I don't take a gun, I just keep a low profile, saying GD, I keep it to myself, I know what I am. I just go, walk past. They won't mess with you if . . .

Q: But you got shot. Okay, Sam. What about books? Do you read outside of school?

Jim: Books about law. I know all about laws. I know police can't fingerprint me cause I'm a child, a juvenile. They can't take a beeper away, can't take my money. I know all of that. They can't pressure me or nothing.

Q: What kind of music do you listen to?

Jim: Rap. All rap. Everything. I got all the good tapes. BGE, DFC, all I listen to is music. Whatever sounds good to me.

Q: There's gangsta rap and hard-core rap?

Jim: Yea. I like all of them. If it sounds good. I just don't listen to the words. If I buy a tape and listen to the songs and I say yea, I like this song. And keep going, listen to the whole tape.

Q: What about the violence.? There a lot of sex, violence, obscenities and
          vulgarities . . .
Jim: Well, I listen to the words and I use them on the street. Like, some of
          the rap songs, when you really listen to them, you get knowledge. I'm
          telling you. Some of the words can reverse the whole thing around. Got
          "scrape." You know what that means don't you? He got money. That
          means that other people are scared of him. They got him "scraped" with
          a gun. When you "scrape", you got a gun on you all the time. You
          know got you "scraped." Like you got a lot of money, people are
          jealous of you. They try to kill you. All the big druggers with all the
          money. So they got him "scraped" with a gun all the time.
Q: So you think the rap songs reflect what's going on in the world?
Jim: Yea, they tell you what to look out for and what not to look for. Like
          you don't want to drop out of school in the sixth grade and all that.
          Keep your money when you got it. All that. They don't tell you to go
          out and kill somebody. They just telling you how things can go down
          a 187, somebody can give you a 187, kill you. They tell you what to
          aware of in the streets. Cause by being older guys, they are more
          experienced then the younger guys and they try to tell you that. Because
          where they live they get drive-bys everyday. They try to tell what to
          look for.
Q: Do you think any of them incite people to do things?
Jim: No, I don't think that. Cause the music can't make you put no gun to
          somebody's head. Telling you what to do just listening to it.

Jim's ardent interest in rap is compelled by his desire to become a rap
artist. He fervently memorizes all the verses to the songs, singing and
dancing at any given moment.

Thomas

Tom: *I have seen House Party,* Jason's Lyric and *Low Down Dirty Shame.*
Q: What type of movies do you like?
Tom: Horror, action.
Q: When you watch the action movies, who do you identify with , the
          good guys or the bad guys.
Tom: If they cricket, I like some of the bad guys.
Q: What does cricket mean?
Tom: Like bad cops.

Q: Bad cops are called cricket. So, if they are bad cops, you identify with whom?

Tom: Sometimes the good people.

Q: What about books? Do you go to the library to get books? Do you buy books?

Tom: No.

Q: What about music? What type of music do you like?

Tom: Rap and my dad listens to blues.

Q: What type of rap do you like? The hard-core?

Tom: Yea. It don't mean nothing to me, it do something to the little crazy people. They need to be in Tinley Park. They get all hyped up.

Q: So, do you like the words, the music, or the beat?

Tom: The music and the beat. Not the words.

Q: How do you feel about the negative things they say about women? Does it effect you one way or the other?

Tom: Sometimes. My grandma doesn't like it. Some of those little girls up there call each other bs, so I don't know.

Shashqua

Shas: I seen *Sankofa, Sarifina, Jurassic Park* and *The Crow.* I like Westcraven. Scary movies. And I like Black American movies like *Sankofa* and *Sarifina.* I liked Sankofa. I just don't like the way they treated black people and it hurt me real bad and I just let it go by.

Q: But that was the purpose of the movie, so you could understand about black history, the legacy of slavery. That's what it was all about. Many don't understand where we come from. Okay, do you read books outside of school?

Shas: Yes. I go to the library.

Q: What about music? What do you like?

Shas: Rap. The hard-core. I just like all types of music.

Q: What about the put-downs for women and all the profanity?

Shas: Well, I don't care nothing about that because I know they ain't talking about me. As long as they not talking about me or saying my name, I don't care. I don't got no problem with that, or in my face. It just a song.

Q: Well a lot of times they say rap music influences teenagers today. How do you feel about that?

Shas: Don't nothing influence me. I influence myself.

Keisha

Q: What about books and magazines?

Keis: I.m in a book club, *Sweet Valley High, Seventeen magazine.*

Q: What about music? You said you like rap.

Keis: Yea. I am in the Columbia House Record Club. I order Snoop
          Doggy-Dogg, Dr. Dre, Patra, Patti LaBelle, Aretha Franklin and Anita
          Baker. Sometimes I listen to the clean cut versions *of rap* and
          sometimes, if I like the beat or the person a lot, I'll listen to the other
          version (Gangsta Rap).

Q: What about the words in Gangsta Rap? Do they mean anything to you?

Keis: I just listen to it.

Q: When you listen to the music, are you listening for the meaning of the
          words, the beat, the messages? What do you look for in music? The
          Gangsta Rap has some really rough words and meaning. Is that
          important to you?

Keis: I look for all three, the beat, the message and the meaning. No, *it is not
          important.*

G.T.

G.T.:   *I 've seen Meteor Man* and *Jason Goes to Hell. I like* scary movies.

Q: What about movies like Menace to Society? Do you like movies like
          that?

G.T.:   Yep. They good. Violence and stuff.

Q: Who do you identify when you see movies like *Menace to Society*?

G.T.:   I don't go by that. It doesn't make any difference.

Q: So, when you see the gangs in the movie, who do you want to win?

G.T.:   I really don't care. It's just a movie.

The remaining students also listen to rap and other styles of music.
However, the fact that movies and music are merely sources of
entertainment is the children's common perception. None of the students
perceives movies and music as vehicles to violence, or for that matter as
having any type of influence on their subsequent actions. They indicate
that the statements relating to identification and escalating violence are
media "hype." Several object to the use of obscenities and insist that the
music and beat are their primary interests.

Affirming the general consensus of the students in the study that music and movies are a form of entertainment, a sixteen year old Whitney Young Magnet High School in Chicago, student wrote an English essay, "Should Our Society Respond to Gangsta Rap?" She made several interesting points regarding the media's preoccupation with the "perils" of rap music.

> Rap does not cause violence. Parents of White Suburban teenagers have this idea of a typical suburban child-a well-mannered, straight A student that acts like a preppy little kid. They figure that if they move to a more expensive neighborhood, their child will behave in that fashion. Wait a minute! Their suburban child listens to Snoop Doggy Dogg, Bone, and Outkast. He wears khakis three sizes too big and has a fade. What do his parents do? They go out and blame rap because it has "corrupted the mind of their child." They fear that their child might go out and commit a drive-by or some violent act because of rap, and that is why rap has and is continually getting the negative rap in our society.

> Gangsta rap has been the blame for many of our problems today. Rap is just a recorded account of what goes on in the hood. The media exploits rap, and should leave it alone and let it remain as a form of entertainment. (McCant, 1994).

Another Whitney Young student presents global and philosophical perspective, but both strongly declare that the media and society in general have given rap music an unfair judgment.

> There are two kinds of rap music. There is a negative aspect (talking about guns, drugs and disrespecting people, especially women) and there is a positive aspect. The latter uses Afrocentricity as a positive means of directly affecting their audience, whether young or old. They use Afrocentricity to teach and inspire the young Black community. They teach these young people to change their mentality, change their circumstances instead of accepting the things that they go through.

> "Music by no means can change societal behavior, but it does have the power to spark curiosity and instigate attitudes. The racial attitude in America right now is very tense. Rap music did not cause this, but it

'reported on it' (Jackson, 38). "Collectively rap music has the largest African voice in America (Jackson, 53)." "Rap music was created because so many people were left out or disenfranchised (Allah, 61)." Young minorities, especially young African-Americans, were tired of being treated like outcasts and receiving the worst of everything from everyone. They were seminals and never had the idea that the sub-culture that they created would be as popular as it is today. The way they walk, have fun, talk and dress is being watched by people everywhere and it is influencing and effecting many people. Hip-hop is indeed a subculture, if not a full one.

Rap music's role in society continues to grow. It has become the focal point of American society. White (and Black) politicians attack it. The media degrades it. Wall Street ignores it. Yet it receives the attention that no other single voice (and form) of the Black community receives (Harkins, 1995).

The students explored the issues of media as "culture bearers" in shaping perceptions of their constructed social reality. In reviewing their perceptions of movies, books, magazines and music, one is able to infer that the judgment of popular culture and Hip-hop needs to be reevaluated and a more meaningful approach to understanding and awareness needs to be negotiated.

CHAPTER 6

Reality Is Socially Constructed:
The Causal Network

Reality is socially constructed. According to Berger and Luckmann (1966), "the man in the streets inhabits a world that is "real" to him, although in different degrees of confidence, which this world possesses such and such characteristics . . . He takes his 'reality' and 'knowledge' for granted" (p. 1). However, people are constrained within their own environments. Mills (1959) contends: Athey are bound by the private orbits in which they live . . . Their visions and their powers are limited to the close-up scenes of job, family, neighborhood . . . A (p. 3). Children's reality is also socially constructed and this construction is influenced by the same factors that forge the common sense world of their adult counterparts. However, authority figures, social economic status, others' perceptions, the setting, and many significant factors are also critical in the construction of this reality.

For most black disadvantaged children, however, the legacy of slavery, the color complex, poverty, gangs, violence, and inferior education are additional determinants in the construction of their reality. Reflecting the social constructivist's theoretical framework, these factors are represented in Figure 5 as a network of causal connections (Miles and Huberman, 1994) linking everyday life experiences to the social construction of reality. Miles and Huberman (1994) explain that causal networks allow the collected data to be used in a more meaningful pattern:

"they are mental maps . . . variables [that] control each other in a loop, illustrating how an event triggers subsequent events" (pp. 151-52).

The schema illustrates a coherent linkage between social factors and the ultimate development of social reality for black disadvantaged adolescents. Each "event" suggests its relationship to another component. The code schema below, developed by Bogdan and Biklen (Miles and Huberman, 1994, p. 61), is modified to represent the population studied in this project.

1. Definition of Situation: How people understand, define, or perceive the setting or topics.
2. Setting/Context: Where action takes place, general information, and on surroundings, which allows you to put players in the context.
3. Perspective: The players' ways of thinking about the setting, i.e., "how things are done here."
4. Ways of Thinking: Players' understandings of each other, outsiders, and objects in their world.
5. Process: Sequence of events, flow, transitions, and turning points.
6. Activities: regularly occurring kinds of behaviors.
7. Events: Specific activities occurring infrequently.
8. Strategies: ways of accomplishing things, tactics, methods, and techniques for meeting needs
9. Relationships and social structure: cliques, coalitions, friendships, romances, and enmities
10. Methods: problems, joys, dilemmas of the research process.

The components in the network contribute to how these children understand and respond to their common sense world and each component makes a claim as follows: 1) The definition of the social situation and the setting, in this instance poverty, is essential in shaping the inhabitants' ways of thinking. 2) The circumstances related to poverty create ways of thinking which are determinants in the development of relationships and critical to the social construction of reality. 3) The perspective and ways of "seeing" strongly influence the development of actions, activities, and strategies of the individuals causing, 4) a sequence of events that form the process in which these children function. 5) The development of these strategies creates activities, and events, e.g., gang membership survival techniques, concerning what takes place in their world. 6) The complete linkage effects the perspective that is pivotal in the social construction of reality. 7) The methods were effective for the research in its entirety and for the unfolding

Figure 3. The Causal Network Linking Life Characteristics and Social Factors to the Construction of Social Reality

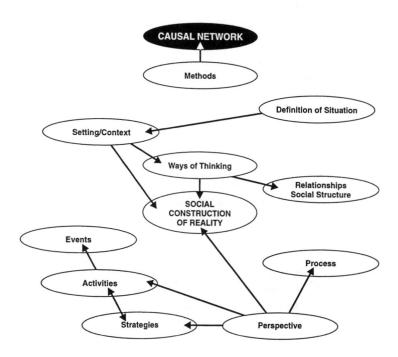

of the causal network. As the components of these children's social reality and the linkages among these are clarified, it is possible to gain a more nuanced perspective into the nature of their reality and the circumstances under which they live.

PROFILE OF THE POPULATION

The twenty children in this study range in age from twelve to fourteen. Thirteen of the students report having direct gang affiliations during research while another five have members of their immediate family in gangs. Only two of the children report neither direct nor indirect gang involvement. The gangs are pivotal in everyday activities in the community, influencing almost every facet of the children's lives. Englewood, ranking ninth of the twelve poorest communities in Chicago, is marked by isolation, drugs, violence, and an exceptionally high drop-out rate.

The students attend a school that is 99.6% African-American, and 84.8% of the school population is classified as low-income. Seventeen of the parents are school drop-outs, eighteen of the mothers dropped out because of pregnancy, eighteen of the parents never married, eight are known to be addicted to drugs or alcohol, and eleven of the families are on general assistance. Except for Dan and Jason, all of the boys have been arrested at least once, and some as many as six times during one year.

At least twelve of the twenty students have been retained for at least one year in school, two repeated the first grade, three the second, four in third, one in fourth, two in fifth, one in sixth, and one in seventh. Three of the children have incomplete school records. With the exception of Tamika, all of the students tested at grade level or slightly above in the first grade and maintained that level during second grade (ITBS). All of the children's scores decreased between third and fourth grades and never recovered. Standardized test scores range from a few months to as many as four years below grade level by the seventh and eighth grades for all of the students except Lee and Dan. Maykeyla, G.T., and Sam are at grade level in math (ITBS) at the time of this research. Surprisingly, the majority of the students maintain excellent attendance.

THE PERCEPTION OF THE PURPOSE OF SCHOOLING

A qualitative study conducted by the Consortium on Chicago School Research (1996) sought to provide a chance for Chicago students to articulate how they perceive the relationship between their school experiences and their lives. According to this report, a large percentage of students in urban schools, "do not achieve because they are not engaged with the school and the academic mission . . . They may comply with school routines but gain little because they do not see the work that they are asked to do as meaningful and worthwhile," (p. 5). These students were unresponsive to the routines, which, in many situations, elicited negative behavior that perpetuated a pattern of misconduct.

Berger and Luckmann (1996) contend that all repeated actions become cast into a pattern that can then become reproduced; these patterns have a historical foundation. In keeping with this claim, many urban children living in poverty areas are bound to develop a historical pattern of underachieving in school. Thus, although the students in School X perceive schooling as necessary, it is not sufficient to meet their needs. This fact becomes evident in their low test scores and their subsequent choices to drop out of school. Often student behavior that is not conducive to learning is an indicator of the extent of effectiveness of their learning environment. The students' behavior, however, fluctuates, conforming to the level of receptiveness of the classroom teacher. That is, the children are quick to perceive the environment as condescending, uncaring, permissive, or positive, and nurturing, and respond to that respective environment.

THE MEANING OF SCHOOLING

The students discuss their school experience and its impact on the construction of their meaning of schooling. Without exception, they agree that schooling is essential; however, their general behavior and lack of commitment to homework and study contradicts their responses and shows a decisive disparity between their aspirations and reality. None of the students views homework as essential, actually required, or effective. Rather, it is a "thing" to be done, or not, without meaningful significance to their lives or futures. As a result of this perception, in many instances they do not do it. In addition, the parents are not in a position to offer "real" assistance since many of them are school drop-outs themselves, unable to provide what they do not themselves possess. Ironically, several of the children speak of gang pressure on them to stay in school and of actual assistance from gang members.

Schooling offers a constellation of incongruities in the minds of these students—for instance, the lack of correlation among ideology, aspirations, goals, expectations, behaviors, and their reality. As an example of this incoherence, is Nicole, who states that Aschool means a lot. I am going to get an education, and when I graduate, I want to finish college and stuff and get me a job," averaged twenty-two and a half days of absence (and as high as forty) in any given school year. For the majority of the children, school is a vehicle to provide for a job in the future but not a means to obtain knowledge nor a source of empowerment. They quickly determine that the material taught in school has no significance to their everyday lives. The instructional work does not engage them nor does it relate to their common sense world. One possible source of this incongruity that needs to be considered is that children living in impoverished areas cannot associate occurrences at home and in the community with the predominantly middle-class framework of instruction provided in school.

This suggests that the preparation of teachers and administrations should be reevaluated, that methodology and curriculum must be reexamined, and that this must occur within the context of the following factors that creates these children's reality:

- Chicago's poverty rate (21.6%) is significantly higher than the national rate
- Poverty is persistent in Chicago
- Chicago school children are disproportionately poor when compared to the national population
- 41% of Chicago's school age population lives in poverty
- The distribution of poverty is uneven in the Chicago land area (Poverty Task Force, 1993)
- A high concentration of poverty predominates in Black and Latino areas

- Of Chicago's school age population, 56% and 28% are Black and Latino (Consortium on Chicago School Research [CCSR], 1996)
- Chicago's drop-out rate, computed from student-level data for 1994 was 42.7 % (CPS, Department of Research, Evaluation and Planning, 1995)
- Gangs present a majority problem within Chicago schools
- Many parents of Chicago school children are school drop-outs

PERCEPTION OF AUTHORITY FIGURES AS EXTERNAL SHAPERS OF SOCIALLY CONSTRUCTURED REALITY

Hopson and Hopson (1992) argue that "a teacher's perception of a student leads directly to an expectation of the student. If the teacher perceives the student as intelligent, then he or she will expect above average work from the children" (p. 154). Conversely, when teachers perceive students as unintelligent, bad, and incapable of learning, they expect below average work and misconduct from the children, and children respond in kind. Regardless of their own ethnicity, teachers who work with black disadvantaged children need to examine their attitudes, beliefs and assumptions about poverty and race for these have grave and lasting effects on school-age children (Burger and Luckmann, 1966, Hobson and Hobson, 1990; McLaren, 1989; Perkins, 1975). Burger and Luckmann (1966) contend that children internalize the world of their "significant others," not as one of many possible worlds, but as *the* world, the "only existent and conceivable world" (p. 134). Emphasizing the profound power that teachers have to shape the reality of children, Maykela—seen as a potential problem because of her brother's history—lives out her teachers' expectations. Maribeth Vander Weele (1994) discusses the "fall-out" from teachers' acts of incompetence and indifference: "Although good teachers are the most essential ingredient in improving education . . . even small numbers of ineffective teachers harm thousands of children for life" (p. 62).

The children, however, are clear in their understanding of "what makes a good teacher." With clarity and perception, they echo sociologist Samuel Betances' idea of "understandable instruction" as a key element that engages students in the learning process within their own framework (1996). Despite the prevailing theory among many educators that disadvantaged children come to school with cognitive, experiential and linguistic deficits (Knapp, Turnbull, and Shields, 1990) these children arrive at school with a wealth of experiential and cognitive knowledge. In their own childlike language, they articulate their conclusion: a humanistic and holistic perspective is essential for effectively educating the total child. In addition, the children believe that a teacher should be amiable, caring, nurturing, tolerant, encouraging, understanding, and provide a sense of affiliation and discipline. However, although they are not opposed to discipline, and believe it necessary, they strongly maintain that discipline should not be administered at the expense of respect nor should it embarrass the student.

Another effective teacher criterion is "not having an attitude"; the teacher-with-an-attitude is mean and disrespectful, hollers, cusses, and is apt to rough students up. In educational practice this sort of teacher labels children, perpetuates inferiority, consigns them to failure, and maintains the status quo (Shujaa, 1994). In sum, Nicole and Dan reflect the group's consensus of what makes teachers effective: "[Teachers are effective] when they want students to learn. When they care. Teachers who have respect for kids, don't curse them or make fun of them. Don't put their hands on them. Get involved with the kids parents. And make sure they do all they work and get an education." In short, the students' summaries would aptly provide a sound framework for selecting effective teachers.

It is interesting to note that the students speak of their alienation in various implicit ways. One student, for instance, talks of wanting other teachers, not only Black teachers. This directly implies that the student is aware that some of their teachers are, in some sense, marginal and that these teachers often cannot provide them with the instruction, modeling, and other elements that they need to "do better" and "be better." Another child cogently points out one of the hallmarking functions of Black English—for confrontation : "When you around a whole lot of black people, be a whole lot of arguments." The children speak these thoughts in deeply dialectal language, difficult to decipher for speakers of Standard English. Clearly, these children are not enfranchised in the speechways of the larger culture (Kochman, 1981).

Although the issue of dialectology and its function in the lives of minority speakers is beyond the scope of this research, it is necessary to address, however briefly, how the perception of Black English as a "linguistically deficient" form of speech affects speakers Black English dialects. First, the term implies lack, imperfection, and incomplete linguistic acquisition and development. Secondly, this implication depends on an idea that linguistic pureness, or a perfect model of English, exists. On purely linguistic criteria, there is no such thing. Rather, these perceptions are based on an inherent misunderstanding of the fluid, changing nature of language and the function of dialects—Standard Educated English included—in all of the public and private processes of a culture and its people. The misguided deficit theory of language shames children who speak Black English, and when children are deemed to be "linguistically deficient," it is not a far jump for them to perceive themselves as inferior, inadequate, and powerless. Children who are shamed about their language soon become ashamed of themselves.

Recent work in descriptive linguistics has found links that associate the development of various Black English dialects to West African languages. Black English dialects, with historical resemblances to Caribbean and West African varieties of English (Dillard, 1972) have a form and structure of their own. Linguist Carmen Tolhurst (1996) contends that Black English includes unique vocabulary elements, various phonological features that systematically replace certain English consonants, and a different, more fully developed verbal system with tense and aspect features that are not found in standard English dialects. If we subscribe to the "deficit" theory of language, which dialect would be deemed deficient on these terms? First, it must be noted that these differences are part of a systematic pattern in Black English, and secondly, that they have correspondences in other languages commonly considered "full" languages—e.g., Japanese, Spanish, etc.

J.L. Dillard (1972) argues that the failure to provide adequate information about Black English is a major hindrance to the educational system. Although research into Afro-American language patterns was not initiated to resolve educational problems, examples of educational practices keep surfacing which show that general social and educational institutions continue to stigmatize black children. In addition, a look at the curriculum of teacher education programs shows that accurate and reliable information on the forms and structures of Black English is not generally made available to educators. While current curricular policy mandates training on multi cultural issues, solid, linguistically-based course work on the history and structure of the English language is required only for high school English teachers—as though teachers whose specialty is not English are unaffected by sociolinguistic issues that dominate students' lives. Clearly, what would be in the best interest of the students—adequate information and training about the nature of language in general, and about the forms and functions of dialects in particular—is not being accomplished.

It must be underscored that deep dialectal forms of English that diverge greatly from educated dialects are the language of many impoverished communities, spoken by parents, siblings, relatives, friends, and neighbors. In an important sense, this constellation of dialects, historically created by a race that was once forbidden to use its native tongue, continues to serve the same historical functions: 1) it cleaves the community unto itself, functioning as a bond; and 2) it is a private kind of talk not shared by the larger culture—except, perhaps, as entertainment, e.g., rap music, Black sit coms, etc.

Not unlike Betances' (1996) assertion that Alower-class people cannot give birth to middle class kids," a community whose language is profoundly dialectal cannot give its children the linguistic repertoire necessary for these children to enter the processes of the larger culture on the same linguistic footing as other children. The domain of language is not different from other domains of the curriculum: the educator is responsible for providing the necessary technical and factual assistance to expand the children's repertoire. In this case the job is not to wipe out their private dialects, but to enfranchise them into the public language of the larger culture—Standard Educated English.

PERCEIVED EFFECTIVE SCHOOLS

For a moment the students stepped outside of the world of gangs, violence, drugs, isolation, and poverty to dream: What if? Envisioning their dream school, they express a hope, however frail, of reaching their goals. They show themselves to be acutely aware and perceptive of their needs and construct incipient blueprints to increase student involvement, develop student self-worth, productiveness, and ultimately, help them not perpetuate and reproduce their poverty and alienation. Miraculously, these children still believe that, given the appropriate educational setting, effective, nurturing teachers, and community support, they can attain productive lives. Rejecting the decay about her, Lee Lee creates an environment that is beautiful and honors the students' right to learn:

It won't have all this graffiti and stuff on it, written on the wall and stuff. And to pass you have to be on your right level because they just pass them because they want to get rid of them. I know you can't stop the rats and roaches. It won't have no windows like this, broken and written all over.

Jason masterfully outlines a process for teacher selection: on site visitations of a perspective teacher would be imperative to evaluate methods of instruction and interaction with the students. "First of all I would not have any mean teachers. I would pick out every teacher. I would see what the teacher is doing. I try to find out what is their background. And if they can do it perfect, I pick'em." Refuting the stereotype of kids who hate school, he suggests that school should be available to students on the week-ends, providing a center to give additional help, utilizing neighborhood resources, and providing a safe retreat. He wants, "A place where kids can go to learn more, like on the week-ends. On week-ends the kids can come to school and do some more work, extra work." Against the prevailing images, these children want more after school activities and twenty-four-hour security; they have correctly understood that schools should be places of safety.

Perhaps it is because the majority of the students are gang members, they all believe that schools should be more knowledgeable about gangs. This implies their repudiation of a lifestyle—if they could only get away—and their belief that effective methods **can** be developed to prevent gang infiltration and provide safety in the schools. These students want schools to assume responsibility for offsetting "street knowledge." By insisting that information be given to students in first grade, they imply that eighth grade is too late to start.

Their visions of the physical plant reveals profound concern for the present conditions of the school. The graffiti, broken and patched windows, rodents and insects, the general degradation and decay would be replaced by cleanliness, desks and equipment in good condition, and sufficient learning material.

The conditions that prevail sustain their sense of inadequacy, worthlessness, and inferiority. Though schools attempt to instill pride via programs of multiculturalism, the children still perceive themselves, their classmates, and other blacks as "just plain bad." They say, "more wild than city kids and more gangs out here." "You around a whole lot of black people, be a whole lot of arguments." Each statement reflects correctly that these children's situation is out of control and desperate.

Finally, the students express concern about their isolation from the core culture. Speaking of the school they envision, these students decree: "it would have black and white"; "I wouldn't want all black teachers." In the best educational tradition, they dream of schools that would provide a route of escape from the constraints of the history, perceptions and environment that dominate their lives.

PSYCHOLOGICAL AND SOCIAL FACTORS RELATED TO SOCIALLY CONSTRUCTED REALITY

Much of the identity of Black America and many of today's disquieting realities are grounded in a history of racism and oppression. Children raised in impoverished communities contend with gangs, violence, poverty, and many other impairing social factors which create negative self-concepts. Perkins (1975) argues that black children are defined by those in power who cannot understand the full dynamics of the black culture and its implications.

> Of course, many white social scientists continue to define the black child from theiralienated perspective and while some of their studies are academically stimulating, they fail to present a clear analysis of the total social factors (capitalism, racism and colonization) which oppress the black child. Instead, most of the studies onlyreinforce the traditional theories of pathological behavior which have been used todefine the behavior of black children (p. viii).

Perkins (1975) addresses the factors surrounding the development of a negative self-concept in African-American children, underscoring the conspiracy of the environment and a larger social order which has not correctly or effectively analyzed the issues. Garbarino (1991) compares this environment to "war zones", so no less than other children living in the heart of conflict—e.g., Ireland, Bosnia, Zaire—Black children living in these areas are at great risk. Their everyday existence is permeated by violence and turmoil, so in response, they develop a manner of being and behaving in the world that will ensure safety and survival of some sort. In fact, they hope for life. Therefore, these mechanisms must not be viewed as pathological; rather, in the deepest sense, they are life-sustaining and life-affirming. From this environment they develop their perceptions of self: who they are and where they fit into the larger social scheme.

PERCEPTION OF SELF IN RELATION TO ENVIRONMENT

Many studies have shown that physical safety and psychological security are essential foundations for a child's total development (e.g., Zinmeister, 1990). The child's self-definition is contingent on the establishment of these preconditions; however, in impoverished communities, these foundations are at risk. Children define themselves in relationship to their environment and the actions of others. Gangs are pivotal determinant factors in this self-definition. The Chicago Crime Commission (1995), generated a report, *Gangs Public Enemy Number One,* which outlines gang structure (p. 38, see figure 6) and some organizational fundamentals of the Chicago street gangs.

> Street gangs are a major cultural and economic force in our communities . . . Today, more than 125 gangs claim territory in the Chicago land area, with gang membership estimated at well over 100,000 . . . Over the years . . . gangs have merged into two major groupings, the "Folks" and the "People" . . . Drive-by shootings often occur as a result of a "Folk" or "People" being spotted in an enemy's territory . . . hand signs are used . . . as a form of non-verbal communication. A gang's hand sign is always given in the up position. If a gang sign is given in the down position, it shows a gesture of

disrespect, possibly resulting in retaliation in the form of a drive-by shooting (pp. 3-8).

Jim narrates a form of retaliation.

> They did something to one of our "Folks" and the older "Folks" sent one of us out to take care of our business . . . I won't try to kill them, just hurt them, but if they die, they die . . . ain't nobody do nothing to you unless you disrespect 'em, Just disrespect their Nation and they be like, we know you in this gang but don't disrespect any of our Nation or do anything to our APeople. And it's over.

Safety and survival are primary issues in the Awar zones." Nicole outlines "maneuvers" to ensure her safety in the "game" she plays called AIt":

> . . . [Y]ou know, it's like, if you getting into a real fight and then you end up walking off and the girl end up pulling a gun out, it's seeing how fast

Figure 6. Gang Structure (Courtesy of the Chicago Crime Commission)

There are approximately 40 major active street gangs operating within the Chicago area. Structure depends on size of membership and the extent of illegal activity the gang is involved with. The structure c.. p. 183 depicts a well organized street gang.

GANG STRUCTURE

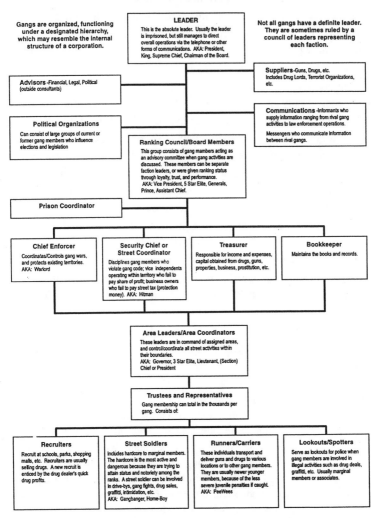

Gangs are organized, functioning under a designated hierarchy, which may resemble the internal structure of a corporation.

LEADER
This is the absolute leader. Usually the leader is imprisoned, but still manages to direct overall operations via the telephone or other forms of communications. AKA: President, King, Supreme Chief, Chairman of the Board.

Not all gangs have a definite leader. They are sometimes ruled by a council of leaders representing each faction.

Advisors -Financial, Legal, Political (outside consultants)

Suppliers -Guns, Drugs, etc. Includes Drug Lords, Terrorist Organizations, etc.

Political Organizations
Can consist of large groups of current or former gang members who influence elections and legislation

Ranking Council/Board Members
This group consists of gang members acting as an advisory committee when gang activities are discussed. These members can be separate faction leaders, or were given ranking status through loyalty, trust, and performance. AKA: Vice President, 5 Star Elite, Generals, Prince, Assistant Chief.

Communications -Informants who supply information ranging from rival gang activities to law enforcement operations.
Messengers who communicate information between rival gangs.

Prison Coordinator

Chief Enforcer
Coordinates/Controls gang wars, and protects existing territories. AKA: Warlord

Security Chief or Street Coordinator
Disciplines gang members who violate gang code; vice independents operating within territory who fail to pay share of profit; business owners who fail to pay street tax (protection money). AKA: Hitman

Treasurer
Responsible for income and expenses, capital obtained from drugs, guns, properties, business, prostitution, etc.

Bookkeeper
Maintains the books and records.

Area Leaders/Area Coordinators
These leaders are in command of assigned areas, and control/coordinate all street activities within their boundaries. AKA: Governor, 3 Star Elite, Lieutenant, (Section) Chief or President

Trustees and Representatives
Gang membership can total in the thousands per gang. Consists of:

Recruiters
Recruit at schools, parks, shopping malls, etc. Recruiters are usually selling drugs. A new recruit is enticed by the drug dealer's quick drug profits.

Street Soldiers
Includes hardcore to marginal members. The hardcore is the most active and dangerous because they are trying to attain status and notoriety among the ranks. A street soldier can be involved in drive-bys, gang fights, drug sales, graffiti, intimidation, etc. AKA: Gangbanger, Home-Boy

Runners/Carriers
These individuals transport and deliver guns and drugs to various locations or to other gang members. They are usually newer younger members, because of the less severe juvenile penalties if caught. AKA: PeeWees

Lookouts/Spotters
Serve as lookouts for police when gang members are involved in illegal activities such as drug deals, graffiti, etc. Usually marginal members or associates.

you can run between you and the girl who pulled the gun on you and trying to shoot you. They try to shoot you and you can run fast.

Jim and Nicole describe occurrences which are familiar for all of these children. Asked when they felt safe, almost without exception the children respond, "In the house." Conversely, when asked about feelings of danger, they respond, "When I'm outside;" "When you leave out of the house, that's a risk on your life;" "When you go in the wrong neighborhood." Severed from the larger social order, this constricted environment only allows for a narrow self-definition. The territorial map in chapter 4 , figure 3, reveals the extent of isolation and the limits in which they exist. Their behavior adapts to the immediate needs of safety and survival. Though deemed pathological (Perkins, 1975) by some, their behavior is highly adaptive, for these children are engaging in a struggle for survival, and the gangs represent and provide—however inadequately—family, security and empowerment. Like the streetcorner men in Tally's *Corner*, these children need a sanctuary so that they can face oppression and failure. In the terms of Elliot Liebrow (1967), they create a new system in which failures are rationalized as successes and weakness become strengths. In their own ways, children such as Jim with his status in the GDs, establish modes of self-respect and power. The most popular boy in the school, Jim's qualifications include: six times arrested, imprisoned, multiply-shot, but a survivor. These "attributes" endow him respect and status in the eyes of his classmates. Jim discusses his feelings about his popularity.

Q: Why do kids look up to you?
Jim: I don't know why they look up to me. Cause you know, I ain't shy, if I don't like something I just say it like it is. They look up to me, I don't know why, cause I been in jail. They think I'm tough. I be happenin' and all that, telling them songs and they say how do you know all the words? And I say I know it by heart. I don't say I can't be warped, but I don't let nobody set up there and make me look like a little wimp.
Q: Do you think of yourself as being tough?
Jim: Jus' like anybody else, I can be beat up. I can be hurt, burnt, shot.
Q: How do you feel that they look up to you, think you're tough?

Jim: Make me feel nothing. I don't get paid for them lookin' up to me. The crossing guard, say Jim, you the most popular kid in school. I don't know why. Just another kid in school that they think is popular. You got the good clothes on. She be telling me and Sam, you the most popular two boys in school. All the girls like you'all . . . I don't tell'em what to do, I just come to school, if they like what I do that's on them

Jim is not an exception, for the majority of the boys in the class have been arrested at least once, and what happens to these children once they enter the juvenile processes has also been established. Although gangs, lack of resources, drugs, decay, prostitution, and the like, continue to define them, still, they are children. Who will take responsibility for them?

EXPOSURE TO OTHER PEOPLE'S REALITY

According to Stephen Steinberg (1981), ethnicity forms the basis for social consciousness and influences behavior. However, the very nature of ethnicity constructs patterns of isolation, initially for the poor, which also affect consciousness and influence behavior. This latter consciousness and behavior are not characteristic of any specific ethnic group but are indicative of poverty, and those effected are primarily African-Americans and Hispanics.

Steinberg (1981), defines ethnicity as "ways of thinking, feeling, and acting that constitute a culture" (p. ix). Although it is recognized and accepted that cultural groups each have their own uniqueness and peculiarities, he stresses that "culture does not exist in a vacuum. On the contrary, culture is in a constant flux and is integrally a part of the larger social process" (p. ix). Certainly, children who live in impoverished communities are socially and residentially isolated, allowing only limited socialization with other ethnic groups. The children in the study have minimal contact with people of other cultures. Their friendships are exclusively within their own communities. Not only does limited exposure prevent their understanding and appreciation of other cultures and create mistrust and prejudice, but it precludes the children from entering into the social processes of the core culture in which they are not embedded. These perceptions are not formed by a single experience but are a sum of their collective experiences.

THE COLOR COMPLEX ENIGMA

Black historians Mike Pflug of the Carter G. Woodson Library and Charles Branham of the DuSable Museum corroborate that the authenticity of *The Willie Lynch Speech of 1712* is still in question. Reportedly given to a group of slave owners, the speech outlines methods of controlling the African slave population. Although unknown in origin, the speech was widely used and quoted. Excerpts of the speech deal with the machinations which gave rise to the color complex that still affects Black Americans:

> First, I shall thank you, The Gentlemen of the Colony of Virginia, for bringing me here. I am here to help you solve some of your problems with the slaves . . . I have experimented with some of the newest and still oldest methods for slave control . . . In my bag here, I have a fool-proof method of controlling your black slaves. I guarantee everyone of you that if installed correctly it will control the slaves . . . I have outlined a number of differences among the slaves and I take those differences and make them bigger. I use fear, distrust, and envy for control purposes . . . Take the simple little list of differences and think about them. On top of the list is "Age" but it is there only because it starts with an "A;" the second is "Color" or shade, there is Intelligence, Size, Sex . . . fine hair, coarse hair. Now that you have the list of differences, I shall give you an outline of action—but before that I shall assure you that distrust is stronger than adulation, respect or admiration.
>
> The black slave after receiving this indoctrination shall carry on and will become self refueling and self generating for hundreds of years, maybe thousands.
>
> . . . You must use dark skin [sic] slaves vs. light skin slaves and light skin slaves vs, dark skin slaves. You must use females vs. males, and the male vs. female. Gentlemen, these Kits are your keys to control. Use them . . . My plan is guaranteed, and the good thing about this plan is that if used intensely for one year the slaves themselves will remain perpetually distrustful.

Acknowledging the dispute in authenticity, this speech nevertheless provides a basis by which to understand the politics of color and subsequent stereotypical images existing in today's black culture. Today's black children could have been the direct audience, still victims of the message that forged a negative idea of the self which has persisted in the black race. The children echo the message: "I like light skin' girls. Oh, ain't nothing wrong with it (being dark skinned), I just like them lighter than me. Not real, real dark. Like Nate is real dark, can't have no girl dark like Nate. Because you can't see. I ain't seen no pretty dark girls yet." or Keisha's remark, "I'm color-struck (spoken with pride). I am going to say light skinned . . . I don't know, they just don't look right, too dark. Medium complexion. They can be dark but not like they stayed in the sun all the time, not too, you know." The children's preferences are remnants of the practices of slavery when light skinned women and men could serve as house servants while their darker complexion kin served in the fields. The standards of beauty associated with light skin are described as "nice" facial features (small and even) and "good" hair—traits most similar to white features. In fact, there came a time when the words *African* and *savage* became synonymous and interchangeable. Latif and Latif (1994) elaborate:

"Civilized" came to mean "white" or "European." It meant living in a house like white people, wearing clothes like white people, being able to speak like white people. To be African was to be dirty, ugly, subhuman. American born slaves turned from such identity in disgust, and looked for something else, anything other than an African, to call themselves (p. 172).

The self-hatred, spawned and perpetuated by a history of slavery, continues to haunt the inner selves of African-Americans today. Although not as dominant as it once was, the children still respond to a negative valuation which prefers light over dark, fine hair over coarse, and uniform features over variable or salient ones. The negative self-concept and preoccupation with shedding "Black" features are reinforced even within the Black community, which tends to identify beauty with white, largely Northern European standards. Surely, racism and historical assumptions continue to affect the color complex propelled by the beauty industry whose success depends on perpetuating ideals of beauty that require "adjustment."

THE EFFECTS OF SOCIALLY CONSTRUCTED REALITY IN RELATION TO A PERCEIVED FUTURE

Collective experience is formed within the association of past and present events from which a memory bank is established. "With regard for the future, [collective experience] establishes a common frame of reference for projection of individual actions" (Burger and Luckmann, 1966, p. 103). Yet, astonishingly, although the children have endured a preponderance of negative experiences, their ability to hope and dream is not destroyed. Their career goals add legitimacy to their lives and their choices refer to and arise from the larger social order. They want to be doctors, lawyers, architects, entertainers, teachers, and President of the United States, however unlikely these dreams may be given their circumstances. Yet, not unlike the cartoon quip in figure 4, "What do you want to be when you grow up?" their immediate goal is to be "Alive." Weighed down by occurrences within their immediate experience, these children are anxious for themselves and members of their families.

Asked, "If you had three wishes, what would they be?" the majority of the children choose to stop gang activity and killings, and initiate safety within the community. These wishes are significant in their communitarian orientation and altruism, revealing a complex and disquieting knowledge of their reality.

THE ROLE OF MASS MEDIA AND POPULAR CULTURE IN SHAPING PERCEPTION OF CONSTRUCTED SOCIAL REALITY

Black popular culture transcends time. Before other forms of self-expression were used, even before enslavement, blacks responded to the rhythmic beat. It was a primal, ancient means of communication. Feet tapping, fingers rapping, heads moving, bodies swaying and dancing to African drums that provided the rhythmic patterns in Gospel, Blues, Jazz, Be-Bop, Rock' n Roll, Du-Wop, Rhythm 'n Blues, and Hip-Hop, music was the major vehicle to confront, cope with, and find answers to life's realities. It has been the traditional black voice. If black music is made the scapegoat for the "moral decline" of modern culture, what is an entire population to understand about itself and its history? What are its children to understand?

The children take issue with the perceptions of the larger society in relationship to the popular culture and the shaping of their reality. They consider movies and rap music to be forms of entertainment and expression although they admit, "[S]ome movies are about us, me and somebody else." Placing popular culture in perspective, they maintain, "[Y]ou know that was a movie so you know how that was. You can't do like that on the street. It doesn't happen like that for real."

Jim explains his interpretation of rap music,

> I listen to the words. Like some of the rap songs, when you really listen to them, you get knowledge . . . they tell you what to look out for. Like you don't want to drop out of school in the sixth grade and all that. Keep your money when you got it. They don't tell you to go out and kill somebody. They just tell you how things can go down. They try to tell you what to look out for.

Rose (1994) provides a philosophical interpretation, but the fundamental message is the same—oral expression and diversion.

> Poor people learn from experience when and how explicitly they can express their discontent. Under social conditions in which sustained frontal attacks on powerful groups are strategically unwise or unsuccessfully contained, oppressed people use language, dance, and music to mock those in power, express rage, and produce fantasies and subversions. These cultural forms are especially rich and pleasurable places where oppositional transcripts, or the "unofficial truths" are developed, refined, and rehearsed. These cultural responses to oppression are not safety valves that protect and sustain the machines of oppression. Quite the contrary, these dance, languages, and music produce communal bases of knowledge about social conditions, communal interpretations of them and quite often serve as the cultural glue that fosters communal resistance (p. 99).

Although rap music is a form of social critique, the children state that they enjoy the beat and the music does not motivate them to violence. Nicole says, "Ain't no music going to make you do nothing. You got a mind of your own and can't nobody sit there and say I was listening to this type of music, and that's what made me do such and such." Lee Lee, who listens to the "message" adds, "Yea. Sometime, I like it because I don't be knowing what they are saying and it sounding good. I just like the beat." Sam also counters social perception: "I listen to the beat . . . No. It influence you to do nothin', cause it don't tell you to go out there and do it. You have your own mind. If you go out there and do it, you want to do it."

Collectively the children say that while they hear the message, they primarily enjoy the rhythm, the beat, the diversion. Paraphrased, their consensus states: We have our own minds, and a movie or song does not and will not arouse us to violence. If we are involved in violence, it is because that is a choice that we made. *Listen: Do You Hear What I Hear?*

IMPLICATIONS AND RECOMMENDATIONS

From this study, many implications can be determined. The questions were constructed to evoke certain aspects of black disadvantaged adolescents' lives and ways of "seeing" that would offer insight on how they socially construct their world. They expressed hopes, aspirations and anxieties. The results are applicable to the specific population in the study—students who represent a microcosm of inner city youth in impoverished areas.

PEDAGOGICAL IMPLICATIONS AND RECOMMENDATIONS

The children entered school at grade level in math and reading and initially maintained grade level through second grade. They came to school with a set of collective experiences and a particular, well-developed, rich dialect—spoken by their parents, siblings, friends and neighbors—which is referred to as Black English. Contrary to the judgment based on negative research models of "cognitive deficits," these children appear not to enter school with cognitive, experiential, and linguistic deficits since they do not test below grade level in the early years. However, after receiving public school education for approximately two years—in the third and fourth grades—their scores begin to drop. Rarely do they recover. Researchers and educators must confront the difficult question: what caused the differential after they entered the system?

It is a truism that the children are already impoverished upon entering school. Elements of drugs, violence, gangs, etc., are in evidence in their environment. Therefore, to assert that poverty alone creates and perpetrators this deficit is invalid. Analyzed carefully, this line of reasoning argues that once the children enter the system and "education" begins, their learning lulls. Yet, somehow, they learn *in spite* of their schooling.

Suggesting that deficits are created because of a style of teaching, an environment, and a context rather than because of a lack of ability on the students' part. This implies that programs currently in existence must shift their emphases in the direction of "effective child centered-education," using instructional material that relates in a significant manner to the students' lives. Educational centers and school-based centers should be organized where students can receive additional technical and social assistance within the community. In addition, parental educational and assistance centers must be established, for parents cannot help provide students with what they themselves do not possess. These centers would operate after school and on week-ends.

With this in mind, several issues need further exploration. Incorporating and carrying out programs that focus on the deficiency at the initial stage of development would require frequent and timely reviews of standardized test scores, grades, and behavior for each student. Within this framework, the current role of school counselors and social workers would need to be re-evaluated so that they could provide more effective assistance.

The children correctly understood a causal connection between teacher attitude and student productivity. Proving what research states, the students saw that uncaring, ignorant, and insensitive teachers quell learning. Teaching, then, requires not only an effective addressing of issues concerning instruction but also of feelings, values, and attitudes of the students. This suggests that many of the teachers are ill-equipped to provide meaningful programs for this population and that much of what is taught does not relate to what occurs in the students' home environment and community. How can teachers learn to bridge the differential between a middle-class curriculum and the students' environment? Teacher training institutions must instruct prospective teachers on how to adjust a curriculum to make it meaningful for the child. This is one of the most important goals of education for these and other children in urban settings.

SOCIAL IMPLICATIONS AND RECOMMENDATIONS

The so-called American "ideal" actually has its origin in conquest, slavery, and exploitations. With the exception of Native Americans, no American can claim a unique ethnic American heritage, since Americans are not "ethnically rooted on American soil" (Steinberg, 1981, p. 6). Racism, inequality, and exclusion, integral components of the "American tradition," have created and affected the poor. Generally born to that "station" in life, they develop a life-style and adopt values that are appropriate and constant for that setting. In labeling this life-style pathological, it is easy for the larger culture to effectively deny its complicity in creating and perpetuating the life of the poor. In addition, it is easier to preclude the poor as being capable of obtaining adequate training, job opportunities, and wages that can sustain a family.

This study reveals that the children in these communities are recipients of negative labeling processes, and as such, they have low-self-worth and their lives are plagued by negativism and inferiority. Their communities are combat zones in a war for survival where adoption of safety and survival techniques is critical. These children cannot travel from community to community or school to school without fear of being injured or killed. Repeatedly, they stress the anxiety which is produced because of a lack of safety. "Prisoners" within their own communities, they fear for their lives and the lives of their family members. They are exposed to violence and execute violence as evidence of their discontent.

However, their issues have broader social implications. One of the most salient is the need for government-developed programs that provide opportunities for these families and their children. The children's dialog stresses the necessity for drug programs and more stringent legislation and its enforcement for drug dealers. Since guns are accessible even to small children, ownership and sales of guns must be harshly curtailed. Neighborhood and school areas must be mandated "dry," removing easy accessibility of harmful substances to children. Other government priorities must focus on methods to deal with crime and violence in these communities. According to the information presented in chapter one, from the Uniform Crime Report for the United States Chicago Police Department's Annual Report (1993), clearly crime is on the rise and the offenders are getting younger.

The data clearly suggest that cities such as Chicago, in conjunction with the United States Government, must design more effective and collaborative plans to curb persistent poverty. Inclusive within those plans, opportunities must be provided to benefit families and children. More funding must be allocated to education; forms of financial relief must be made available to parents with college-aged students; jobs and increased medical benefits must be made available; continuous and effective war on crime, drugs and violence, and better legislation for gun control must be carried out. Although the minimum wage has been increased, a continuous process of review should be initiated so that parents can take care of their families without having to resort to desperate means.

FURTHER RECOMMENDATIONS

Based on the findings of this research, the following recommendations are made for further research: This study is broad in scope. Each theme developed from this study could be examined in-depth by other researchers. The lives of disadvantaged minority children need to be the focus of more qualitative research. From such research, we can learn more about the construction of children's reality—their goals, dreams, anxieties, and fears—leading, hopefully to developing creative "learning" environments to enhance skills, ensure their ability to enter the larger social process, increase their sense of self-worth and empower them to attain full lives. However, critical to this understanding, those who conduct educational research must *listen* to the voices of these children and understand that they come "equipped" with a wealth of pre-existing knowledge. In addition, they must rid themselves of preconceived perceptions of disadvantaged children that have existed for too long. Such research should investigate the "natural resources" of minority children and then suggest appropriate educational strategies.

Pilot Study

For the purpose of this study, a pilot was conducted. The subjects were seventh grade students from a magnet high school with a seventh and eighth grade academic center The students were multi-racial and multiethnic, between the ages of eleven and twelve. The academic center program has an enrollment of approximately two hundred and ten students. The school is located in a historical section of Chicago and the majority of the students are from middle to upper middle class socioeconomic levels.

The pilot study provided highlights of certain differences in educational, social backgrounds, social values and lifestyles of the two diverse groups. It also resulted in improved conceptualization of the interview instrument. Some questions were clarified, rephrased and modified that would have possibly produced undesirable responses.

The students were informed that they were taking part in a sample study. They were asked to be critical and forthright; to ask for clarification of any questions they did not understand; and to provide suggestions for modifications. They were told that their participation in the pilot study would help to produce improved questions for the research study.

PERCEPTION OF SCHOOLING

School children construct their perception of the elements and factors that connect and shape the reality between schooling and their lives. They responded to questions that focus on the "purpose" of schooling.

Q: You spend a great deal of time in school. What does school mean to you. Do you think it is different being a student and not being a student? How is it different? What do you think about kids that are not in school?

B/F: It is different to be a student and not be a student. Students in school are getting themselves an education and pressing towards their goal of what they want to be. In my opinion they're on the right track. Students who are not in school anymore need their education. I don't know their reason for not being in school, but they need to. It would make life easier for them (later on in life).

B/F: . . . One person is learning something and the other is not. I think it is really sad that some people are not in school. They are not getting an education or anything for that matter.

A/F: Some kids are naturally smart, but you've got to go to school to sharpen your abilities. I think kids who don't go to school are careless or stupid. School is very important.

W/F: When you are in school you focus on different things when you are out of school. kids who are out of school should go back, because even though it is tough, it will pay off later.

W/F: In school you are learning more and more everyday. You are also making more friends and learning to socialize more. I think that people who are not in school can also get involved in drugs and gangs.

W/F: Kids that are not in school are just people that are not aware that not being in school can ruin their lives.

H/F: When you are a student you have working ability and you are being well educated. Children who are not in school will end up living in poverty and not getting a good job to support themselves.

W/F: Kids should be in school because they need an education to succeed in life.

W/F: Children that are not educated will not become successful.

P/M: Non-students have a harder life and turn to crime.

H/F: Being a student is a bigger responsibility. Those who aren't in school may have no job or can't afford much. I feel that people with no education have less advantage than those who are in school.

The students were asked whether or not they considered the knowledge received in school useful in their everyday lives.

Q: Are the things you learn in school useful to your everyday life? If so give some examples.

B/F: Yes, I talk better—meaning my vocabulary and speech. For math, when I cook, I understand what I have to do more clearly and I understand my measurements. There are other things too.

B/F: Yes, in the store you have to be able to read and knowing math can help you not be cheated. Also in school you learn several things about racism, etc., and you can help stop those things if you know about them.

B/F: Yes—a new vocabulary, how to critical think.

K/F: Some of the things we do connect with my everyday life, but others I don't know when I will use them again. The vocabulary words we have are very useful, every once in awhile I will hear one of the words we have studied and recognize it. Problem solving will also be useful in the future.

W/F: The school is teaching me more about the environment and it also teaches me about things such as stereotyping so I am ready to face all the racism in the outside world.

H/F: It depends. Some stuff like math is most helpful because you use math at the grocery store, balancing check books, cutting pie in equal pieces.

W/F: Yes, they are, I need math to determine a study schedule and plan my time wisely.

W/F: Yes. Because it helps me to understand the world around me better and it gives me knowledge.

B/F: Yes. I am able to teach those younger than me in my family new things as well as those older than me.

B/M: Some of the things I learn in school are useful such as math and comprehending with people using vocabulary.

The students were also asked to plan a school that would meet their needs. The answers primarily focused on internal organization, curriculum, and excelling. Although some reference was made to the physical plant, it was only in relation to physical structure enhancements of was already available. Surprisingly, teachers or teacher's attitudes were not an issue. However, many of the children were content with their current school and the education they were receiving

Q: If you could plan a school the way you wanted it to be , what would it look like inside and out, what would it have? Would it be like this school? Or would it be completely different? How would your school be?

H/F: I would plan it so that each room is really big. Then I would make it so that all the teachers are the best in the city. Each student would have their own computer at their desk connected to the teacher's computer. All work would be done on the computer so you don't waste paper.

A/F: I would start at 10:00 A.M., so that I wouldn't have to wake up at 6:00 A.M. every morning. But other than that, it would be the same.

B/F: Well, my school would have a test to get in. It would go from sixth grade to a senior high school . . . In science we would have 1½ hours to do our lab instead of 50 minutes. In social studies we'd have VCR to take us to different place and times. That sort of fun and we still learn.

B/F: Everyone would have the same ethnicity, they would be from the same environment. The teachers would be very smart and there would be two counselors per class.

B/F: It would be the same as it is now except less homework and we were able to go outside for lunch and you could choose who you sat by.

P/F: I think if I could plan a school it would be very similar to the way *this school* is organized.

W/F: The school would be small (1 story high, 1/4 of a block long). It would be tidy, clean, people would be courteous of each other there, it would give well pay to the teachers, low school entrance fee and it would give well education.

W/F: I like the school I am at right now. I probably wouldn't change anything (except less homework!).

W/M: I'd have gym and computers all day.

All of the children in the pilot study believed schooling was meaningful to their present and future lives. They also perceived the knowledge received in school as useful, with a significant correlation between what is learned and its relationship to their future.

PSYCHOLOGICAL AND SOCIAL FACTORS RELATED TO SOCIAL REALITY CONSTRUCTION

In relation to everyday experiences, the students were asked to give an example of their daily activities.

Q: One of the things I am interested in understanding is your everyday experiences. Give me an example of your everyday life. What do you do when you go home?

B/F: Have a snack. Do part of my homework. Go to an activity. Eat dinner. Do the rest of my homework. Get ready for bed. Go to sleep.

B/F: When I go home *from school*, I get a snack and do my homework while talking on the phone. Or Tuesday and Thursday I go to karate and Friday tennis. If I feel like it I go outside.

K/F: When I get home I usually rest or have a snack then start my home work. When I finish or during reading breaks I might play with my gerbils, work on my computer, read a book, or watch T.V.

W/F: When I go home, I walk my dog, watch television, talk on the phone, go to friends houses, do my homework, eat dinner.

W/F: When I go home I usually play the piano a little, watch some T.V., have a snack, dinner, then I go outside and play, after I come back in to help my mom with chores and to do my homework.

W/F: I go skating in the morning before school. When I get home I watch a little T.V. and have a snack then sit down and do my homework. After homework I either watch T.V. or do something in my room.

H/F: When I go home I'll have a small snack, hold my baby sister, do my homework, watch T.V., eat dinner, take a shower, go to bed.

W/M: I do my homework and go rollerblading.

W/F: I'm a very busy person. I'm involved in many sports: swimming, soccer, basketball, ballet, jazz. I go out to play, I relax, I play board games, T do homework, I eat candy (I love candy!) . . . I sometimes do chores and errands.

P/M: Eat, watch T.V., do homework.

A/F: I get a snack, watch TV, or go outside, and do my homework, then eat dinner, then sit around with my family and then go to sleep.

C/M: I start on my homework. Playing sports with my family.

B/M: When I go home I jog three miles, lift weights and then go outside and play or go to the library. I come home around dark do my homework if I haven't done it at the library, eat dinner then go to bed.

Without exception, homework was a significant part to each child's everyday experience. They were also very involved with aspects of family and participated in numerous activities. Whereas, social activities were placed in a secondary perspective . However for this group of students, gangs and issues of safety were not problematic in their common sense world but proved to become concerns on a global scale. The students also had an expanded sense of "space." They had done extensive travels both in and outside of the United States. These experiences developed respect and appreciation for the many ethnic races and cultures they encountered on a daily basis.

In relation to a perceived future, the students were asked how and where do they see themselves ten years from now? Who do they admire most? If they had three wishes, what would they be? All of the children saw themselves as college graduates with productive future employment. College for these children, is not a question of, are you going to college, but where are you going to college? They contribute these successes and future endeavors to the support of their families.

The wishes presented another realm to expand their visions. The majority of the students foresaw a world free of poverty, violence, pollution, and suffering.

Q:	Who do you admire most?
W/F:	Phobe Mills, she follows her dreams and never underestimates her abilities.
B/F:	Janet Jackson—because I like her attitude toward—racism, illiteracy, and bigotry.
K/F:	I admire my grandfather the most. He always was, and still is a hard worker at everything he does.
W/F:	My fifth grade teacher because she was such a wonderful teacher.
W/F:	My parents because I can always go to them with questions and problems.
H/F:	My dad, because he is a hard worker, a good friend, a great person and supporter of a family of six.
P/M:	My parents. They are always there for me. They are great parents. They want the best for me.
C/M:	My uncle. Because he understand my problems and helps me.
B/F:	I admire my parents because they are understanding and lovable. They brought me into this world. I feel they are honest people.
B/M:	I admire my parents most because they keep me going and they are always there. I am thankful for them.
Q:	Based on your experiences so far in life, Where do you think you will five years, ten years from now? And, if you were allowed three wishes what would they be?

W/F: I will probably be in college. *If I had three wishes*, my dad would never have had a heart attack and heart problems—because it is hard to see him so unhappy and grouchy all the time; that I would be on the '96 Olympic women's gymnastic team—I love the sport. I wish I could go far and be recognized for my talent and love for the sport; I wish I had no worries—so my life would be care-free. I would be assured a road to happiness, that whatever goes wrong it would always work out.

B/M: Ten years from now I will be in the NBA. If I were allowed three wishes, my first wish would be that my whole family and I could all be promised eternal life in heaven because I believe that Jesus is the Savior, my second wish would be that I had my own room because I share a room with my brother who is very messy And my third wish would be that I got an A in every class for the rest of my educational career including college.

V/F: Ten years from now I'll probably be graduating college and going to medical school. If I got three wishes, I would wish to stop pollution, poverty and save the environment because without pollution there wouldn't be a hole in the ozone layer and animals and people wouldn't die.

K/F: Either going to college or finishing up college. Then settling down and getting a job. First I would wish for a nice big house by the ocean. Then I would wish for no crime or gangs in the city because I think there is too much all ready. And everything money can't buy.

C/F: I will be in high school or college in 5/10 years from now. Everyone would live peacefully, there was no shortage of food or money, and no more crime. You wouldn't argue as much, you would have plenty to eat, and you wouldn't be afraid of crime.

A/F: In five years, I will be finishing my term at high school. In ten years, I will be graduating from UCLA with a masters degree and getting married. *If I had three wishes*, for my mothers leg to get better and her back, for war to stop, for everyone to be happy.

C/M: I think I will be in college 10 years from now. I would wish for world peace because people in the world are suffering. I would wish for a big house, because I want to have my own room. I also wish I could see my great-grandmother, I want to find out what she is like.

B/F: In five years I think I'll be graduating from high school and in ten years , I think I'll be graduating or out of college. If I'm out of college I'll probably have a job. My first wish would be that my sister Tabitha hadn't gone out on August 1, 1994 because that's the night she died in a car accident. My second wish would be that schools and after school activities had a lot of money and could practice everyday because some recreational things and schools need money to become more up-to-date. My third wish would be that no one in the whole world was living in poor and dirty places.

B/F: Five years from now I'll be a senior then I plan to go to a predominantly black college and afterwards go to medical school. *I wish for* world peace, end poverty and homelessness, and for me to have a million dollars. War, poverty and homelessness are very big problems that need to be solved. Life would be much easier financially for my family if I had a million dollars.

W/F: Five years high school senior, ten years college. 1) A big house by the lake 2) I want to marry a prince 3) a computer.

W/F: In high school/college. World peace—too much violence. No poverty because poverty is sad. Tons of toys and clothes—have fun.

P/M: Five years from now—high school; ten years from now college. To become very rich, because I like money. To go to Harvard because education is important. To live a long time.

B/F: Five years—high school; ten—college. 1) World peace—I abhor how there are so many wars in this world. 2) No gangs—I'm tired of hearing people firing guns at night 3) No pollution—I don't like it when my mother is taking me somewhere and I see garbage everywhere.

THE ROLE OF THE MASS MEDIA AND "POPULAR CULTURE" IN SHAPING PERCEPTION OF CONSTRUCTED REALITY

The questions about popular culture and mass media had to be completely restructured in order to produce more meaningful responses.

Key: A/F A/M—Asian Female/Asian Male
        B/F B/M—African American Female/African American Male
        H/F H/M—Hispanic Female/Hispanic Male
        K/F K/M—Korean Female/Korean Male
        P/F P/M—Pakistan Female/Pakistan Male
        W/F W/M—White Female/White Male
        C/F C/M—Chinese Female/Chinese Male

Wolf's Artwork

Q: You draw a lot of guns. Tell me your feelings about guns and why you have so many guns in your drawings, see figure 7?

Wolf: That's what I like I like guns.

Q: What do you like about them?

Wolf: They shoot and kill. Sometimes it makes me feel happy.

Q: Wolf can you explain your pictures? Tell me about figure 8.

Wolf: (Laughing) Oh, somebody getting shot. A gang war.

Q: What about figure 9?

Wolf: Gang war too.

Q: What is happening in figure 10?

Wolf: This is when I was on the Westside. I sorta had dreams like this. And this is suppose to be me right here, *holding the gun.*

Q: Who is that under you?

Wolf: Somebody I done shot. And he's a hostage and I shot him and took his money.

Q: Is that blood up under this one?

Wolf: Yea.

Q: Who's Mr. Big in figure 10?

Wolf: That's him right here. A big time gangster.

Q: So you took care of him. Now this one, figure 11? Where are you? Are you in this one?

Wolf: Nope that's my brother.

Q: The one in the stripe suit is suppose to represent your brother? What's he smoking?

Wolf: A blunt.

Q: What's a blunt? A reaper?

Wolf: (Laughing) Yea.

Q: What going on here. I see somebody else. This is a gun here?

Wolf: Yea. He was going to get him payback.

Q: He doesn't have a face? Is that because you didn't finish it or does that mean something?

Wolf: He ain't got no face because he in the shadow shooting and you can't see him.

Q: O'k, so they don't know who that is? Who is this?

Wolf: That Mr. Big's cousin. Shot him with it?

Q: What is this (pointing to the rectangular figure in illustration) ?

Wolf: That's a picture.

Q: What do you do with you drawings? You draw a lot. Didn't somebody say something about the Art Institute? Did they send you to the Art Institute?

Wolf: They send my pictures.

Q: And what happened?

Wolf: They didn't say who won yet.

Figure 7

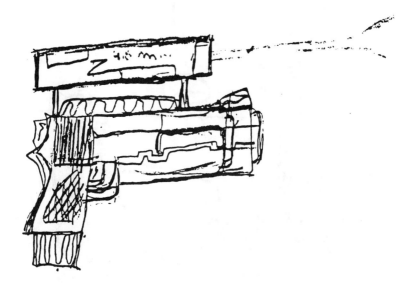

Figure 8

Figure 9

Figure 10

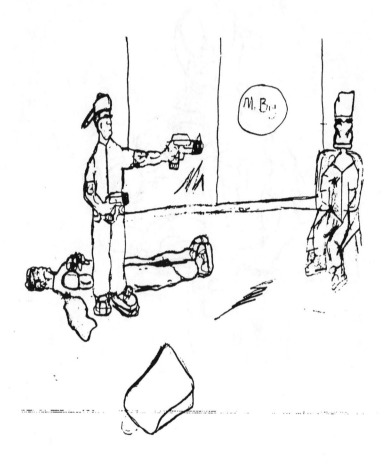

Figure 11

References

Akbar, Na'im. *From Miseducation to Education*. Jersey City: New Mind Publications, 1982; reprint 1984.

———. *Chains and Images of Psychological Slavery*. Jersey City: New Mind Productions, 1984.

Agar, Michael H. *The Professional Stranger: An Informal Introduction to Ethnography*. San Diego, CA.: Academic Press, 1980.

Al-Mansour, Khalid. *Betrayal: By Any Other Name*. San Francisco, CA.: The First African Arabian Press, 1993.

Althusser, Louis. *Lenin and Philosophy: and Other Essays*. New York: Monthly Review Press, 1971.

Andreas, A.T. *History of Cook County Illinois*. Chicago: A.T. Andreas Publisher, 1884.

Aronowitz, Stanley. *False Promises: The Shaping of America Working Class Consciousness*. New York: McGraw-Hill Book Co., 1973.

Atkinson, Pansye. *An African-American's View Brown vs. Topeka: Desegregation and Miseducation*. Chicago: African American Images, 1993.

Baker, Houston. *Black Studies Rap and the Academy*. Chicago: The University of Chicago Press, 1993.

Beasley, Paul L. "The Relationship Between Students' Views About the Purpose of School and Race, Socioeconomic Status, Educational Aspiration and Academic Self-Concept." Ph. D. diss. The University of Tennessee, 1988.

Beckom, Jesse Jr. *Gangs, Drugs & Violence: Chicago Style*. Chicago: Gangs, Grugs and Violence Prevention Consultants, 1993.

Bell, Janet Cheatham, ed. *Famous Black Quotations*. New York: Warner Books, 1986.

Bennett, Lerone Jr. *Before the Mayflower: A History of Black America.* New York: Penquin Books, 1961, 6th ed. 1988.

Benson, Janice E. Hale. *Black Children: Their Roots, Culture and Learning Styles.* Baltimore: The John Hopkins University Press, 1986.

Berger, Peter L. and Thomas Luckmann. *The Social Construction of Reality: A Treatise in the Sociology of Knowledge.* New York: Anchor Books, 1967.

Blassingame, John W. *Slave Testimony: Two Centuries of Letters, Speeches, Interviews, and Autobiographies.* Baton Rouge: Louisiana State University Press, 1977.

————. *The Slave Community: Plantation Life in the Antebellum South.* New York: Oxford University Press, 1979.

Boyce, Elizabeth Robinson. "An Exploratory Study of Two In Service Training Programs for Twenty Teachers On Race and Poverty in the Inner City." Ph. D. diss., Boston University, 1972.

Bossard, James H.S. and Eleanor Boll. *The Sociology of Child Development.* 4th ed. New York: Harper & Row Publishers, 1966.

Bourdieu, Pierre, Jean-Claude Chamboredon, and Jean-Claude Passeron. *The Craft of Sociology: Epistemological Preliminaries.* Translated by Richard Nice. Beate Krais, ed. . New York: Walter de Gruyter & Co., 1991.

Boudieu, Pierre and Jean-Claude Passeron. *Reproduction: In Education, Society and Culture,* trans. Richard Nice, London and Beverly Hills: Sage Publications, 1977.

Bowles, Samuel and Herbert Gintes. *Schooling in Capitalist America.* New York Basic Books, 1973.

Brahnam, Charles, historian at the Dusable Museum. Interview by author, 11 September 1994, Chicago. Tape recording. Dusable Museum.

Campbell, Edward D. C. Jr. and Kim Rice, ed. *Before Freedom Came: African-American Life in the Antebellum South,* Richmond Virginia: The Museum of the Confederacy and University Press of Virginia, 1991.

Campbell, J.P. "Gangsta' Rap in the African Village," *Freedom Rag,* Vol N2, (Fall 1994):10-14.

Chicago Fact Book Consortium, ed. *Local Community Fact Book Chicago Metropolitan Area.* Chicago: The Chicago Fact Book Consortium University of Illinois, 1984.

Chicago Crime Commission. *Gangs Public Enemy Number One.* Chicago: Chicago Crime Commission, 1995.

Chicago Intervention Network, comp. *Gang Prevention Information: Gang Violence.* Chicago: City of Chicago Department of Human Services, 1990.

Chicago Police Department. Chicago Police Department Annual Report 1992. Chicago: Chicago Police Department, 1993.

Chicago Police Department, comp. *Gangs Don't Let Them Take Over!* Chicago: Chicago Police Department Neighborhood Relations/Preventive Programs, n.d. Division

Clark, Kenneth B. *Prejudice and Your Child.* Connecticut: Wesleyan University Press, 1963.

Collins, Patricia Hill: *Black Feminist Thought: Knowledge, Consciousness, and Politics of Empowerment.* New York: Routledge, 1991.

Coleman, James S. *Equality of Educational Opportunity.* Washington: U.S. Department of Health, Education, and Welfare, 1966, PB-5983-4-SB N-T.

Comer, James P. "Educating Poor Minority Children," *Scientific American, Vol. 259,* (November 1988): 42-48.

Comer, James P. And Alvin F Poussaint. *Raising Black Children.* New York: Plume Books, 1992.

Cremin, Lawrence A. *The Transformation of the School: Progressivism in American Education 1876-1957.* New York: Vintage Books, 1961.

Cripps, Thomas. *Slow Fade to Black.* New York: Oxford University Press, 1977.

Cronbach, Lee J. And Patrick Suppes, eds. *Research for Tomorrow's Schools: Discipline Inquiry for Education.* London: The Macmillan Company, 1969.

Crucial Conflict. *The Final Tic.* Compact Disc September 8, 1996 UD-53006, Pallas Records.

Cunningham, Hugh. *The Children of the Poor.* Cambridge: Blackwell, 1991.

David, Jay, ed. *Growing Up Black: From Slave Days to Present.* 2nd. ed. New York: Avon Books, 1992.

DeCosta, Sandra B. "Not All Children Are Anglo and Middle Class: A Practical Beginning for the Elementary Teacher." *Theory Into Practice* Vol 23 No.2 (Spring 1984): 155-62,

Dent, Gina, ed. *Black Popular Culture.* Seattle: Bay Press, 1992.

Denzin, Norman K. *Sociological Methods a Sourcebook.* New York: McGraw-Hill Book Company, 1978.

Department of Planning and Development. *1990 Census of Population and Housing— Report #2, Social and Economic Characteristics of Chicago's Population Community Area Profiles.* Chicago: Department of Planning and Development, 1992.

Department of Planning and Development. *1990 Census of Population and Housing—Report #5 Demographic and Housing Characteristics of Chicago Englewood Community Area #68 Profile.* Chicago: Department of Planning and Development, 199.

Department of Research, Evaluation and Planning. *Special Report: School-level Drop-out Trends 1989-1994.* Chicago: Chicago Public Schools, 1995.

Devise, Pierre. "Descent From the Summit: Race and Housing in Chicago Since 1966 (Discrimination, Illinois." Ph.D. diss., University of Illinois at Chicago, 1985.

Davis, Judy Mitchell. "Toward A Community Conscience." n.d. Personal Collection, Judy I. Mitchell-Davis.

Dillard, J.L. *Black English: Its History and Usage in the United States.* New York: Vintage Books, 1973.

Douglass, Frederick. *Narrative of the Life of Frederick Douglass: An American Slave.* New York: Signet Books, 1968.

DuBois, W.E.B. *The Education of Black People: Ten Critiques, 1906-1960.* edited by Herbert Aptheker. New York: Monthly Review Press, 1973.

————. *The Souls of Black Folk.* edited by Candace Ward. New York: Dover Publications, Inc., 1994.

DuSable Museum of African American History. Exhibits. Chicago

Dyson, Michael Eric. *Reflecting Black: African-American Cultural Criticism.* Minneapolis: University of Minneapolis Press, 1993.

Eidman-Aadahl, Elyse Anne. "Where the Talking Starts: Speaking Publicly About Race and Teaching." Ph. D. diss. University of Maryland College Park, 1993.

Elkins, Stanley M. *Slavery: A Problem in American Institutional and Intellectual Life.* Chicago: The University of Chicago Press, 1959, 3rd. Ed. 1976.

Ellison, Ralph. *Invisible Man.* New York: Vintage Books, 1947.

Erikson, Erik. *Childhood and Society.* New York: W. W. Norton & Company, Inc. , 1950.

————. ed. *Youth: Change and Challenge,* New York: Basic Books, 1963; reprint, *The Challenge of Youth.* New York: Anchor Books, 1965.

————. *Identity and the Life Cycle,* New York: W.W. Norton & Company, 1968.

Fanon, Frantz. *The Wretched of the Earth,* trans. Constance Farrington. New York: Grove Press, 1963.

————. *Black Skin White Masks.* New York: Grove Weidenfield, 1967.

Federal Bureau of Investigation U.S. Department of Justice. *Uniform Crime Reports for the United States 1993.* Washington: U.S. Government Printing Office, 1993 94-401P.

Feinberg, Walter and Jonas F. Soltis. *School and Society.* New York and London: Teachers College Press, 1985.

Foster, Edward Michael. "Childhood Poverty and the Underclass: Unraveling the Effects of Constraints and Preferences." Ph. D. diss. The University of North Carolina at Chapel Hill, 1991.

Foster, Michelle. "Savage Inequalities: Where Have We Come From? Where Are We Going?" *Educational Theory* Vol 43, No. 1 (November 1993): 23-32.

Freidman, Leon. *Argument*. New York: Chelsea House Publishers, 1969.

Freire, Paulo. *Pedagogy of the Oppressed*. 20th ed., New York: The Continuum Publication Co., 1993.

Garbarino, James, Kathleen Kostelny, and Nancy Dubrow. *No Place To Be A Child: Growing Up in a War Zone*. Massachusetts: Lexington Books, 1991.

George, Nelson. *Buppies, B-Boys, Baps & Bohos: Notes on Post-Soul, Black Culture*. New York: Harper Perennial, 1992.

Gergen, Kenneth J. and Davis E. Davis, ed., *The Social Construction of the Person*. New York: Springer-Verlag New York Inc., 1985

Gibbs, Nancy. "Shameful Bequest to the Next Generation." *Time*. 8 October 1990, 42.

Giroux, Henry A. *Ideology, Culture, and the Process of Schooling*. Philadelphia: Temple University Press, 1981.

———. *Theory & Resistance in Education: A Pedagogy for the Opposition*. New York: Bergin & Garvey, 1983.

Glasgow, Douglas G. *The Black Underclass: Poverty, Unemployment and Entrapment of Ghetto Youth*. New York: Random House, 1981.

Goldstein, Naomi Carol. "Why Poverty is Bad for Children." Ph. D. diss. Harvard University, 1991.

Goss, Linda and Marian E. Barnes, ed. *Talk That Talk: An Anthology of African-American Storytelling*. New York: Touchstone Books, 1989.

Grant, Gerald. *The W.O.R.L.D. We Created at Hamilton High*. Cambridge: Harvard University Press, 1988.Greer, T.J. *The Culture of Destruction: Why Our Black Children are Not Learning*. Chicago: The Karnak Company, 1991.

Guga, Egon G. and Yvonne S Lincoln. *Naturalistic Inquiry*. Newbury Park: SAGE Publications, 1985.

———. *Fourth Generation Evaluation*. Newbury Park, CA.: Sage Publications, 1989.

Gutek, Gerald. *Education in the United States: A Historical Perspective*. Englewood Clifts, N.J. : Prentice-Hall, Inc.

Hacker, Andrew. *Two Nations: Black and White, Separate, Hostile, Unequal*. New York: Ballantine Books, 1992.

Hall, Bobby Ray. "A Study of At-Risk Characteristics of Those Students Who Moved Beyond the At-Risk Group." Ph. D. diss. University of Virginia, 1991.

Hansberry, Lorraine. *A Raisin in the Sun*. New York: Signet Books, 1958.

Hare, Nathan and Hare, Julia. T*he Hare Plan: To Overhaul the Public Schools and Educate Every Black Man, Woman and Child*. San Francisco, CA.: The Black Think Tank, 1991

Harris, Middleton A., Levitt, Morris, Furman, Roger and Smith, Ernest. *The Black Book*. New York: Random House, 1974. *

Hill, Pascoe G. *Fifty Days on Board a Slave Vessel*. Baltimore, MD.: 1993.

hooks, bell. *Black Looks: race and representation*. New York: Random House, 1981.

————. *Yearnings: race, gender and cultural politics*. Boston: South Press, 1990.

Hopson, Darlene and Derek Hopson. *Different and Wonderful: Raising Black Children in a Race-Conscious Society*. New York: Simon & Shuster, 1992.

Hughes, Langston and Melton Meltzer. *Black Magic: A Pictorial History of the African-American in the Performing Arts*. New York: A Da Capo Press, 1967.

Jackson, Robert Scoop. *The Last Black Mecca: Hip-Hop*. Chicago: Research Associates, 1994.

Johnson, Charles. *Shadow of the Plantation*. Chicago: The University of Chicago Press, 1934.

Johnson, LouAnne. *My Posse Don't Do Homework*. New York: St. Martin's Paperbacks, 1992.

Jordan, Winthrop D. *The White Man's Burden: Historical Origins of Racism in the United States*, London and New York: Oxford University Press, 1974.

Katz, Michael B. *The Undeserving Poor*. New York: Pantheon Books, 1989.

Kerlinger, Fred N. *Foundations of Behavioral Research*. New York: Holt, Rinehart and Winston, Inc., 1964.

Keyes, Johnny. *Du-Wop*. "n.p.," 1987.

Kimmel, Douglas C. and Irving B Weiner. *Adolescence: A Developmental Transition*. New Jersey: Lawrence Erlbaum Associates, Publishers, 1985.

Kitwana, Bakari. *The Rap On Gangsta Rap*. Chicago, IL.: The Third World Press, 1994.

Kluger, Richard. *Simple Justice*. New York: Vintage Books, 1977.

Knapp, Michael, Brenda J. Trunbull and Patrick Shields. "New Directions for Educating the Children of Poverty, " *Educational Leadership*, 48 (June 1990): 4-8.

Kochman, Thomas. *Black and White: Styles in Conflict*. Chicago: The University of Chicago Press, 1981.

Kotlowitz, Alex. *There Are No Children Here*. New York: Anchor Books, 1992.

Kozol, Jonathan. *Savage Inequalities: Children in America's School*. New York Crown Publishers, Inc., 1991.

Kunjufu, Jawanza. *Developing Positive Self-Images & Discipline In Black Children*. Chicago: African American Images, 1984.

————. *Countering The Conspiracy To Destroy Black Boys*. Vol. 1, Chicago: African American Images, 1985.

————. *Countering The Conspiracy To Destroy Black Boys*. Vol 11, Chicago: African American Press, 1986.

————. *Countering The Conspiracy To Destroy Black Boys*. Vol 111, Chicago: African American Press, 1990.

————. *Hip-Hop vs. Maat: A Psycho/Social Analysis of Values*. Chicago: African American Images, 1993.

Lane, Ann J. ed. *The Debate Over Slavery: Stanley Elkins and His Critics*. Urbana: University of Illinois Press, 1971.

Latif, Sultan A. and Naimah Latif. *Slavery: The African American Psychic Trauma*. Chicago: Latif Communications Group, Inc., 1994.

Lawson, Bell E. *The Underclass Question*. Philadelphia: Temple Press, 1992.

Lemann, Nicholas. *The Promised Land: The Great Black Migration and How It Changed America*. New York: Vintage Books. 1992.

Leslau, Charlotte and Wolf Leslau, comp. *African Proverbs*. New York: Peter Pauper Press, Inc., 1962.

Liebow, Elliot. *Tally's Corner*. Boston: Little, Brown and Company, 1967.

Lindenberger, Jan. *Black Memorabilia Around the House*. Schiffer. 1993.

Lobosco, Antionette. "Individual, School and Community Correlates of High School Graduation." Ph. D. diss. University of Illinois at Chicago, 1992.

London, Rebecca and Deborah Puntenney. *A Profile of Chicago's Poverty and Related Conditions*. Chicago: Center for Urban Affairs and Policy Research, Northwestern University, 1993. WP-93-1.

Luttrell, Wendy "Working-Class Women's Ways of Knowing: Effects of Gender, Race and Class," *Sociology of Education* 62 (January 1989): 32-46.

Lynch, Kevin. *The Image of the City*. Cambridge: The M.I.T. Press, 1960.

Madhubuti, Haki and Safisha Madhubuti. *African-Centered Education*. Chicago: The Third World Press, 1994.

Majors, Richard and Janet Mancini. *Cool Pose: The Dilemmas of Black Manhood in America*. New York: Lexington Books, 1993.

Mead, George Herbert. *Mind, Self and Society*. Chicago: University of Chicago Press: 1934.

McLaren, Peter. *Life in Schools: An Introduction to Critical Pedagogy in the Foundations of Education*. New York: Longmur. 1989.

Mellon, James, ed. *The Bullwhip Days: The Slaves Remember, An Oral History*. New York: Avon Books, 1988.

Memmi, Albert. *The Colonizer and The Colonized*. Boston: Beacon Press, 1965.

Miles, Matthew B. and Michael A. Huberman. *Qualitative Data Analysis*, 2nd ed., London: Sage Publications, 1994.

Mills, C. Wright. *The Sociological Imagination*. New York: Oxford Universities Press, 1959.

Morganthau, Tom, Vern Smith, Howard Manly, and David L. Gonzalez. "Children of the Underclass." *Newsweek*. 11 September 1989, 16.

National Alliance of Black School Educators. *Saving Our African American Children*. Atlanta: National Alliance of Black School Educators, Inc., 1994.

Nightingale, Carl Husemoller. *On The Edge: A History of Poor Black Children and Their American Dreams*. New York: Basic Books, 1993.

Office of Policy Planning and Research. *The Negro Family: The Case for National Action*. Washington: United States Department of Labor, 1965, PB 5983-11-SB 740-42T.

Ogbu, John U. *Minority Education and Caste: The American System in Cross-Cultural Perspective*. New York: Academic Press, 1978.

Ogle, Patrick, comp. *Facets: African-American Video Guide*. Chicago: Facets Multimedia, Inc., 1994.

Oppenheim, A.N. *Questionnaire Design, Interviewing and Attitude Measurement*. London and New York: Pinter Publishers 1992.

Paskman, Dailey. *Gentlemen, Be Seated: A Parade Of American Minstrels*. New York: Clarkson N. Potter, Inc./Publisher, 1976.

Patton, Michael Quinn. *Qualitative Evaluation and Research Methods*, 2nd ed. Newbury Park: Sage Publications, 1990.

Perkins, Eugene. *Home Is The Dirty Street: The Social Oppression of Black Children*. Chicago: The Third World Press, 1975; reprint 1991; reprint 1990.

———. *Explosion of Chicago's Black Street Gangs: 1900 to Present*. Chicago: The Third World Press, 1987, 2nd ed. 1990.

———. *Harvesting New Generations: The Positive Development Of Black Youth*. Chicago: The Third World Press, 1985.

Powell-Hopson, Darlene and Derek Hopson. *Different and Wonderful: Raising Black Children in a Race-Conscious Society*. New York: Fireside, 1992.

Price, Richard. *Clockers*. New York: Avon Books, 1992.

Rainwater, Lee and William L. Yancey. *The Moynihan Report and the Politics of Controversy*. Cambridge: The M.I.T. Press, 1967.

Rawick, George P., ed. *The American Slave: A Composite Autobiography Georgia Narratives*. Vol 12-13, Connecticut: Greenwood Publishing Company, 1971.

———. *The American Slave: A Composite Autobiography Unwritten History of Slavery*. Vol 18, Connecticut: Greenwood Publishing Company, 1972.

Reams, Bernard D. And Paul E Wilson, ed. *Segregation and the Fourteenth Amendment in the States: A Survey of State Segregation Laws 1865-1953;*

Prepared for United States Supreme Court in re: Brown vs. Board of Education of Topeka. New York: William S. Hein & Co., Inc., 1975.

Reed, Adolph Jr. "The Underclass As Myth and Symbol: The Poverty of Discourse About Poverty" *Radical America* 24 (January 1992): 21-42.

Rose, Tricia. *Black Noise.* Hanover and London: University Press of New England, 1994.

Reed, Sally and Craig R Sauter. "Children of Poverty." *Kappan* 71 (June 1990): 1-12.

Roediger, David R. *The Wages of Whiteness: Race and the Making of the American Working Class.* New York and London: Verso, 1991 reprint 1992 and 1993.

Rogers, Dorothy. *The Psychology of Adolescence.* New York: Appleton-Century-Crofts, 1962.

Russell, Kathy, Midge Wilson, and Ronald Hall,. *The Color Complex: The Politics of Skin Color Among African-Americans.* New York: Anchor Books, 1992.

Ryan, William. *Blaming the Victim.* New York: Vintage Books, 1971, revised 1976.

Saalakhan, Mauri'. *Why Our Children Are Killing Themselves.* Maryland: Writer's Inc.-International, 1990.

Sacks, Howard L. and Judith Rose Sacks. *Way Up North In Dixie: A Black Family's Claim to the Confederate Anthem.* Washington: Smithsonian Institution Press, 1993.

Schroeder, Ken, ed."Reaching Out for the Disadvantaged," *The Educational Digest* 58 (September 1992).

Sebald, Han. *Adolescence a Sociological Analysis.* New York: Appleton-Century-Crofts, 1968.

Sebring, Penny Bender and others. *Charting Reform in Chicago: The Students Speak.* Chicago: Consortium on Chicago School Research, 1996.

Shujaa, Mwalimu, ed. *Too Much Schooling Too Little Education: A Paradox of Black Life in White Societies.* With a Forward by Haki R. Madhubuti. New Jersey: Africa World Press, Inc., 1994.

Simmons, Richard K. *The Crucial Element In The Development Of Black Children.* Chicago: Richard K. Simmons, 1985.

Sinclair, April. *Coffee Will Make You Black.* New York: Hyperion, 1994.

Slaughter, Diana. "The Home Environment and Academic Achievement of Black American Children and Youth: An Overview." *The Journal of Negro Education.* 56 (1987): 3-21.

Social Science Institute, Fisk University. *Unwritten History of Slavery.* Social Science Institute, Fisk University. Nashville: Microcard Editions, 1945.

Stack, Carol B. *All Our Kin: Strategies for Survival in a Black Community*. New York: Harper Ccolophon Books, 1970.

Stampp, Kenneth. *The Peculiar Institution: Slavery in the Antebellum South*. New York: Vintage Books, 1964.

Stanfield, John H. and Dennis M. Rutledge, ed. *Race and Ethnicity in Research Methods*. Newbury Park: Sage Publications, 1993.

Staples, Robert. *The Black Family: Essays and Studies*. 5th ed. California: Wadsworth Publishing Co., 1994.

Steinberg, Stephen. *The Ethnic Myth: Race, Ethnicity and Class In America*. Boston: Beacon Press, 1981.

Stevens, Floraline I. "Opportunity to Learn and Other Social Contextual Issues: Addressing the Low Academic Achievement of African American Students." *The Journal of Negro Education* 62 (Summer 1992): 227-31).

Stith, Deborah Prothrow. *Deadly Consequences: How Violence is Destroying Our Teenage Population and a Plan to Begin Solving the Problem*. New York: Harper Perennial, 1991.

Strauss, Anslem and Juliet Corbin. *Basics of Qualitative Research: Grounded Theory Procedures and Techniques*. Newbury Park and London: Sage Publications, 1990.

Taylor, Susan. "A Promise At-Risk." *Modern Maturity*. Aug.-Sept. 1989, 32-41.

Thomas, Deborah Bauldee. "At-Risk Early Adolescent Females: An Ethnography of Their School Experiences." Ph.D. diss. Florida State University, 1992.

Thomas, Jim. *Doing Critical Ethnography*. Vol. 26, Newbury Park: A Sage University Paper, 1993.

Tolhurst, Carmen, linguist at Trinity College. Interview by author, 10 August 1996, Illinois.

Tomblin, Jimmy. "Ratings of Teacher Performance." Ph.D. diss., Northwestern University, 1979.

Tribble, Israel Jr. *Making Their Mark: Educating African-American Children*. Silver Springs: Beckham House Publishers, 1992.

Turner, Patricia A. *Ceramic Uncles & Celluloid Mammies: Black Images and Their Influence on Culture* . New York: Doubleday, 1994.

U.S. Department of Labor. Office of Policy Planning and Research. *The Negro Family: The Case for National Action*. [Washington, D.C.]: U.S. Department of Labor, Office of Policy and Research, March, 1965.

White, Joseph L. *The Psychology of Blacks: An Afro-American Perspective*. New Jersey: Prentice Hall, Inc., 1984.

Willis, Paul. *Learning to Labor*. England: Saxon House, !977.

Wilson, Amos N. *Black-On-Black Violence: The Psychodynamics of Black Self-Annihilation In service Of White Domination.* New York: Afrikan World Infrosystems, 1990; reprint 1993.

——. *The Developmental Psychology of The Black Child.* New York: Africana Research Publications, 1978; reprint 1987.

——. *The Falsification of Afrikan Consciousness.* New York: Afrikan World Infosystems, 1993.

Wilson, William Julius. *The Truly Disadvantaged: The Inner City, The Underclass, and Public Policy.* Chicago and London: The University of Chicago Press, 1987.

Whitman, Mark, ed. *Removing a Badge of Slavery: The Record of Brown v. Board of Education..* New York: Markus Wiener Publishing, Inc., 1993.

Wittrock, Merlin C. ed. *Handbook of Research on Teaching.* 3rd. ed. New York: MacMillan, Inc., 1986.

Wolf, R.L. and B. Tymitz. "Ethnography and Reading: Matching Inquiry Mode To Process." Reading Research Quarterly 12 (1976-77):

Woodson, Carter G. *The Mis-Education of the Negro* 6th ed., Trenton, N.J.: African World Press, 1991.

——. *The Education of the Negro.* New York: A&B Books Publishers, 1919.

Woodstock Institute Staff. *The 1992 Community Lending Factbook.* Chicago: Harris Trust and Savings Bank, 1994.

Wright, Richard. *Native Son.* New York: Harper & Row, 1940; restored ed., With an Introduction by Arnold Rampersad. New York: Harper Perennial, 1993.

Yin, Robert K. *Case Study Research: Design and Methods.* London: Sage Publications, 1994.

Zinsmeister, Karl. "Growing Up Scared." *The Atlantic* June 1990, 49-66.

Zubrow, Judith Meeker. "The Pedagogy of Adolescent Peer Relations: Searching with Inner-City Adolescents for Critical Consciousness." Ph. D. diss. University of Pennsylvania, 1993.

Index